SS: HELL ON THE WESTERN FRONT

THE *WAFFEN-SS* IN EUROPE 1940–1945

SS: HELL ON THE WESTERN FRONT

CHRIS BISHOP

SPELLMOUNT
Staplehurst

British Library Cataloguing in Publication Data:
A catalogue record for this book is available
from the British Library

Copyright © Amber Books Ltd 2003

ISBN 1-86227-185-2

First published in the UK in 2003 by
Spellmount Limited
The Old Rectory
Staplehurst
Kent TN12 0AZ

Tel: 01580 893730
Fax: 01580 893731
Email: enquiries@spellmount.com
Website: www.spellmount.com

Editorial and design by
Amber Books Ltd
Bradley's Close
74-77 White Lion Street
London N1 9PF

Project Editor: Charles Catton
Editor: Caroline Curtis
Design: Jerry Williams
Picture Research: Lisa Wren

Printed and bound in Italy by: Eurolitho S.p.A., Cesano Boscone (MI)

Picture credits

POPPERFOTO: 110. **Private Collection:** 92. **Süddeutscher Verlag:** 6–7, 8, 11, 13, 14, 16, 18,
21, 22, 25, 26, 28, 29, 30, 32–33, 34, 37, 38, 39, 44, 46, 51, 58–59, 61, 67, 68, 71, 72, 73, 74–75, 78,
80, 81, 83, 84, 85, 86, 88, 89, 91, 94–95, 97, 100, 105, 108, 109, 114–115, 121, 123, 124, 131, 132,
133, 135, 137, 138, 140–141, 142, 144, 157, 159, 160–161, 167, 169, 172, 175, 177, 179, 180, 181,
182, 184. **TRH Pictures:** 1, 10, 15, 19, 41, 42, 45, 48, 49, 53, 54, 55, 56, 60, 64, 65, 69, 76, 96, 99,
103, 106, 111, 112, 116, 117, 118, 122, 126, 127, 128, 146, 147, 148, 149, 150, 153, 155, 156,
162, 164, 168, 170, 171, 174.

CONTENTS

ORIGINS OF THE WAFFEN SS

They were the original 'Men in Black', the personification of the Nazi state. In their sombre uniforms adorned with swastikas and death's heads, the members of the *Schutz-staffeln*, or SS, cast their shadow over Germany in the 1930s, and they grew in power during the war. Offering the Führer loyalty to the death, SS members were committed to National Socialism long after it became obvious that the Nazis were pulling Germany down into ruin.

Even today, they have a curiously compelling image: black-clad Aryan supermen, executors of the Final Solution, the cruel and merciless soldiers of the Nazi state, who were armed with the latest weapons that Germany's scientists and engineers could devise. Like many commonly held notions, this picture of the SS does not tell the whole story. The SS did wear black, but only in the pre-war years. SS men were responsible for some of the worst atrocities of the war – but they were also Germany's toughest soldiers.

Left: Hitler's SS bodyguard, the *Leibstandarte*, parades past its master on his birthday in 1939. Born out of a need for hard men to protect Nazi political meetings, the SS grew into an all-powerful state within a state.

INSPIRED BY HITLER

The original shape and form of the SS owed much to Adolf Hitler. It was he who formed the specially selected bodyguard units that would evolve into the SS; gave them their sense of being chosen men; selected men who took pride in their unquestioning obedience and who would do anything he asked – whether legal or not.

The origins of the SS date back to the early 1920s, when for the first time the National Socialist German Worker's Party (NSDAP) was making its presence felt in the rough-and-tumble of Bavarian politics. Violence played a major part in the politics of the time, so a paramilitary

Below: When Germany went to war in 1939, the SS was being transformed from a political guard organization into a fully fledged fighting force operating alongside the German Army. Trained and equipped as a purely military formation, the *Waffen* or Armed SS would grow into a million-strong private army which often provided the *Wehrmacht's* spearhead.

wing was set up by the Nazis for street fighting. By the end of 1922, this had become the *Sturmabteilung,* or the SA.

Hitler was nominally in command of the SA, but could not count on the loyalty of the ordinary storm troopers. Most were army veterans or former *Freikorps* men, who gave their loyalties to their own leaders. As a result, Hitler set up his own personal bodyguard in May 1923. Known as the *Stabswache,* or headquarters guard, it consisted of men whose loyalty was presented unswervingly to Adolf Hitler. Hitler called them 'my first group of toughs, ready to fight at any time'. The *Stabswache* did not last long, and was replaced by the *Stosstrupp Adolf Hitler* (Adolf Hitler Shock Troop). Led by two of Hitler's most trusted comrades, Joseph Berchtold and Julius Schreck, it included Rudolf Hess and Josef 'Sepp' Dietrich in its number.

The *Stosstrupp* had been at the forefront of the Beerhall Putsch, though it disbanded during the temporary eclipse of the Nazi party following

Hitler's failed coup in 1923. After Hitler returned from imprisonment and political exile he resolved to form a similar unit, initially consisting of only eight men, under the command of

---

Distinctive uniforms and insignia set the highly-disciplined SS apart from the brawling, brown-shirted masses of the SA.

Julius Schreck. At Hermann Göring's suggestion, the unit, and those which followed, were known as *Schutzstaffeln*, or Protection Squads. The name was quickly abbreviated to 'SS'.

When the *Stosstrupp* was formed, its members adopted a black cap and distinctive insignia to set themselves apart from the brown ranks of the SA, and the newly formed SS continued in the same way. The cap eagle held a *Totenkopf*, or death's head, in its claws rather than the red, black, and white national cockade. *Totenkopfs* adorned the smart uniforms of Hitler's *Leibstandarte-SS* guard during the party rallies of the 1930s, and were still being worn at the end of the war, when camouflaged *Waffen-SS* soldiers made their last, futile defence of Berlin against the overwhelming might of the Red Army. But it was as the chosen symbol of the *Totenkopfverbande* – the concentration camp guards – that the death's head acquired its horrific associations.

However, the *Totenkopf* was not chosen for its ghoulish appearance: rather it was a way of linking the SS with famous military units of German history. As a symbol of mortality, the skull and crossbones can be found on graves and headstones all over the world. It is also an ancient military symbol, since war is absolute and allows no half measures between defeat or victory. For the soldier, the death's head carries a potent message – death or glory – and it consequently became the cap badge or insignia of elite formations that were prepared to fight to the death.

The first protection squads were never more than 10 strong. One was located in each of the Nazi Party's districts, or *Gaue*. Julius Schreck insisted that the SS squads be created from reliable, mature men, aged between 25 and 35, who were sober, fit, and with no criminal record – a stipulation that disqualified many of the rank-and-file members of the SA.

In 1926, Joseph Berchtold, who had taken three years to recover from wounds taken at Hitler's side during the Munich Putsch, replaced Julius Schreck as the head of the SS. Berchtold returned to an unhappy organization. The elitist beliefs of the SS were resented by the rank and file of the SA, and to head off a revolt Hitler had made the SS subordinate to the *Oberste SA Führung*, or SA High Command. This, in turn, did not sit well with the members of the SS, who felt that they were being treated badly by the SA. However, there was one instance of the Führer's favour: in 1926 Hitler gave the SS the keeping of the *Blutfahne*, the banner stained with the blood of the 'martyrs' of the 1923 putsch.

Berchtold resigned in 1927, disheartened by Party backstabbing, and was replaced by Ehrhardt Heiden. Heiden had no more success in fighting the SS corner than his predecessor, but he did make one far-reaching decision: he appointed a young veteran of the Beerhall Putsch as his deputy. This former protégé of two of Hitler's rivals, Ernst Röhm and Gregor Strasser, was none other than Heinrich Himmler. Although Hitler gave birth to the SS, it was Himmler who provided the executive ability and gave it the structure that enabled it to grow.

THE MAN WHO MADE THE SS

Heinrich Himmler remains one of the most enigmatic of the bizarre figures who reached the top in the Third Reich. This man, who could not stomach executions, made the Final Solution possible. Throughout his life he suffered from psychosomatic illnesses, including headaches, dyspepsia and hysteria.

Born near Munich on 7 October 1900, he was the son of a former tutor to the Bavarian royal family, and was brought up in a devoutly Catholic home. His service as a cadet clerk at the end of World War I gave him a taste for keeping records. He would later apply this skill to compile dossiers on potential rivals within the Nazi Party. He joined the party in its early days and participated in the Beerhall Putsch in 1923 at the side of his mentor Ernst Röhm – the future leader of the SA.

In 1925 Himmler became acting *Gauleiter* in Lower Bavaria, and from then until 1929 he worked as propaganda leader of the Party. In 1928 he married 35-year-old Margarete Boden, and they set up a poultry farm near Munich. His wife encouraged his interest in homeopathy,

mesmerism and herbalism; it was onto these harmless enthusiasms that he would graft a more sinister fascination with racial purity.

Himmler became deputy leader of the SS in 1927. Then in January 1929 Ehrhardt Heiden resigned the leadership, and Himmler was appointed *Reichsführer*. Almost immediately, he started moulding the organization into a very different shape from that envisaged by the Führer. Few members of the SA leadership had any respect for the quiet, bespectacled, apparent nonentity, and none dreamed that he would be able, even with Hitler's support, to change the subservient position of the SS within the SA. But Himmler had ambitions for his new command.

As an avid student of Germanic history, Himmler had been enthralled by stories of the Teutonic Knights, who in the fourteenth and fifteenth centuries had brutally spread German culture and religion among the Slavs to the east.

Below: One of the earliest incarnations of what would eventually become the SS was the *Stosstrupp* Hitler, formed before the Munich Beerhall Putsch in 1923. Led by Julius Schreck (centre, with moustache), they succeeded Hitler's original bodyguard, the *Stabswache*. Hitler described them as 'my first group of toughs, ready to fight at any time'.

Himmler wanted to create a new order of Teutonic Knights to continue the job – an order to match his romanticized ideals of the Germanic race.

The new *Reichsführer* had two main aims. First, he wanted to use the SS to protect the Party. To this end he established a small intelligence section, which under Reinhard Heydrich was to become the feared *Sicherheitsdienst*, or SD. SS units from all over Germany were expected to forward reports on political opponents, as well as on groups such as Freemasons and Jews.

Secondly, Himmler saw in the SS a 'sworn community of superior men'. They were to become the purifiers of the German race, a gene pool from which the perfect Aryan could be produced. He tightened entry procedures considerably, weeding out some of the street thugs who had been in the

Above: Politics in Weimar Germany was a brutal business, with political debate all too often evolving into brawls and all-out street battles. The most vicious fights were usually between the Communists and the extreme nationalists led by the Nazis. Here, uniformed police have broken up a fight between SA and SS men and Communist Party paramilitaries.

organization from the beginning and provided a strict health and fitness standard that all new recruits had to meet. Indeed, Himmler examined personally photographs of all new applicants, looking for signs of Mongoloid, Negroid or Semitic features. The new SS members were to be supremely fit, with unblemished Germanic ancestry going back three generations, and above all, to be as obedient and loyal as a Jesuit – but without the Jesuit habit of asking awkward questions.

Himmler's romantic dream of a race of blue-eyed, blond heroes was to be achieved by cultivating an elite according to 'laws of selection' based on criteria of physiognomy, mental and physical tests, character and spirit. His 'aristocratic' concept was consciously to breed a

---

Himmler's aim for the SS was to create a new order of Teutonic Knights, who would impose 'Aryan' culture on the rest of Europe.

---

racially organized order that would combine charismatic authority with bureaucratic discipline. The SS man would represent a new human type – warrior, administrator, scholar and leader, all in one – whose messianic mission was to repopulate Europe.

From the outset, Himmler introduced the principle of racial selection to the SS. Married SS officers were expected to set an example to lower ranks and to the German nation by fathering at least four healthy children. Anyone unable to do so should sponsor 'racially and hereditarily worthwhile children'.

But if SS men were required to do their duty as fathers – in or out of marriage – there was also a duty on loyal young Nazi women to bear racially pure children. After the outbreak of war, Himmler issued a notorious procreation order that 'it will be the sublime task of German women and girls of good breeding to become mothers to children of soldiers setting off to battle'.

The State-registered human stud farms of the *Lebensborn* project, or Fountain of Life, were designed to help create the cannon fodder of the future. The *Lebensborn* centres played host to young women selected for their perfect Nordic traits, who displayed regular Aryan features and could prove their descent over several untainted generations. One girl caught up in a moment of rather startling zeal for the Nazi concept of motherhood was untroubled by the idea of an extra-marital birth. She announced to the surprised passengers on a local Bavarian train in the

autumn of 1937: 'I am going to the SS *Ordensburg* Sonthofen to have myself impregnated.' Sonthofen was one of four *Ordensburg*, or 'Order Castles', which were a sort of university for the future elite of the Nazi Party.

The gossip in the Third Reich was that the 13 *Lebensborn* maternity homes dotted through Germany from Hohehorst near Bremen to Hochland in Bavaria were part SS brothel and part racial stud farm, and that they employed permanent *Zeugungshelfer*, or 'procreation helpers', to ensure that only the most Aryan of conceptions took place. Himmler took an active interest in the programme, commenting that: 'We only recommended genuinely valuable, racially pure men as *Zeugungshelfer*.'

The *Lebensborn* association was first registered in September 1936 under the auspices of the *Rasse und Siedlungshauptamt* (RuSHA, or SS Central Office for Race and Resettlement). Writing in 1939, Günther d'Alquen, editor of the SS newspaper *Das Schwarze Korps* (The Black Corps), explained:

The Lebensborn *association consists primarily of members of the SS. It provides mothers of large families with the finest obstetrical treatment in excellent maternity homes, as well as facilities for rest both before and after confinement. It also affords an opportunity for pre- and extra-conjugal mothers of good stock to give birth under relaxed conditions.*

SUBORDINATE TO THE SA

By the time Hitler came to power, the SS had grown to be 25,000 strong, though this was a drop in the ocean compared to the millions of SA members. Nevertheless, the SS was regarded as an elite within the Nazi Party, and it gave Himmler the platform on which to build his perfect state within a state.

From the first, the SS had differentiated itself from the storm troopers by wearing black caps and its own insignia. However, when Himmler was appointed its commander, he made further changes. Above all, the adoption of an all-black uniform with silver trim made the SS stand out

even more from the brown-shirted masses of the SA. To this ready visibility were added fiercely high selection standards and strict training, emphasizing loyalty to the Führer above all else. Thanks to Himmler's intelligence-gathering operation, however, their brown-shirted colleagues continued to regard the SS as toadying informers.

One function of the SS was to do the Führer's dirty work, and it was believed widely in Germany that the Berlin SS was responsible for the Reichstag fire of 27 February 1933. Nonetheless, the fire was blamed on Marinus van der Lubbe, an unemployed Dutch bricklayer, who was arrested in the Reichstag building. Van der Lubbe was short-sighted and simple-minded, but during the trial held in Leipzig between 21 September and 23 December 1933, Hermann Göring was able to portray him as a dedicated Communist agent. Under the terms of a special retroactive law, the *Lex van der Lubbe*, the unfortunate man was beheaded on 10 January 1934.

Above: Following Hitler's release from prison after the failed Munich Putsch, the Nazi Führer established a new security force called the *Schutzstaffel* or Protection Squad. The original eight-man unit is seen here. Seated at the table with Hitler are (from right) his adjutant Julius Schaub, SS leader Joseph Berchthold, and photographer Heinrich Hoffmann.

The Reichstag fire was used as the pretext for the arrest of about 4000 people, mainly Communist functionaries. The Reichstag Fire Decree was issued, which abrogated fundamental laws. The Communists' campaign for the Reichstag was halted, and the Social Democrats' (SPD) seriously curtailed. Whoever was behind the fire, it gave Hitler an immense boost in power – the Führer proclaimed that the fire was 'a sign from heaven' even while the Reichstag was burning.

The true growth of the SS began after Hitler seized power in 1933. Himmler was appointed police chief in Bavaria, a position that he used as a platform to bring all German law enforcement agencies, both uniformed and plain-clothed, under SS control. The power of the SS was consolidated in June 1934, when Hitler used the black shirts to destroy the leadership of the rival SA in the 'Night of the Long Knives'.

The relationship between the Party and the SA had been uneasy even before Hitler came to power. There was little love lost between the beer hall thugs and ineffectual ideologues like Rosenberg or sinister schemers like Heydrich and Himmler. In 1931 the Berlin SA had mutinied over Hitler's order to stop its escalating campaign of street violence, which was politically counterproductive. SA leader Walther Stennes refused to comply and his men smashed up Party offices in the capital. Expelled, he later joined Otto Strasser's splinter group in Prague and eventually escaped to China, leading Chiang Kai-shek's bodyguard.

Ernst Röhm had fallen out with Hitler even earlier. While Hitler had been in Landsberg Prison, he defied the Führer's orders and allied the SA to other right-wing paramilitaries, creating a new organization, the *Frontbann*. Hitler feared losing control over the SA: Röhm saw himself as the champion of the front-line soldiers betrayed in 1918, the embodiment of the nihilist *Freikorps* spirit. Disenchanted, he left Germany to become a mercenary in South America but was soon invited back: his organizational skill was unquestionable. But a year after Hitler became Chancellor, the revolution seemed no nearer.

RIVALRY WITH THE SA

What Röhm and his cohorts really believed in is difficult to fathom. They were an embittered generation, having seen countless comrades die in a war that won them nothing. They wanted power and initially believed Hitler – once an ordinary soldier too – was the man to get it for them. However, Röhm and the SA leadership soon began to talk of initiating the full revolution themselves, of becoming the 'brown flood that would submerge the grey [i.e. party] rocks', making no further compromise with industrialists, bankers, the church or the officer class. But Hitler would strike first, conducting a swift and merciless purge.

In the spring of 1934, Hitler was still obliged to govern with some respect for constitutional niceties. Although he had demanded and received totalitarian powers, his regime was not yet fully established. Indeed,

Left: Although nominally part of the SA, the SS behaved like an independent organization. Hitler signified his approval of the SS by giving them the responsibility for guarding the *Blutfahne*, the Swastika banner carried in the Munich Putsch which was stained with the blood of Nazi dead. Here it is used to 'consecrate' SA standards at the 1934 *Parteitag* (Party Day).

Right: Much of the military success achieved by the *Waffen*-SS was due to Himmler's choice of former army general Paul Hausser to oversee the military training of the organization. A gifted staff officer, Hausser ensured that the members of the new Armed-SS would be trained to army standards, with even greater levels of fitness.

he was still vulnerable to a firm move by President Hindenburg or the Army. Determined to succeed Hindenburg as president, he realized it was essential that no rival candidate be allowed to emerge. All Germany knew the president was ailing; at 87 years old, he was poised to retire to his estates for the summer, probably never to return to the capital.

To achieve a smooth succession, Hitler had to travel a little further along a tightrope of his own making. For five years he had maintained a precarious equilibrium between the left wing, avowedly socialist elements of the Nazi Party, and the bankers, industrialists and senior Army officers. Without them, he knew that government, let alone German re-armament, would be impossible. Now, however, he had to choose between the men who had dedicated their lives to his struggle, and the plutocrats who were prepared to support him for their own short-term selfish interests.

Prominent among those old comrades who stood in Hitler's way was Ernst Röhm, *Stabschef* of the SA. Röhm had spent two years in exile as a military adviser in Bolivia, but was invited back by Hitler at the end of 1930. Hitler needed Röhm's undoubted brilliance as an organizer, and knew he could rely on the passionate loyalty of this brutal, battle-scarred pederast.

Röhm's recruiting and organizing skills quickly bore fruit: so quickly, in fact, that the authorities reacted against the expansion of the SA, banning the wearing of paramilitary uniforms late in 1931. Nevertheless, the SA grew to an intimidating size, smashing Communist resistance exactly as Hitler had planned.

Paradoxically, it was Hitler's victory in the elections of January 1933 that doomed Röhm and his cohorts. As Chancellor, Hitler was now seen dressed incongruously in top hat and tails, consorting with the very class enemies that the SA leadership had sworn to wipe out. The organization became restive, vocal in its demands for more revolutionary measures, and it was not long before loose tongues attracted the attention of the most sinister of Hitler's followers.

SS PLOTS AGAINST THE SA

Reinhard Heydrich, head of the *Sicherheitsdienst*, kept incriminating files on many Germans, especially other leading Nazis. He compiled a thick dossier on the SA, and it made for fascinating reading. While drunk, Röhm and his henchmen criticized the Führer in the crudest terms, damning him for selling-out to the capitalists; many senior SA figures joined their leader in all-male sex orgies. Hitler was perfectly aware of Röhm's sexual orientation, and had hitherto exercised an unusual tolerance, having been

Above: One of the few members of the Nazi Party with a power base that could threaten Hitler, Ernst Röhm was an organizer of genius who had turned the SA into a multi-million strong paramilitary force. The Army looked on Röhm's revolutionary ideas with alarm, and gave active assistance when Hitler unleashed the SS against his old comrade-in-arms.

assured that it was men and not boys who shared Röhm's bed.

Heydrich, however, passed the dossier to his ambitious chief, Heinrich Himmler – whose whole SS organization was itself a branch of the SA. He also informed Hermann Göring, who appointed Himmler Chief of the Prussian Secret State Police Office, the grandly titled assassination squad that Himmler would transform into the Gestapo.

Meanwhile, the Army too had heard Röhm's demands to merge it with the SA – and have Röhm at its head. As early as February, Hitler had already had to warn Röhm publicly, making him sign a formal agreement with General von Blomberg to restrict SA activity. Moreover, wider public opinion was unhappy at the posturing antics of the Brownshirts. President Hindenburg, leaving Berlin for his estates and conscious that he was going home to die, confessed to Vice-Chancellor Franz von Papen 'things are going badly'.

On 4 June 1934, Hitler summoned Röhm to a meeting, in which they talked long into the night. Whether Hitler genuinely sought to avert a terminal breach with Röhm, or was merely lulling him into a false sense of security remains a mystery. Hitler was an opportunist, but he was equally capable of the most Machiavellian long-term planning. The upshot was that Röhm ordered the SA to go on leave for a month, while he himself took a break with his senior commanders at the spa town of Bad Wiessee.

On 21 June, Hitler visited the ailing Hindenburg, who sat gruffly in a wheelchair and let General von Blomberg do most of the talking. It was a short meeting, just four minutes by one

---

Ernst Röhm's ideas of a National Socialist revolution alienated the Führer, who saw the Brownshirts of the SA slipping from his control.

---

account. The general threatened to order martial law, to bring the Army on to the streets and deal with the SA. This would have been a body blow for Hitler, who remembered only too well how the Army had crushed his attempted coup in Munich. If it came to a fight, the Army would easily be able to dispose of the SA, and destroy National Socialism in the process. Hitler spun on his heels and flew back to Berlin.

The next morning he called to the Chancellery Viktor Lütze, one of the few senior SA men he could count on, and declared Röhm had to go. Hitler then promised General von Blomberg that he would suppress the SA leadership. Whether Röhm's fate was to be expulsion from the party, exile or something more drastic, Hitler was undecided. Not so Himmler and Göring. Their powerful rival's fate was now sealed by Heydrich's report: the dossier of mutinous talk and unnatural vice would be enough to bury Röhm.

Military units went on the alert all across Germany. Significantly, the SS was reported to be on the Army's side, and orders were passed that SS men needing extra weapons could draw them from military bases.

Himmler waited until Thursday 28 June. Hitler was out of the capital, at Essen to attend the wedding celebrations of one of his *Gauleiters*. There Himmler telephoned him with a string of fabricated reports, which sent Hitler into a blazing rage. Göring, who was with him, fanned the flames until he got permission to fly back to Berlin and prepare to behead the SA.

Hitler then called Röhm and announced that he would speak to the SA commanders on Saturday 30 June. Röhm was pleased, believing the Führer's visit to their conference was a gesture of public support for the Brownshirts.

Hitler spent Friday night at a hotel in Bad Godesberg, and ordered Sepp Dietrich, leader of his SS bodyguards, to descend on Bad Wiessee and arrest Röhm. But after more fabricated reports from Himmler, including one that the SA were preparing to launch a *coup d'état* the following afternoon, Hitler decided to take charge himself. Commandeering a Junkers Ju 52 airliner, he took off shortly after 2 a.m.

Hitler was accompanied by a small entourage: his bodyguard Emil Maurice, his 19-year-old secretary Crista Schröder, drivers Julius Schreck and Erich Kempka, Joseph Goebbels, Rudolf Hess, adjutants Wilhelm Brückner and Julius Schaub, a few plainclothes police officers and SS men – and the Judas of the SA, Viktor Lütze. Hitler was in such a blind fury that when he landed in Munich he did not wait for the following aircraft, which was packed with SS men. Instead, he leapt into a Mercedes and ordered Kempka to head for the Ministry of the Interior.

There, a little after 4 a.m., he summoned the two most senior SA men in the city, and arrested them the moment they arrived. The bewildered Brownshirts were hustled off to Stadelheim Prison, where an SS firing party was waiting.

THE SS GOES INTO ACTION

In Berlin, Sepp Dietrich had assembled and armed more than a thousand SS men at the former Cadet School barracks at Lichterfelde, where the *Leibstandarte* had made its home since the end of 1933. Some flew to Munich to assist Hitler at Bad Wiessee; the rest awaited the codeword *Kolibri*, or 'hummingbird'.

Hitler's party drove immediately to Bad Wiessee, where the SA had hired a small pension. There were no sentries, no indication that this was the headquarters from which a coup was about to be launched. Indeed, everyone was in bed. Röhm was woken by someone knocking at the door of his room. Hitler marched inside, gun in hand. 'Ernst,' he said, 'you are under arrest.' The astonished SA chief was told to dress. He continued to protest his innocence as Hitler rapped on another door. Inside, 37-year-old *Obergruppenführer* Edmund Heines was discovered in bed with another man: his young driver. Hitler exploded. Stamping and screaming at them, he demanded their immediate execution. The two lovers were dragged outside and shot.

Röhm and his surviving minions were thrown into jail in Munich, to be joined by other local SA

Below: The SS won a turf fight with the SA for control of the concentration camp system established after the Nazis came to power at the beginning of 1933. Under the brutal tutelage of Theodore Eicke, the camp guard organisation quickly showed the dark side of SS fanaticism. Here, Eicke addresses political detainees at the newly-established Dachau in December 1933.

leaders rounded up by Rudolf Hess. Hitler called Göring in Berlin and gave the codeword. Thus began *Die Nacht der Lange Messer*, 'The Night of the Long Knives'. Göring and Himmler organized the arrest of SA members in the capital. All were taken to the *Leibstandarte* barracks at Lichterfelde and shot by *Leibstandarte* firing squads in droves, many still protesting dumbly their loyalty to the Führer. Göring's death squads murdered former chancellor General von Schleicher and his new wife, shooting the couple down in front of their 14-year-old daughter. His associate General Bredow was gunned down too. The 73-year-old Gustav Ritter von Kahr, the man who had crushed the Beerhall Putsch nine years previously, was dragged from his home and beaten to death.

Also condemned to death was Franz von Papen, who had spoken out recently against the regime. The silver-tongued von Papen talked his way out of it, but his speechwriter was tortured and then shot. Gregor Strasser was shot in an adjacent cell. Another man who knew too much,

Father Bernhard Stempfle, was abducted and killed, and the truth of Hitler's relationship with his own niece Geli was buried with him.

Röhm sweated in his cell throughout the following day, hoping his Führer would save him. But at 6 p.m. on 1 July he was handed a newspaper announcing his arrest – and a revolver loaded with a single bullet. Röhm refused to commit suicide and was shot by *SS-Gruppenführer* Theodor Eicke, Inspector of concentration camps.

NIGHT OF THE LONG KNIVES

The phrase *Die Nacht der Lange Messer* has the kind of dramatic style characteristic of the fertile mind of propaganda chief Joseph Göbbels. Göbbels was a latecomer to what began as a conspiracy against Hitler's old comrades, and turned into a general settling of scores. Like most of his statements, it was an inversion of the truth. Most

Above: To the outside world, the pre-war SS presented an impressive image. In their smart black uniforms, they provided security at the great Nazi events of the 1930s, from the Harvest Festival at Bückeberg to the Nuremburg rallies. But while the General SS were doing their duty, the Armed-SS was being created as a military force under the personal control of the Führer.

of the killings took place during the day, and were carried out with pistols and sub-machine guns. The number of dead – estimates range from 80 to as many as 1000 – was tiny by comparison with Hitler's later crimes, but it set the stage for the complete subjugation of Germany. In the wake of this massacre, Hitler would declare himself literally above the law of the land. And all Germany cheered him for it.

Hitler would face other enemies within Germany over the next 10 years, but no longer was it elements within the Party that posed the most serious threat. After the massacre of the SA leaders, the NSDAP's political significance was diminished. Membership was no longer a means to power but was simply a route to personal advancement. In time, it became more an agent of control than a political party.

After the Night of the Long Knives, the SS grew rapidly. In the process it split into three main groups – the *Waffen*, or Armed SS; the *Totenkopfverbande*; and the *Allgemeine*, or 'General', SS.

The *Allgemeine-SS* initially took control of both the police and the *Sicherheitsdienst* (security service or SD). By the mid-1930s, the *Sicherheitsdienst* had informers all over Germany, with some 50,000 individuals reporting on anti-Nazi activi-

---

The second major step in the SS road to power, after beheading the SA, came about when Himmler took control of the German police.

---

ties. The SD played a central role in the genocidal campaigns of the *Einsatzgruppen* and in the administration of the Holocaust. It competed with the *Abwehr* – Military Intelligence – in intelligence work until July 1944, when Admiral Canaris, the *Abwehr*'s head, was arrested and the SD also took control of espionage abroad. Across occupied Europe, the SD co-ordinated operations against the resistance, working with the Gestapo.

For an organization of such formidable power, the SD had very humble origins. It was created in the summer of 1931 by the then 27-year-old Reinhard Heydrich. There would be another 18 months of frantic political action before Hitler became Chancellor, and the purpose of Heydrich's team – just three men to start with – was to spy on their fellow Nazis. At a meeting in the Munich Brown House, the Nazi headquarters, Heydrich claimed the NSDAP was riddled with spies and traitors. Heydrich was authorized to set up an intelligence desk in each SS district, reporting to him. He established the SD in a rented

apartment, which was filled steadily with index cards that made up an A–Z of Nazis, packed with salacious detail about their private lives, business dealings and political friendships.

However, it was only when Himmler took control of the state's security apparatus that the ordinary German's respect for the SS changed into distrust and fear. Originally a small party organization, the *Sicherheitsdienst* grew to encompass all secret police functions. Himmler had been appointed chief of the German police after Hitler's accession to power, and had worked through the 1930s to bring all security and law-enforcement organizations into the operational control of the SS. In 1939 the establishment of the Main State Security Office – the RSHA, or *Reichsicherheitshauptamt* – meant that he had succeeded. It was said that Heydrich had incriminating evidence on virtually every German citizen in his voluminous files. Gathered by a huge network of informers, the information fed to the SD allowed the Nazis to nip any opposition movements in the bud.

The *Allgemeine-SS* was also responsible for administering the rapidly growing SS economic empire, and took a leading role in investigating and promoting Himmler's racial theories. The *Allgemeine-SS* retained the characteristic black long after other SS branches had switched to grey or brown uniforms.

Himmler sought to increase his power by offering honorary membership in the *Allgemeine-SS* to people of influence. By attracting prominent industrialists, academics, landowners and former military officers, Himmler allayed some of the population's fear of the Nazis. In the early days, at least, the disciplined *Schutzstaffel* was seen as being more acceptable than other Nazi groups.

CONCENTRATION CAMP GUARDS

The most sinister SS group was the *Totenkopfverbande* – the Death's Head Guards. These brutal units were created in 1933 after the SS won a turf fight with the SA over who should be in control of the concentration camps. The first camps were being built almost as soon as the Nazis came to

Above: The Nazis were masters of spectacular public events. The SS always played prominent parts, as here at the 1936 *Parteitag* where they form up at the head of the massed torch-bearing ranks of the SA. The wall of searchlights framing the scene was created by a young architect named Albert Speer, whose creative skills were to take him to the heights of power.

power, and it was at Dachau that the *Totenkopf* guards evolved many of the systems and techniques by which the SS terrorized Europe.

They were very different from the ferociously disciplined members of the armed SS. Tasked with guarding and running Nazi concentration camps, the *Totenkopfverbande* took pride in

their total lack of military virtues. The guards took their cue from one of their early commanders, Theodor Eicke. A psychopathic killer even before being recruited by Himmler, he had been a failure as a soldier and a policeman. In his Death's Head Guards – recruited from unemployed malcontents, embittered farmhands and simple thugs – Eicke found willing pupils for his brand of brutality.

Control of the camps gave Himmler access to a large pool of slave labour, which proved useful in the growth of SS industrial power. Himmler wanted the SS to be economically independent, and from the start he encouraged SS business. SS control of the camps meant that it was primarily responsible for the implementation of the 'Final Solution', a task it performed with gusto. Following the crackpot racial theories that permeated the upper reaches of the SS, the genocidal murder of millions of Jews was seen simply as a necessary means of purifying the Aryan race.

BIRTH OF THE ARMED SS

The Armed SS came into existence at the same time as the *Schutzstaffel* was gaining friends and influence. Hitler's bodyguard, the *Leibstandarte*, was the first unit of what would become the

Below: The most obvious manifestation of the militarization of the SS was in the formation of Hitler's bodyguard, the *Leibstandarte-SS Adolf Hitler*. From its ranks came many of the key commanders of the *Waffen*-SS, including Joseph 'Sepp' Dietrich and Joachim 'Jochen' Peiper, seen here accompanying *Reichsführer-SS* Himmler during an inspection.

Waffen-SS. Both Hitler and Himmler, neither of whom trusted the German generals, saw it as a military force loyal personally to the Führer, which he could use as a counterweight to the Army. In public, Hitler stated that the most important role of the SS was the protection of the Führer, but in private it seems that he agreed with Himmler's view, which was that the SS existed to guarantee Germany's internal security, just as the *Wehrmacht* protected the state from external threats.

The Armed SS was the largest branch of the organization. It would eventually number some 39 divisions, and one million men of 15 nationalities passed through its ranks. Its premier formation, the *Leibstandarte Adolf Hitler*, provided guards of honour for visiting VIPs before the war. In the spring of the 1940, the organization was renamed the *Waffen-SS*, and during the war took part in 12 major campaigns, gaining a

reputation for tough fighting qualities and aggressive leadership.

Initially the Armed SS was made up from Hitler's bodyguard together with a number of *Politische Bereitschaften*, or Political Emergency Squads. These had been established in the early 1930s as strong-arm units designed to use violent measures against political opponents. On 16 March 1935, the day that Hitler abrogated the Treaty of Versailles and reintroduced conscription, the emergency squads were merged into a single unit, and were henceforth known as *SS-Verfügungstruppe*, or Special Duty Troops. The name was usually shortened to *SS-VT*.

The first Armed SS guard unit, though, was the *SS-Stabswache Berlin*, later renamed the *SS-Sonderkommando Zossen*, and later still the *Wachtbataillon Berlin*. Hitler announced its final name, the *Leibstandarte SS Adolf Hitler*, or SS Bodyguard Regiment Adolf Hitler, at the Nuremberg *Parteitag* in September 1933. Two months later, on the tenth anniversary of the Munich Putsch, the *Leibstandarte* paraded in front of the *Feldherrnhalle* in Munich and took an oath of personal allegiance to Adolf Hitler – an oath which was to make his bodyguard the Führer's personal Praetorian Guard, and which to some extent made them independent of the rest of the SS:

> I vow to you, Adolf Hitler, as Führer and Chancellor of the Reich, my loyalty and courage. I swear to you, and to those you have personally named in authority over me, obedience unto death. So help me God.

In its short but violent existence, between March 1933 and May 1945, the *Leibstandarte* grew from a bodyguard of 120 men protecting the Führer to an outsized armoured division more than 20,000 strong, equipped with the most modern weapons that German industry could produce.

'SEPP' DIETRICH

The man who did most to shape the character of *Leibstandarte* was its first commanding officer, Josef 'Sepp' Dietrich. In German, *dietrich* is slang for a skeleton key, so to honour their com-

mander the division adopted a shield with a key as its insignia.

Sepp Dietrich was born in Bavaria in 1892. A veteran of World War I, he joined the SA in 1923, just in time to take part in the Munich Putsch, for which he was dismissed from the police. After drifting from job to job, he became a full member of the Nazi Party in 1928. For a time he was Hitler's driver, which earned him the nickname *Chauffeureska* from his patron. Dietrich joined the expanding SS in 1930. In March 1933 he was given command of the *SS-Stabswache* Berlin.

Hitler once described Dietrich as being a mixture of cunning, ruthlessness and hardness – a word much used in National Socialist propaganda. He was certainly very tough, and instilled a unique fighting spirit into the Armed SS. He was popular with the men he commanded because he cared for their welfare. However, he was not as highly regarded by the professional Army officers with whom he served as the SS expanded.

In its early days, the main purpose of the *Leibstandarte* was ceremonial – standing like black statues outside the main buildings in Berlin or executing crisp drill movements as honour guards for visiting VIPs. It was responsible for security in an area about 5km (2 miles) square around Hitler's Bavarian retreat, the Berghof.

Ceremonial duties were only part of the story, however. The *Leibstandarte's* capacity for violent action was never far from the surface. In June 1934 Dietrich and his men – using weapons and transport supplied by the Army – were instrumental in destroying a major threat to Hitler's domination of the Nazi party in the infamous 'Blood Purge', the Night of the Long Knives.

When it was decided to set up a private Nazi army, the *Leibstandarte* provided the core of the new Armed SS. In December 1934 it was expanded to regimental size and began to move away from its political bodyguard function to a more conventional military role. As Hitler's personal armed force, the *Leibstandarte* played a leading role in the bloodless occupation of the Rhineland in March 1936, the Führer's first military move beyond the boundaries of the Reich.

Hitler told his reluctant Generals that 'If the army does not want to take the risk, a suitable spearhead force will be provided by the *Leibstandarte*.' In the event, the SS Company that advanced on Saarbrücken met only with cheering crowds, and not the French tanks that the Army feared.

Two years later, in March 1938, a battalion under Sepp Dietrich played a similar part in the invasion of Austria. General Guderian, commander of the XVI Corps welcomed the SS presence, primarily because the battalion was motorized and could keep up with his light Panzers, which were undergoing their first operational test. However, SS involvement in the *Anschluss* went much further than providing troops to support the Army.

NAZIS IN AUSTRIA

As in Germany, political life in Austria after World War I was polarized. The uncompromising slogans of left and right contributed greatly to the uncertainty following the dissolution of the Austro-Hungarian Empire. Extremists like the Austrian Nazis had their fire stolen in the early 1930s, when Austria drifted from democracy to authoritarian government, first under Engelbert Dolfüss and then Schuschnigg. Nevertheless, on 25 July 1934, a group of Austrian Nazis, backed and armed by the SS, seized the Viennese Chancellery and attempted to proclaim a government. Dollfüss, whom they had taken prisoner, was murdered. The rebels then appealed to Hitler for support, but the Führer could do nothing because the Fascist leader in Italy, Benito Mussolini, had sent heavy forces to the Brenner Pass to invade Austria in the event of a German intervention. However, with Hitler growing ever more confident at home and abroad, it was only a matter of time before the aims of Austria's Nazis were realized.

When German troops crossed the border on Saturday 12 March 1938, they were welcomed with flowers and Nazi flags. A *Leibstandarte* battalion raced towards Linz, to await their Führer. Hitler arrived later that day to a rapturous reception in his hometown. A similar ovation greeted him in Vienna, scene of his dismal young manhood. As his big black Mercedes-Benz travelled the country's roads, adoring onlookers knelt to scoop up bits of earth the cars tires had touched. He was escorted by SS men dressed in army field-grey, but retaining their *Totenkopf*-adorned black caps.

In Vienna a Nazi government, headed by Arthur Seyss-Inquart, was established, and collaborated with Hitler in proclaiming the Anschluss on 13 March. As for Schuschnigg, he was arrested by the Nazis and interned in a concentration camp, to be released only in May 1945.

By the time of the *Anschluss*, the Armed SS had grown dramatically. In addition to the 2600 men of the *Leibstandarte*, there were two *SS-VT Standarten*, or regiments, derived from the *Politische Bereitschaften*. The regiments were given the names *Deutschland* and *Germania*, and after the annexation of Austria a third *Standarte* was raised and given the name *Der Führer*. Like the *Leibstandarte*, the *SS-VT* units were trained and equipped as motorized infantry.

At this time, there was considerable confusion about the true status of the Armed SS, and the high command of the Wehrmacht was getting worried about the increasing size of a force that seemed to have been set up in opposition to the Army. On 17 August 1938, Hitler issued a directive in which he made it clear that the SS-VT was

'...a permanent armed force at my personal disposal. It is neither a part of the army nor is it part of the police. In emergencies, it is to be used for two purposes, which are:
1. In the event of an external emergency the SS-VT is to be available to the Commander-in-Chief of the Army within the structure of the armed forces. Operationally, it will then be subject to military law and military orders, but politically it will remain a branch of the NSDAP.
2. At home in cases of emergency and in accordance with my instructions, it will be under the direct control of the Reichsführer-SS.'

OCCUPATION OF THE SUDETENLAND

On 1 October 1938, the SS were again on the march, being used alongside the *Wehrmacht* as it

rolled into the Sudetenland, the western and northern border areas of Czechoslovakia. These had a German-speaking population of three million, but after World War I, the area of Bohemia had been awarded to Czechoslovakia according to the terms of the Treaty of Saint-Germain-en-Laye agreed between Austria and the Allies. The Nazis had long cast covetous eyes on the area's rich mineral resources and also its major munitions factories at Pilsen.

The indigenous Nazi movement, the *Sudeten Deutsche Partei* (SdP) created by Konrad Hen-

Above: Adolf Hitler returns in triumph to Vienna, the city in which he had struggled to make a career as an artist before World War I. The Armed SS had played its part in the Nazi annexation of Austria: the *Leibstandarte* operated as a motorized unit under the control of Guderian's Panzers as the German armed forces swept into the country in March 1938.

lein, had long pressed for the Sudetenland to be united with Germany. In 1933 the Czech government banned the 9500-strong SdP, but this served only to encourage it. In 1934 Henlein held his first mass meeting and gathered 20,000 people, and by 1938 membership had grown to 1.3 million.

Citing the will of the German-speaking people, Hitler prepared to invade, a piece of brinksmanship that brought the British, the French, the Italians and the Czechs to the conference table in Munich. Allied appeasement meant that the Czechs were forced to accede to the Führer's

Below: Men of the General or *Allgemeine-SS* men hold back cheering crowds in the Wilhelmstrasse as Hitler returns to Berlin following the Anschluss. Members of the General SS were distinct and separate from the Armed SS, but with the expansion of the organization during World War II many of the SS *Standarte*, or regiments, were absorbed into the *Waffen-SS.*

demands, and on 1 October, German troops, led by elements of the *Leibstandarte* and all three of the *SS-VT Standarte*, moved in.

By March, convinced that the British and French would not act, Hitler occupied the rest of Czechoslovakia. Renamed the Protectorate of Bohemia and Moravia, it was ostensibly ruled by diplomat Konstantin von Neurath. However, the real power lay in the brutal hands of *SS-Obergruppenführer* Karl Hermann Frank, who used the SS to round up and imprison any Czechs who seemed likely to resist German rule.

KRISTALLNACHT

Inside Germany, the SS had already shown its darker side. On the night of 9/10 November, only a month after SS troops had marched alongside

the Army into the Sudetenland, SS men were intimately involved when Nazi anti-Semitism exploded into the violence of *Kristallnacht*.

Organized by the SS and the Gestapo, and carried out by the SA and by ordinary Germans, this was a pogrom that took place the length and breadth of Germany. The ostensible cause of the rioting was the assassination in Paris of German diplomat Ernst vom Rath by Herschel Grynszpan, a German Jew. Grynszpan had intended to kill the German ambassador in protest against the deportation of his parents to Poland along with 10,000 Jews. The tragic irony was that his victim vom Rath was totally opposed to Nazism, and was under Gestapo surveillance.

When he received the news of the killing, Hitler was in Munich, at a meeting of Nazi leaders. Dr Josef Göbbels, after a brief private conversation with the Führer, stepped up to the podium to announce the assassination. The murder of vom Rath, he announced, had sparked anti-Jewish rioting in Kurhessen and Magdeburg-Anhalt. The Führer, he continued, had decreed that if the rioting spread, it was not to be discouraged.

The result was that the rioting spread from the Rhineland to East Prussia within hours. What began as scattered local disturbances by SA toughs were taken over and co-ordinated by the Gestapo and the SD. Stormtroopers and SS men were ordered to destroy Jewish synagogues, homes and businesses. The rioting snowballed, reaching a scale not seen in Germany since the Middle Ages. The next morning streets and pavements all over Germany were covered with broken glass, hence the name *Kristallnacht*, or 'Crystal Night'.

SS ANTISEMITISM

Heinrich Müller, the head of the Gestapo, instructed Gestapo offices to liaise with local police to ensure that Jewish properties were destroyed but not looted (an act that would have been criminal, after all). Müller was himself following orders that came from Reinhard Heydrich, who at 01:20 on 10 November sent a telegram from Munich to all police and SD head-

quarters 'regarding measures against the Jews tonight'. Acknowledging the weight of international opinion, he added 'foreigners, even if they are Jews, are not to be attacked'. Heydrich instructed the police not to interfere – except where incendiary attacks on synagogues threatened other buildings – and to arrest Jews.

The SS security service, the *Sicherheitsdienst* or SD, coordinated the anti-Jewish pogrom which swept through Germany in November 1938.

Once it became clear that the police had been ordered to stand aside, that the authorities were giving *carte blanche* to beat, rape or kill Jews, gangs of like-minded thugs felt free to attack Jewish homes, business and synagogues. Those Germans who did try to stop the violence were arrested; 22 were subsequently charged with interfering in lawful demonstrations. Over a million men and women roamed the streets that night, many drawn by the burning synagogues that proved an irresistible spectacle. By the morning of 10 November, 191 synagogues had been gutted by fire; 76 of them were subsequently demolished. Also destroyed by fire were 171 Jewish-occupied apartment houses, while some 7600 Jewish-owned businesses had been looted and destroyed.

The human cost is harder to quantify. There were 236 deaths, including 43 women and 13 children. About 600 people were seriously injured and thousands more suffered beatings of varying severity. The number of rapes, however was covered up: after all, Nazi ideology decreed that no Aryan should sully himself with Jewish flesh. Indeed, five men were expelled from the Nazi Party for violation of the Nuremberg racial laws – but not for the crime of rape, for which they received no punishment at all.

In the wake of *Kristallnacht*, the Nazis intensified their anti-Semitic policies, prohibiting Jews from entering theatres, cinemas, and even sitting on park benches. 'Gestapo' Müller ordered his

men to target wealthier Jews for arrest. More than 20,000 were taken into custody by the police and the SS, and released only on payment of heavy fines. Many, however, could not afford the fines and were instead despatched to Buchenwald concentration camp, where around 8000 lost their lives.

The spectacle of a medieval pogrom in a supposedly civilized European nation aroused an international outcry. In America, where anti-Semitic prejudice had kept some conservative elements in favour of Hitler, condemnation was universal. The German ambassador in Washington reported gloomily that the Hearst newspaper empire was now hostile, as was J Edgar Hoover and the FBI. The next week, President Roosevelt

Above: A company commander of the *Leibstandarte-SS Adolf Hitler* talks to Sudeten Germans in Wenceslas Square in Prague following the German occupation of Czechoslovakia in March 1939. The *Leibstandarte* and all three of the *SS-VT Standarte* had taken part in the initial occupation of the German-speaking Sudetenland six months previously.

lambasted the Nazi regime at a press conference. Hitler took little notice: his ignorance of the United States blinded him to the danger of poisoning relations with the world's most powerful industrial economy. Even Ribbentrop, described accurately by Molotov as 'a man of monumental density', realized the effect that *Kristallnacht* would have on public opinion in England.

Hershel Grynszpan was never brought to trial. Charged with murder, he was still languishing in jail when France surrendered in June 1940. The Gestapo deported him to Germany but abandoned plans for a public trial after Grynszpan claimed he had had a sexual relationship with vom Rath. No evidence of his final fate has come to light. He is presumed to have been executed later that year.

HONOUR AND LOYALTY

Although noted for their fighting spirit, SS men were ideological warriors above all else. Their motto was *Mein Ehre heisst Treue* – 'My Honour is Loyalty'. That loyalty was beyond question, and the prime recipient of their absolute belief was the man to whom they swore a personal oath of allegiance, Adolf Hitler. They were trained to be hard, often showing a willingness to commit atrocities. That said, their belief in the cause also meant that *Waffen-SS* units generally fought with suicidal courage and with a disdain for death.

Before the war, the SS was an exclusively volunteer force, and its physical entry standards were high – though the educational standards of

Below: Hitler and Himmler listen as Felix Steiner, commander of the *SS Standarte Deutschland*, describes the progress of a military exercise shortly before the invasion of Poland. Steiner, a World War I veteran who had been Paul Hausser's assistant in the early days of the Armed SS, was largely responsible for creating the organization's aggressive spirit in battle.

Above: SS men were among the first troops in action on 1 September 1939, as Germany invaded Poland. SS men in the free city of Danzig were especially active as they sought to take control of the Polish Corridor between East and West Prussia. Here, members of the *SS-Heimwehr Danzig* take cover behind an armoured car as the Nazis fight to take control of the post office.

the average SS man was surprisingly low, much lower than those of the conscripts in the regular army. Physical standards for the *Leibstandarte* were especially high: Dietrich wanted men not boys, and would not accept anybody younger than 23 years of age. The minimum height was 1.8m (5'11") and recruits had to be in perfect health: a single tooth filling was a ground for rejection. The prospective *Leibstandarte* member also had to prove pure Aryan heritage back at least three generations.

Young men volunteered for the Armed SS for a number of reasons, but the desire to join an elite force ranked high. Most SS men were from the country, used to living in relatively primitive conditions, and in combat they proved to be much more adept at fieldcraft than Army men, who were conscripted mostly from cities. Enlistment was for four years (though NCOs were expected to serve for 12 years and officers had to commit to 25 years).

Training was along regular army lines, though the SS emphasized fitness even more than the *Wehrmacht*, and sports played a greater part in the SS man's life. Aggression was highly prized, and exercises emphasized speed and ferocity of attack.

The man behind the SS training programme was *Brigadeführer* Paul Hausser. A former General Staff officer in the Army, Hausser had joined the *Stahlhelm*, a right-wing ex-serviceman's organization, and had risen swiftly through the ranks of the SA when the two groups merged. Transferring to the SS after the seizure of power, he was appointed commandant of the first SS officer cadet school.

SS indoctrination produced superbly aggressive fighting men – though many army officers thought them reckless rather than aggressive.

In October 1936, Hitler promoted Hausser to command the *SS-VT* Inspectorate. Hausser had two key assistants: Cassius Freiherr von Montigny, a former U-Boat commander who was a ferocious disciplinarian; and Felix Steiner, a veteran of World War I. Steiner, who was to go on to become one of the outstanding SS commanders of World War II, was a former Stormtroop officer in World War I. He modelled the attitude of the SS on that of the assault troops of 1918: lightly armed, fast moving, disciplined and extremely aggressive. In general he was successful, though all too often in battle, ruthlessness overcame discipline, and aggression often pushed too far towards recklessness. The same qualities that made the SS such excellent fighting men also meant that they were more prone to committing atrocities than any other military organization.

Basic training took place in the areas where each *Standarte* was based. In the early days this meant Hamburg for *Germania*, Munich for *Deutschland* and Berlin for the *Leibstandarte*. Military training for the *Totenkopf* units took place at Dachau. Unless they had previous Army experience, would-be officers had to serve for at least two years as an *SS-Mann* before applying for officer training. Officer cadets were trained at

two purpose-built facilities at Brunswick and Bad Tolz. While there were plenty of volunteers for the rank and file, few former combat officers joined the SS, and the lack of real command experience in battle was to result in very high casualty levels in the early campaigns of the war.

The training regime was straightforward. Recruits were roused at 06:00 for an hour's physical training. After breakfast, the SS men went on to the military part of their training: first, familiarization with weapons, moving on to marksmanship training once the instructors were sure that the recruit could strip, clean, and reassemble his rifle even when wearing a blindfold. Once the *SS-Mann* had learned how to shoot, he moved on to field manoeuvres, where the SS placed much greater emphasis on assault techniques than the regular army. Later in the course the trainees learned unarmed combat and bayonet/knife fighting. Sport played a major part in the physical conditioning of SS volunteers, boxing being particularly favoured by the instructors. Route marches and cross-country runs were also regular features, stamina being highly prized in the SS.

After lunch, the men cleaned their barracks, polished their boots and mended clothes before going out on further training sessions. The *Leibstandarte*, being parade soldiers, necessarily had more drill practice than other *SS-VT* units. In addition to the normal SS training, the *Leibstandarte* also had to master ceremonial drill – so much so that other units gave them the nickname 'asphalt warriors'.

Ideology played a major part in SS training. Every week the recruits had to attend several lectures, during which they were indoctrinated with the SS creed. Central to that creed was the idea that the SS was a brotherhood dedicated to creating a new Aryan world, the vanguard of the master race whose destiny it was to rule that world. They were also exposed to Heinrich Himmler's pseudo-Teutonic mythology, but there is some evidence to suggest that few of the fighting SS paid more than lip service to the *Reichsführer's* fantasies.

WAR IN THE WEST

Adolf Hitler had a passion for war. The Führer considered it to be the means by which men, nations and races are tempered to achieve greatness. 'War,' he declared, 'is for man what childbirth is for woman.' It was not only natural, an integral part of the human experience, it was a duty.

'As a boy,' he wrote in *Mein Kampf*, 'I longed for the chance to prove that my patriotism was not mere talk.' As a volunteer with the List Regiment of the Bavarian Army, he was given the chance to prove his thesis. He turned out to be a courageous soldier, his bravery under fire winning him an Iron Cross First Class in 1917. He treasured the medal to the end of his life; it was often the only decoration on his tunic. He also kept a front-line soldier's cynical regard for the generals, those bewhiskered, monocled aristocrats who had presided over four years of carnage on the Western Front.

Heinrich Himmler was an enthusiastic follower of his Führer, and espoused many of his beliefs, not least those about the ennobling experience of combat. Like Hitler, he felt an instinctive distrust for the professional Prussian aristocrats of the officer corps. However, unlike

Left: The SS had performed well in Poland. Now men like this anti-tank gun crew in Belgium were given the chance to prove they could handle a much larger campaign, as the War in the West exploded into life.

the senior members of the Nazi Party, he had no combat experience from the Great War. As a result, the sense of inferiority that he felt acted as a spur in his creation of the Armed SS. Nobody would be able to doubt the *Reichsführer*'s warrior credentials if he stood at the head of the Teutonic Knights, the warrior elite of the Aryan Third Reich. But for the rest of the world to accept his men as a true elite, they would have to be blooded in real combat. That blooding came quickly.

INVASION OF POLAND

In September 1939, Hitler unleashed his forces against Poland, leaving no more than a small covering force in the west to face the French Army of 70 divisions, which was supported by 3000 tanks and had, in theory, complete air supremacy – assuming the *Armée de l'Air* was indeed ordered to fight. Hitler, though, gambled

Above: Rotterdam burns after the Luftwaffe mounted a massed bombing raid on Holland's major port. The *Leibstandarte* and all three *SS-VT Standarten* had been driving towards the city before the attack – which was unnecessary because the Dutch had already agreed to stop fighting. Nine hundred were killed in the raid, and more than 80,000 were made homeless.

that the French would do nothing, and the gamble paid off. The huge French Army sat still, while a small British Expeditionary Force was shipped to northern France.

The Armed SS played its part in the war in Poland, proving that it had a fighting spirit to match anything that Prussian tradition had instilled into the regular army. The *Leibstandarte* in particular fought hard, serving as a motorized regiment attached to von Rundstedt's Army Group South. The *Leibstandarte* was part of the 10th

Army, under the command of General von Reichenau, a fanatical Nazi.

Casualties were high, however, as the attacking philosophy instilled into the SS by Felix Steiner meant that commanders often threw caution to the winds in order to achieve their aims. Army commanders were particularly critical of the leadership capabilities of junior SS officers. The darker side of SS fanaticism also showed itself when the *Leibstandarte* artillery company murdered 50 Jews in a synagogue. The Army wanted the perpetrators arrested and tried, but Himmler argued, successfully, that SS men should face SS discipline. The killers were never brought to justice.

The three *SS-VT Standarte* also fought in Poland, as individual regiments attached to

Wehrmacht formations. Himmler was dissatisfied with this arrangement, and eventually won a concession from the Army that the SS would serve in wholly SS formations, though he agreed to their remaining under ultimate *Wehrmacht* control when in combat. After the campaign in Poland the *SS-VT* units were withdrawn to East Prussia, where they were to be merged into a new *SS-VT* division.

Below: The first stage of the German campaign in the west saw Bock's Army Group B driving in to Holland, partly to secure the northern flank of the main offensive, but also to draw the Allies northward out of their prepared defensive positions. Once this had been done, Rundstedt's Army Group A would force through the Ardennes, racing for the Channel to cut off the Allies.

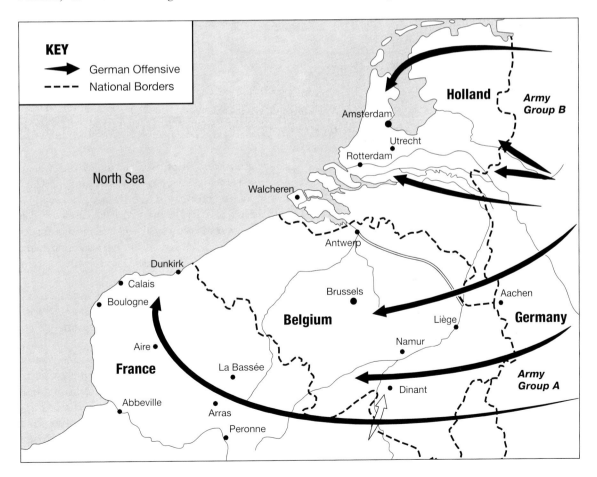

For some time, the *Reichsführer* had been pressing to expand the Armed SS. In this he was supported by the head of the *SS-Hauptamt*, *Obergruppenführer* Gottlob Berger, who was responsible for recruiting. The performance of the SS units in Poland meant that in October 1939 Hitler gave Himmler permission to raise two new divisions. However, Army opposition was intense, and since the Army had by law the right to conscript all German nationals, the SS struggled to find the manpower it needed. There were, however, two sources of recruits that were under Himmler's control.

THE *TOTENKOPF* DIVISION

Originally classed as part of the Armed SS, Theodore Eicke's *Totenkopfverbande*, the concentration camp guards, had in effect become a separate organization. Although the Death's Head units were an important part of the SS, they were very different from the ferociously disciplined members of the Armed SS. Tasked with guarding and running Nazi concentration camps, the *Totenkopf* men took pride in their total lack of military virtues.

The guards took their cue from their commander, Theodor Eicke. This failed soldier hated Army officers almost as much as he hated Marxists and Jews. In his Death's Head guards, he found pupils eager to learn his personal brand of brutality. In October 1939 Eicke was given permission to raise a field division from the Death's Head *Standarte*, five of which were then in existence at Dachau, Mauthausen, Sachsenhausen, Buchenwald and Frankenberg. On 1 November 1939, the *SS-Totenkopf* division was officially raised, and began training at Dachau. A number of *SS-VT* troops were transferred into the division to provide a core of well-trained, combat experienced troops. They were needed, since the new division was plagued with disciplinary problems. In December 1939 further reinforcements came from the former *Totenkopf Standarte Götze*, which had seen combat with the *SS-Heimwehr Danzig* in the early stages of the Polish campaign.

The *Totenkopf* Division had to struggle to acquire weapons from the army. Though the Generals had to some extent come to accept the *Leibstandarte* and *SS-VT* as real fighting men, they regarded the *Totenkopf's* former concentration

---

The success of the SS in Poland inspired Heinrich Himmler to expand the Armed SS by forming new divisions, against Army objections.

---

camp guards as paramilitaries or police at best, and as simple thugs lacking in any military virtue at worst. It took a direct order from Hitler before the Army could be persuaded to supply the new SS unit with artillery and anti-tank guns.

The other source of at least partially trained manpower under Himmler's control was the police. On June 17, 1936 the *Reichsführer-SS* had taken control of the unified German police service. Now he used that control to transfer 15,000 members of the uniformed *Ordnungspolizei* into a new division. Raised as the *Polizei* Division at Truppenübungsplatz Wandernas, near the Black Forest, the unit was not strictly part of the SS at this stage, though it was definitely under Himmler's control. Its members continued to use police insignia and rank badges until the division came fully under SS administration early in 1941.

Used as occupation troops in Poland, the *Polizei* Division began to receive more intensive military training in February 1940. However, the men were older, less fit and much less ideologically inspired than other SS units, and the division was only partially equipped, and with weapons that were obsolete or captured.

By the spring of 1940, the *Leibstandarte* and the three Armed SS divisions had been moved westwards, ready to take part in the next stage of the war. By now known unofficially as the *Waffen-SS*, Himmler's private army was far bigger and more capable than it had been only six months before. Even so, its three and a half divisions were a very small part of the *Wehrmacht*'s order of battle, which could call on 135 or more divisions deployed by the Army.

The *Waffen-SS* had been wearing field grey uniforms like the army since before the outbreak of war. However, unlike Army units, its soldiers were also equipped with a range of well-designed camouflaged smocks and helmet covers – which were later to become complete camouflage uniforms.

The *Leibstandarte* was the only armed SS unit to retain the black uniform (and the white summer uniform) beyond 1939. However, these were worn only for ceremonial duties, and in battle members wore standard *Waffen-SS* uniforms. In the field, however, Hitler's bodyguards were distinguished from other *Waffen-SS* formations by cuff titles worn on the left sleeve of uniform jackets. The *Leibstandarte* cuff title consisted of a strip of black ribbon with a woven silver border and a facsimile Hitler's signature. In day-to-day usage, the regiment's full title – *Leibstandarte SS Adolf Hitler* – was usually contracted to *LSSAH* or *LAH*.

WEHRMACHT MOVES WEST

The 'Phoney War' in the west lasted throughout the winter, ending only when German forces invaded Denmark and Norway, forestalling an Allied landing by a

matter of days. These territories thus secured, Hitler was able to send his armies west.

His plans did initially meet resistance. The German Army was determind to avoid the stalemate of 1914, when the Kaiser's armies had poured through Belgium and into France, marching hard for Paris. Marching was the operative word, in those early days of the internal combustion engine. The troops got close to the French

Right: At Hitler's command, the SS and particularly the *Leibstandarte* were used as the Wehrmacht's spearhead troops whenever possible. In Holland the *Leibstandarte* and the SS-VT Division headed the drives on Rotterdam and Amsterdam. Hitler wanted his personal Praetorian Guard to figure prominently in any German victories.

capital, but the Allies rallied in time to stop the Imperial Army short of its target. The battlelines now drawn, trenches spread from the North Sea to the Swiss frontier, and after four, long, bloody years Germany was beaten.

Little surprise, then, that the German Staff did not share Hitler's enthusiasm for another West Front. The German forces of 1940, though, had several advantages. True, the bulk of the Army was still made up of foot soldiers, supported by horse-drawn logistics, but these now marched in the wake of a fast-moving Panzer force, which was itself supported by its own mechanized

Below: Officers of the LSSAH negotiate with local Dutch commanders after it has become clear that there is little the Dutch Army can do to stop the German advance. However, the Dutch resisted in other areas, and that resistance caused a considerable number of delays to the German timetable. Even so, final surrender could not be delayed for long.

infantry and artillery. Overhead, the *Luftwaffe* deployed the most experienced fighter pilots in the world, which seized control of the skies for both the dreaded Stuka dive-bombers and the massive force of medium bombers that were to clear the way for the advancing *Wehrmacht*. Within a week, German forces broke the back of enemy resistance. Within a fortnight, the British were evacuating their soldiers, and France was at Hitler's mercy. Finally, the humiliation of 1918 was avenged – and it was the Führer's master strategy that had done it, not the General Staff.

The original Army plan for the invasion of Western Europe was based on Germany's opening attack in World War I, but was actually less ambitious than the Schlieffen Plan of 1914. The generals intended to occupy Belgium and France's northern industrial regions, but no further. They had no intention of repeating the ill-fated march on Paris attempted in 1914. They also believed that the ratio of forces and the power of modern defence admitted no other strategy; new objectives would require a further campaign in 1941.

ANGLO-FRENCH PLANS

On the other side of the line, both the British and French High Commands were also fighting the last war. The Allies expected just such an assault, violating the neutrality of Holland and Belgium, and as a result they planned to push the main field armies northwards to meet the Germans head-on.

Hitler had first ordered the attack in the autumn of 1939. However, it took time to switch the bulk of the German Army from the East to the West, and in any case the *Wehrmacht*'s divisions needed time to recuperate and refit after the Polish campaign. As the months passed, the Führer began to feel uneasy about the

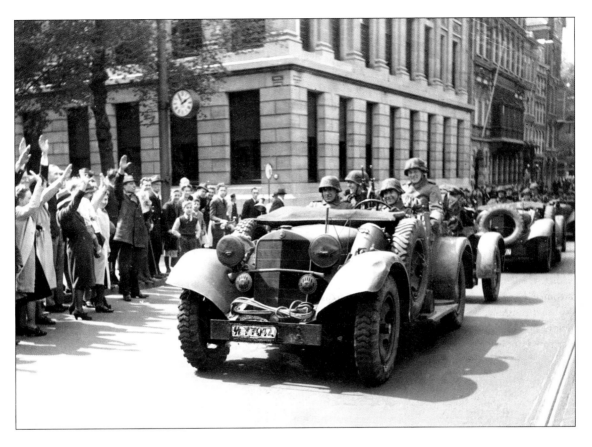

plans put forward by the General Staff. He had fought in Belgium, among the shattered villages around Ypres, where a million British and German soldiers were killed in 1917. He knew the ground, and how artillery bombardments reduced that ground to a quagmire. Futhermore, countless small rivers and streams offered endless obstruction to an invader. Surely, he argued it would be better to attack further south, perhaps through the forested hills of the Ardennes?

The generals looked down their noses at the idea, condemning it as one that came from an amateur strategist. At the very least, the hilly, heavily wooded forest of the Ardennes would slow the tanks on which their new style of warfare depended. At the worst, the Panzer divisions would be gridlocked in the few narrow roads that approached and passed through the region. And yet, by the time the postponed offensive was

Above: Although the Armed SS units had been diverted south after the drive on Amsterdam had been bogged down by a series of blown bridges, a contingent was sent to Amsterdam for the victory parade after the Dutch capitulation. Holland was to prove a fertile recruiting ground for the SS in years to come, though it would also offer serious resistance to the occupiers.

ready to roll in the spring, Hitler discovered that there were some officers who shared his vision.

General Erich von Manstein was chief-of-staff to General von Rundstedt, commander-in-chief of Army Group A in the West. Von Manstein had studied the Ardennes region and come to the same conclusion as the Führer. He discussed the idea with Germany's most influential tank expert, General Heinz Guderian. The two men argued for a radical strategy: to rush German Panzer divisions along the narrow forest tracks and out onto the gently rolling hills of northern France. Bursting into open country, these would then punch through the enemy before the defences were ready for them.

There was an obvious counter-argument: it would be difficult to bring enough artillery with these fast-moving formations. Indeed, other German commanders envisaged a pause while the guns were brought forward to allow a World War I-style battle to take place along the Meuse River. Guderian and his tank men, however, remained sanguine, confident they could storm the French defences. Moreover, the *Luftwaffe*'s bombers, especially its fearsome Ju-87 Stuka dive-bombers, would provide close support in place of artillery.

Hitler adopted the Manstein plan and changed the orders to his commanders in the West. Von Manstein would receive due credit in time, but the orthodox generals resented having a relatively junior officer's plan thrust upon them, and posted him to command an infantry corps in the rear.

One thing Hitler could not change was the odds. Although Germany enjoyed superiority in the air, with 4000 aircraft against 3000 Allied, the *Wehrmacht* had only 141 divisions with which to attack 144 Allied divisions. The Allies had some 3383 tanks compared to the German total of 2335 – and many of these were light tanks of limited fighting capacity.

ALLIED ARMIES MOVE NORTHWARD

When the German offensive began, the Allies followed their agreed strategy, pushing their best troops across the border to take up defensive positions along the Dyle River between Antwerp and Namur. However, the Ardennes front was not left unguarded: the French 9th Army assembled along the Meuse River around Sedan. (Here, in 1870, the French Emperor Napoleon III had been decisively beaten by the Germans, going into captivity with his surviving soldiers while revolution broke out in Paris.) The French Commander-in-Chief, 68-year old General Maurice Gamelin, expected German units to emerge from the Ardennes at some stage in the battle. But

since he did not anticipate anything more than a light, probing force, the 9th Army was stretched more thinly than other French armies.

THE ATTACK IS LAUNCHED

On 9 May 1940, all German forces received the codeword *Danzig*, which set in motion one of the most devastating advances in military history. Shortly after 02:30 on 10 May, 64 German troops crossed the Dutch frontier to spearhead Germany's invasion of the Low Countries. Three hours later, glider-borne troops dropped over the Belgian border to capture and demolish the huge fortifications at Eben-Emael. The imposing concrete-and-steel fortress fell to a crack unit of *Fallschirmjäger* (paratroops), who landed by glider right on the roof of the fortress.

At 05:45, the 30 infantry divisions of General Fedor von Bock's Army Group B moved out of the Rhineland, heading for the Low Countries. In the centre, the 44 divisions of General Gerd von Runstedt's Army Group A advanced towards the Ardennes, with the lead being taken by seven Panzer divisions under General Ewald von Kleist. Army Group C, commanded by General Wilhelm Ritter von Leeb, faced the strongest French defences in the south, its primary task being to pin down the 400,000 French troops manning the Maginot Line.

The bulk of the Armed SS was deployed in this operation. *Leibstandarte* was attached to the right flank of the 227th Infantry Division with von Bock's forces, which also controlled the *SS-VT* Division. The *Totenkopf* Division was held back as part of von Runstedt's reserves, while the *Polizei* Division was assigned to Army Group C, where it would remain largely inactive for more than a month. By now, the Armed SS was almost invariably known as the *Waffen-SS*, though the title would not become official until early in 1941.

In immediate opposition to the Germans was an Allied field force of 20 divisions, comprising five of the British Expeditionary Force (BEF), eight of the French First Army on their right, and seven of the French Seventh Army up on the coast around Dunkirk.

Above: Sepp Dietrich, one of Hitler's most loyal followers, commanded the *Leibstandarte*. Here he interrogates an officer captured on the Dutch/Belgian border after most of the SS units in the Netherlands were ordered to wheel southwards. They were directed towards the Allied armies advancing northwards through Belgium from the French border.

Bock, a fanatical career soldier of the old school, was one of the most senior generals in the German Army at the outbreak of war. Commanding the German forces that occupied Austria and Army Group North during the invasion of Poland, he then took command of Army Group B.

Once the attack was launched on the morning of 10 May, German forces stormed across Holland and Belgium, just as the Allies had expected. Although von Bock's Army Group was in part a feint, designed to draw attention from the real punch by Rundstedt's army group, it nevertheless had an important military function. Army Group B drew the Allied armies from the defensive posi-

tions they had prepared arduously in France during the bitterly cold winter of 1939–40. By the evening of 14 May, the Allied line was formed after British and French troops moved forward to join the Belgian Army. Roads choked by refugees fleeing ahead of Bock's advancing infantry hampered their movements. And once again the *Luftwaffe* was tasked with establishing air superiority and supporting ground operations. The *Blitzkrieg* on the Low Countries gave Allied troops their baptism of fire by Stuka dive-bombers and they soon came to associate the eerie nerve-shaking howl from the Stukas' sirens with death and destruction from above.

The Allied defensive line stretched from the Scheldt to Namur. Three divisions of the French Army held the northern sector. The 80km (50 miles) south-east to Louvain were held by 13 divisions of the Belgian Army. Between Louvain and Wavre the front was held by the BEF and from Wavre to Namur by six divisions of the French First Army.

Some of the battalion and brigade commanders were dismayed by the poor positions they now occupied, especially compared with those they had just left. Yet whatever worries these relatively junior officers may have had, they were nothing compared to those of divisional and higher commanders, who were beginning to receive news of alarming developments to the south.

MASSIVE FEINT

After sucking the Allied mobile forces northwards, Bock was tasked with securing Holland before moving southwards into Belgium and France, providing the anvil to the hammer of the Panzers heading for the French coast.

The first task for the Germans was to take key fortifications around which the Dutch and Bel-gian defences were based. The imposing concrete-and-steel fortress at Eben Emael had already fallen to a glider assault. Other paratroopers were needed to secure the bridges that made it possible to operate across Holland's vast canal network, before driving for the major Dutch cities near the coast.

The *Leibstandarte* was the first SS unit into action. The regiment crossed the Dutch border

Below: Members of the *SS Totenkopf* Division paddle a light infantry gun on a ferry across the Meuse. The *Totenkopf*, a newly formed division, had little part to play in the early stages of the push through the Ardennes, being held in reserve for von Rundstedt's Army Group A. Before long, however, Theodore Eicke's division would be in the thick of the action.

just after dawn on 9 May, capturing the bridge at de Poppe before the Dutch border guards could blow it up. Opening the barriers, the initial assault group waved through the regiment's vehicles and tanks – the *LSSAH* was the first SS unit to incorporate a Panzer company, a fact that made both the *SS-VT* and the *Totenkopf* somewhat jealous of the 'Asphalt Soldiers'.

From de Poppe, the *Leibstandarte* advanced at great speed towards its next objective – the bridge over the Ijssel at Bornebruck near Zwolle. Covering 80km (50 miles) in just six hours, the Regiment's reconnaissance units arrived at Bornebruck, only to find that the Dutch defenders had destroyed the crossing. Nevertheless, the SS troopers improvised rafts from barn doors and forced their way over, establishing a bridgehead on the other side. They seized the town of Hooen, and drove forwards another 80km (50 miles) towards Amsterdam. It was now that *Obersturmführer* Hugo Krass won the first Iron Cross of the western campaign, commanding a raid that penetrated about 96km (60 miles) into Dutch-held territory and capturing over 100 Dutch troops in the process. The Germans were moving so fast that the Dutch Army was caught completely by surprise – in one instance, the leading SS troops captured a Dutch infantry unit while it was having its lunch!

Meanwhile, the *SS-VT* division had been split. The *Der Führer* regiment fought alongside the *Leibstandarte* as the German 10th Corps pushed through the Grebbe defensive lines en route to Amsterdam. The other two regiments, *Deutschland* and *Germania*, were attached to the 9th Panzer Division. Operating further south, the units were tasked with pushing through heavily mined polders on the approach to Rotterdam. First combat came against Dutch units reinforced by French troops who had driven through Belgium, and the *Deutschland* regiment performed very well in heavy fighting around the port of Flushing.

The Dutch destruction of the key bridges across the Ijssel meant that the German push towards Amsterdam was slowed considerably.

Since Hitler did not want his 'show troops' to get bogged down, they were moved south on 13 May to join with the *SS-VT* regiments and the 9th Panzer Division in the drive on Rotterdam. German *Fallschirmjäger* had already captured the key Moerdijk bridges intact, and the way into

---

Armed SS units proved their ability to advance very rapidly during General von Bock's offensive against Holland and the Low Countries.

---

the city was open. On the morning of the 14th, the SS men accompanying the Panzers relieved the lightly armed paratroopers holding the Moerdijk bridge, having taken over 4000 prisoners during the advance.

Dutch resistance, though patchy, was holding up the German timetable. The German High Command issued an ultimatum, threatening to destroy Rotterdam by artillery and air bombardment unless Dutch resistance ceased. The Dutch, cut off from their British and French allies, had no choice but to comply. However, although the artillery bombardment was cancelled, the orders did not reach the *Luftwaffe*, and Rotterdam was bombed into ruin.

Immediately after the bombing, the *Leibstandarte* moved into the city. At one point, they saw a number of armed Dutch soldiers and opened fire. Unfortunately for the SS men, the Dutch soldiers had been part of a local surrender that was being accepted by *Luftwaffe* General Kurt Student. The *Leibstandarte* fire seriously wounded Student, the founder of the German parachute force, though he survived to lead the invasion of Crete a year later.

The Dutch campaign was all but over, and the German plan was, with a few minor exceptions, working as predicted. Bock's advance into Holland had drawn the Allied forces northwards. Rundstedt's armour had been unleashed through the Ardennes. Now it was time for the *Leibstandarte* and *SS-VT* along with the rest of Army Group B to strike south, rolling down on the

British and French forces while the Panzer forces cut them off from the south.

SS SIDELINED

The SS had no part to play in the opening stages of the drive through the Ardennes. The *Totenkopf* Division had been assigned to General Max Weichs' Second Army, though the Army commanders had felt that a newly formed, untried division would be of little use in the campaign, and in the early phases of planning had expected that the SS men would never play more than a reserve role. However, when Weichs inspected the division early in April, he was pleasantly surprised. Theodore Eicke, the divisional commander, had put the *Totenkopf* through an intensive period of training in February and March. By April he had begged, stolen and borrowed enough modern equipment to ensure that the division could match the best regular army mechanized unit. The hard training produced another effect on the thuggish former camp guards who made up much of the division: disciplinary cases, which had been running higher than in any other SS unit, were reduced considerably.

Weichs, a devout Catholic, had long been a critic of the agnostic, even pagan SS. However, his inspection showed that he could use the SS division in the front line, so he changed his plans. The division was to remain in reserve at Kassel for the first days of the campaign, but the aristocratic Army General would now not hesitate in calling it into action if necessary.

INITIAL SUCCESS

The push through the Ardennes started well. The 44 divisions of von Runstedt's Army Group A headed down the dirt roads through the forest in alarmingly dense columns, encountering little resistance from the Belgian troops in the area. Military traffic police have seldom had a more decisive impact on a campaign: thousands of vehicles kept to schedule and by the evening of 12 May, German spearheads had reached the river Meuse River. While the *Totenkopf* men awaited their call to action, Kleist's Panzer spearheads,

Above: Wilhelm Mohnke was one of the founding members of the *Leibstandarte SS*. During the French campaign in 1940, he took command of the regiment's *II Bataillon*. Troops under his command committed one of the first atrocities in the west, killing 80 British PoWs in cold blood. Although investigated after 1945, he was not tried for war crimes, for lack of evidence.

under the command of Heinz Guderian, were fighting through the key battle of the campaign, at Sedan.

The French infantry divisions around Sedan were mostly reserve formations, with only a handful of regular officers or NCOs. The *poilus* – ordinary soldiers – had received little more than basic training. There were five French cavalry divisions in the area, but units made up from light tanks, motorized light infantry and horse cavalry could not stop the German assault. Hammered by professional armoured forces, mostly combat veterans of the Polish campaign, the French formations disintegrated.

On 13 May, Guderian's infantry paddled across the Meuse in rubber dinghies while the French defences were pulverized by 300 twin-engine bombers and 200 Stukas. The dive-bombers attacked with particular accuracy, knocking out key French gun positions. The foot soldiers were across by 15:00. Combat engineers had a ferry operational in an hour, and by 16:30 a bridge was in place and the tanks could cross to the far bank.

By the morning of the next day, Guderian had two bridgeheads. Up at Dinant the 7th Panzer Division – under the command of Major-General Erwin Rommel – had formed yet another bridge-

Below: Troops from the *Totenkopf* Division move a rubber assault boat towards a small river during the French campaign. *Totenkopf* had mixed fortunes in France: badly shaken by a British counter-offensive at Arras, they fought hard in other places, but were also responsible for a number of atrocities, especially against French colonial troops.

head in the face of desperate, but sporadic, French defences.

Early on 15 May, the German flood burst into France. From each of the bridgeheads the Panzers roared out, preceded by swarms of screaming Stukas. These were protected from British and French fighter attack by roving Messerschmitts.

Refugees choked the roads. The fleeing civilians were harried by *Luftwaffe* fighters, bullied by frightened and demoralized soldiers of their own side, or forced into the ditches by strange, ominous, foreign vehicles manned by blond young giants who waved triumphantly at them. The Germans rarely harmed civilians deliberately but left in their wake an impression of total invincibility.

The Allies' strategy unravelled as the Panzer divisions fanned out, racing ahead of their infantry and threatening to cut off the British and French armies in Belgium. French counter-attacks came too little and too late: all the first-line troops had been committed to the northern flank.

That evening, German Panzers were reported only 12 miles from Laon. France's new Minister of National Defence, Daladier, ordered a counter-attack. General Gamelin replied that he had no reserves because the bulk of French strength was locked up in the outflanked Maginot Line. At the same time Gamelin announced that he could no longer take responsibility for the defence of Paris, and he issued orders for a general retreat of all French forces in Belgium.

On 16 May, the *Totenkopf* Division was ordered into Belgium. As a mechanized force, it

Below: On guard patrol through discarded helmets, webbing and equipment at Dunkirk, a German soldier paces through the detritus of a defeated army. Dunkirk was a miraculous escape for the British: defeated, forced ignominiously off the continent, they still man-aged to evacuate the bulk of Britain's army from under the noses of advancing panzers and SS troops.

could keep up with the fast-moving Panzers, so it was sent to join General Hermann Hoth's 15th Panzer Corps, consisting of the 5th and 7th Panzer Divisions. Struggling though roads crowded both with military traffic and fleeing refugees, Eicke's men made slow going. Reaching Le Cateau on 19 May, they entered combat against French tanks and Moroccan troops the next day. In a series of hard engagements, the *Totenkopf* lost 16 killed and 53 men were wounded. However, any respect due to the division's fighting abilities had to be tempered by the *Totenkopf*'s attitude to the French colonial troops they faced: refusing to take 'sub-human Negroes' prisoner, they preferred instead to shoot surrendering Moroccan soldiers.

'WE ARE BEATEN!'

In a devastating indication of French morale, the French premier, Paul Reynaud, woke British Prime Minister Winston Churchill with a telephone

call announcing: 'We have been defeated! We are beaten! We have lost the battle!' Churchill, though, refused to abandon hope. There were still considerable French forces to the south of

---

The Allies had no answer to German *Blitzkrieg* tactics, even though the theory behind them dated back to the last year of the Great War.

---

the German breakthrough, and even larger forces – including the BEF – to the north. Churchill hoped that between them, they could manoeuvre first to channel, and then contain, the German breakthrough. Then they could counter-attack from both sides, cutting the enemy spearheads off from their main sources of supply and support.

The despondent French leaders were reluctant to admit such a scheme was possible unless Churchill sent the entire RAF fighter force from Britain to France. Even then it seemed most likely that the German forces would be on the Channel coast or in Paris – or both – in a matter of days. In that case, the British and French armies to the north most probably faced early disintegration. Worse, unless a general armistice saved them, they also faced possible destruction.

Churchill was right in theory. The extended German formations were moving fast, but were stretched thin, making them vulnerable to a determined Allied counter-attack. On 21 May five British brigades attacked out of Arras, led by 74 Matilda infantry tanks. The Matildas, supported by 60 French tanks and two battalions of infantry smashed into the flanks of the *Totenkopf* and Rommel's 7th Panzer Division.

After a period of unbroken success, the British attack came as an unwelcome shock. An even more unwelcome shock was the fact that the standard German anti-tank guns were useless: the Matildas might have been slow and lightly armed, but their thick armour shrugged off German 3.7cm (1.46in) armour-piercing shells. Eicke ordered his artillery to engage the British over

open sights, but a number of inexperienced *Totenkopf* men fled in panic. The British were forced eventually back by a combination of Ju-87 Stuka attacks and by Rommel's use of the powerful 8.8cm (3.45in) Flak gun in the anti-tank role, but German confidence had been dented severely, and the poor performance of some *Totenkopf* units was an embarrassment to the SS.

By the evening of 23 May, Lord Gort, the British commander, was withdrawing the British brigades further north. Two days later it became evident to him that only a rapid retreat to the coast and evacuation to England would save even a quarter of his command.

Over the next five days the *Totenkopf* pressed forward towards the Lys Canal at Bethune, stubborn British opposition inflicting significant casualties in the process. General Höppner, the Corps commander, did not approve of the SS technique of all-out attack, which brought high casualties and led him to describe Theodore Eicke as a 'butcher, not a soldier'.

MASSACRE AT LE PARADIS

On 27 May, they reached the hamlet of Le Paradis, which was being held by 100 members of the Royal Norfolk Regiment. The British defended their positions with vigour, retreating through a farm complex to make a stand from a large cowshed. The British infantrymen fought off several assaults by *4.Kompanie* of the *Totenkopf*'s *Infanterie Regiment 2* before it became clear that further resistance would be futile.

After a white towel was waved, the Germans stopped shooting. Six or seven of the British edged nervously into the open, whereupon the SS men started firing, shouting at the British to lay down their weapons and come out with their hands up. After some delay, the British survivors emerged from the barn, their hands on their heads.

The *Totenkopf* men searched them roughly, then herded their prisoners down to a field alongside another barn. There the SS men, already smarting from earlier reverses at the hands of the British, decided to take revenge for the 17 killed and 52 wounded they had suffered that day. Two

Above: The reconnaissance detachment (*Aufklärungs abteilung*) of the *Totenkopf* Division probes forwards towards Béthune on 25 May 1940. Short of armoured vehicles as they were, the SS men have captured and pressed into service a Panhard armoured car. Note the prominent crosses designed to prevent the French-built vehicle being shot at by other German units.

machine guns opened up, mowing down the 100 British soldiers in cold blood. Astonishingly, Privates William O'Callaghan and Albert Pooley survived, though wounded. Later taken prisoner by German Army units, they became PoWs, living to tell the tale of the massacre.

It was *Oberstürmführer* Fritz Knochlein who gave the orders for the massacre. Formerly a member of the *Deutschland* regiment, he had transferred to the *Totenkopfverbande* before the war, where he commanded a guard company at Dachau. Several *Waffen-SS* officers did protest at the massacre, but Himmler refused to take action against Knochlein and his men. Knochlein survived the war, eventually being brought to trial by the British. He was hanged early in 1949.

Unfortunately, such protests as there were proved to be the exception rather than the rule.

And just a day later, the parade soldiers of the *Leibstandarte* demonstrated that it was not only the thugs and bullies of the *Totenkopf* who were capable of mass murder.

FRENCH PULL BACK

The French commander, General Gamelin, ordered a retreat – without telling the British. The scale of the catastrophe suddenly became apparent and the French Government prepared to evacuate Paris. Political will was also paralyzed in London, where Winston Churchill had only just replaced Neville Chamberlain as Prime Minister. It was thus left to Lord Gort VC, commander of the British Expeditionary Force, to choose between abandoning the French or hazarding most of Britain's tiny regular army in a last attempt to salvage the situation. But soon even that option was taken from his hands.

Following the defeat and capitulation of the Dutch, both the *Leibstandarte* and the *SS-VT* division were freed to move southwards through Belgium and into France. By 24 May, British and French troops in Flanders had been isolated into a triangular pocket around Dunkirk. An extensive canal network bound the southern end of the triangle, and the two SS formations had reached the Aa canal a little way upstream from the *Totenkopf*. The *Leibstandarte* was now attached to the 1st Panzer Division.

Meanwhile, Guderian's Panzers had reached the coast, and Gort chose to withdraw the BEF to Dunkirk. Trapped in an ever-decreasing pocket, it seemed only a matter of time before the British were annihilated. But at this point Hitler issued his famous 'Stop Order', commanding all troops on the ground to stand in place. This gave the British a breathing space in which a fleet of civilian boats helped the Royal Navy evacuate over

338,000 soldiers, including 100,000 Frenchmen, in nine days.

The reason for the 'Stop Order' is difficult to fathom. It may have been to allow Hermann Goering to make good his boast that the *Luft-waffe* could finish the job, or Hitler might simply have been worried about bogging down his Panzers in the network of canals in the region. In the event, the *Luftwaffe* met with stiff resistance from the Spitfires and Hurricanes of the RAF, and in spite of some successes, it was unable to impede the evacuation significantly.

Sepp Dietrich, never one to obey what he considered to be nonsensical orders, ordered an attack across the canal to take the town of Watten, and the nearby hillock called The Wattenbourg. After

Below: Leibstandarte troopers rest while doing some repairs and weapons maintenance during one of the all-too-brief periods in which the regiment was pulled out of the front line. After Dunkirk, the entire German army was re-arranged ready for the final assault on the remainder of France. The *Leibstandarte* would be assigned to operate with von Kleist's panzers.

an intensive artillery barrage, the *Leibstandarte's* 10th Infantry Company, commanded by a promising young officer named Joachim 'Jochen' Peiper forced a crossing. The *Leibstandarte* men managed to hold on in the face of serious Allied counter-attacks, and before long General Guderian was ordering a full-scale attack towards the town of Wormhout, to the south of Dunkirk.

Perhaps influenced by the success of the unordered attacks, Hitler rescinded his 'Stop Order' on the night of 26 May. *SS-VT* regiments *Germania* and *Der Führer*, which like the *Leibstandarte* had been halted along the line of the Aa, pushed on through the Nieppe forest, suffering numerous casualties in the face of stern defence by the British.

The third regiment, *Deutschland*, had been detached to the 3rd Panzer Division to attack the bridges at Merville. Forcing its way over the canal, the regiment's bridgehead came under attack from British tanks, and was saved only by the anti-tank company from the *Totenkopf* Division that had been following behind. The British continued to shell the SS position, causing

enough of a delay to allow the bulk of the defenders to pull back to Dunkirk, buying time for the huge cross-channel evacuation that was even then getting under way.

The *Leibstandarte* moved faster as it drove towards Dunkirk, but it too had to fight hard for ground. As the German spearhead, drove towards Wormhoudt, it came under attack from three directions, and had to fight through a strong British artillery barrage.

BELGIAN SURRENDER

On 28 May, King Leopold of the Belgians signed an armistice with the Germans and the Belgian Army ceased to exist. This created a large gap on the left of the British defensive positions. It was filled during the night by General Montgomery's 3rd Infantry Division. This operation undoubtedly saved the BEF from annihilation by the Germans.

On the same day, as the leading Panzer and SS units approached Wormhoudt, Sepp Dietrich moved forwards to coordinate a *Leibstandarte* attack. Passing through the village of Esquelbecq, his staff car strayed too far north and came under fire from members of the 5th Battalion, the Gloucestershire Regiment. Dietrich and his adjutant were forced to bail out of their burning car, and took refuge in a nearby ditch. *Leibstandarte* infantry and tank units made several attempts to rescue their commander, but all were fought off. The fierce opposition made the SS men think that they were fighting elite British troops. In fact, most of the opposition was coming from territorials, part-time volunteers.

As two infantry companies and a tank company fought to rescue their commander – or to retrieve his body – the rest of the regiment pushed on to attack Wormhoudt. The village was defended by 331 men of the Warwickshire Regiment, the Cheshire Regiment and the Royal Artillery. By 15:00, after several hours of house-to-house fighting, the *Leibstandarte* had fought its way into the town and by 17:00 had reached the town square. The British were eventually forced out of the town by SS fanaticism and large numbers of Stuka

attacks. They left behind 80 prisoners in the hands of the *Leibstandarte*'s 2nd Battalion.

The SS men were enraged by what they believed was the death of their commander, and were further incensed by the severe wounding of the commander of their own battalion, *SS-Sturmbannführer* Schutzek. At the orders of *SS-Hauptsturmführer* Wilhelm Mohnke, the prisoners were herded into a barn into which grenades were thrown. Any men who tried to break out of the barn were shot. Amazingly, 15 British soldiers survived to be taken into captivity by German Army units. Ironically, while the massacre was taking place, a patrol led by *SS-Oberscharführer* Oberschelp managed to reach and rescue Dietrich, who was still very much alive.

Wilhelm Mohnke would rise eventually to command the 1st SS Panzer Division *Leibstandarte* during the Battle of the Bulge. Neither he nor any of the troops under his command were ever called to account for the massacre. Indeed, as recently as 1988 a German prosecutor decided that there was insufficient evidence to bring the former SS commander to trial.

By dawn on 29 May, the *Leibstandarte* finally reached their objective, only to find that the fierce opposition they expected had melted away. Protected only by a small rearguard, the British had pulled back into Dunkirk.

FRANCE READY TO FALL

The miracle of Dunkirk kept Britain in the war. It still had an army, though most of its equipment had been left on the beach. However, there was no hope for France, who had replaced the ageing Gamelin with the even older General Weygand.

In spite of stiffening resistance in places, the Panzers turned west, moving with incredible speed to secure the Atlantic coast. Others sped south, completely bypassing the Maginot line and leaving more than 400,000 French troops bewildered and demoralized in their suddenly useless fortifications.

On 29 May the Führer told both von Rundstedt and von Bock that their next task would be to 'settle the French Army's account'. Britain could

Above: SS men search a French house for soldiers towards the end of the Battle of France. At this stage in the war, French resistance is limited. Later in the war, a knock on the door by such a group might signal a much more sinister purpose – an anti-Maquis raid, a hostage taking mission, the rounding-up of labourers for the *Reich*'s factories or of Jews for deportation.

wait – or better still, come to terms. Even before the Dunkirk evacuation was over, Bock had assigned his Eighteenth Army to clear up Belgium and press on westwards. The remainder of Army Group B was ordered to take position along the Somme, to the right of von Rundstedt's triumphant infantry and Panzer divisions closing up to the coast. By 4 June, the 10 Panzer divisions of both army groups had been redeployed into five armoured corps, three under von Bock, two under von Rundstedt.

After Dunkirk, the three SS units were withdrawn for a couple of days of rest, before being moved yet again to take part in the Battle of France. The *Leibstandarte* and the two SS divisions were attached to *Panzergruppe Kleist*, which was planning its advance towards the Marne.

The German offensive against the bulk of the French Army was launched on 5 June, with more than 140 divisions outnumbering French troops

in the field by more than two to one. The *Leibstandarte* was attached to the 3rd Panzer Division, which was to form a *Kampfgruppe*, or battle group, with three other divisions to prevent a counter-attack by French and any remaining British troops to the south.

On June 8, the *Leibstandarte* drove through Soissons towards the Aisne. At first, they encountered only token resistance, primarily from the French 11th Division. Piercing the defensive line set up by the new French Commander-in-Chief, General Maxim Weygand, *Panzergruppe Kleist* reached the Marne on 12 June, and the *Leibstandarte*'s 2nd Battalion crossed at St. Avige. Motoring on, the SS troops cut the main railway line to Paris. Taken briefly out of the line for a rest, the *LSSAH* was then attached to the 9th Panzer Division, which was driving southwest. It was while they were resting that they heard the news that Paris had fallen, on 14 May.

HEAVY FIGHTING WITH THE FRENCH

Meanwhile, the *SS-VT* Division had linked up with General von Reichenau's Sixth Army. Crossing the Somme, the division reached the Aire River on 7 June, where it encountered some of the fiercest French resistance of the campaign. Heavy French artillery fire stopped the *SS-VT*'s leading elements in its tracks, and support from Kleist's Panzers did little to change the situation. The German troops forced their way across the river, but the French Army fed more resources into the battle and resistance continued to stiffen.

For the next few hours the remaining French troops hurriedly assembled into 'hedgehogs' around what their commanders considered strategic nodal points to hold back the Germans. They destroyed the leading Panzer formations as they came within range, giving Panzer commanders pause for thought. 'The French are putting up strong opposition,' reported one. 'We are seeing a new French way of fighting.'

Eventually, Kleist was to lose several hundred Panzers destroyed or withdrawn for repair, and the *Panzergruppe* had to be pulled back. It was moved further east, where resistance was lighter and where other German divisions had been more successful. The badly mauled *SS-VT* retired over the Somme.

Next it was the turn of the *Totenkopf* Division, which like Eicke, its aggressive commander, was eager to get into the battle. While the *Leibstandarte* pushed southwest, the *Totenkopf* moved to the head of *Panzergruppe Kleist*, with *SS-VT* bringing up the rear.

The *Panzergruppe* now aimed southeast towards Dijon, its purpose being to cut off any French armies in Alsace. On 16 June, the French tried to break out but were pushed back by *SS-VT*. The division captured more than 30,000 prisoners as a wave of defeatism swept through the French Army.

The *Totenkopf* Division was also capturing prisoners – white prisoners, that is. The atrocities of May, when Eicke's men slaughtered surrendering colonial troops, were to be repeated on numerous occasions in June. However, the division encountered serious resistance only once, at Tarare near Lyon, where the reconnaissance battalion fought a vicious little action against African troops before taking several thousand prisoners.

The *Leibstandarte* continued the chase through central France, taking Clermont Ferrand on 20 June. They overran the large French airbase near the city, capturing hundreds of *Armée de l'Air* aircraft as well as a number of Polish Air Force machines that had fled westwards the year before.

Given another brief two-day rest, the *Leibstandarte* returned to action on 23 June in an assault towards St Etienne. Here they met almost the last of all French resistance: a scratch force of old heavy tanks, impervious to 37-mm anti-tank guns, which had to be driven off by heavy artillery. The *Leibstandarte* eventually entered the town on 24 June.

The *Leibstandarte* advanced from its positions on the Belgian border to Clermont-Ferrand in central France in little more than two weeks.

One further SS formation had by now entered the battle. The *Polizei* Division, which had been formed in October 1939 out of men drafted from the uniformed police, had spent the first month of the war in the West at Tübingen, where it formed part of the reserve for Army Group C. Early in June it was moved towards the Aisne front, where it saw its first major combat between the Aisne River and the Ardennes Canal. Less well equipped than the other SS divisions, the *Polizei* made hard work for itself against tough French opposition near Voncq. On 10 June it entered the Argonne forest, where it overcame a small but determined French rearguard only after bitter hand-to-hand fighting. Nevertheless, it began to cross the Aisne the same day, and saw little further fighting until it was returned to the reserve, where it would remain until recalled to active service on the Eastern Front a year later.

PÉTAIN SEEKS AN ARMISTICE

The fall of Paris on 14 June tore the heart out of the French government. On 16 June, Prime Minister Reynaud resigned, and was succeeded by Marshal Philippe Pétain. Almost the first act of the ancient hero of Verdun was to ask the Germans for armistice terms. By 20 June, German troops had reached the Swiss border in the east, Lyon and Grenoble in the south, and controlled the Biscay coast as far south as Royan.

Italian leader Benito Mussolini, who had declared war on both France and Britain 10 days earlier, urged his soldiers to cross the Franco-Italian frontier and capture Nice before the Germans got there. They were prevented by the events of the following day. At 15:30, a French delegation headed by General Huntziger was led into the very railway carriage at Compiègne in which the 1918 Armistice had been signed, where they were awaited by Hitler and his entourage. Little negotiation took place, for Hitler knew that he had

Below: One of the benefits of invading France is the chance to acquire some of the local produce. SS troops forming part of von Kleist's *Panzergruppe* examine vintage bottles of Champagne they have uncovered. For much of the next three years the chance of sampling such wines would make France a preferred posting for many a German soldier.

Above: Heinrich Himmler congratulates *Gruppen-führer* Paul Hausser and his operations officer, *Sturmbannführer* Werner Ostendorff, on a visit to the *SS-VT* Division in France after the successful conclusion of the battle for that country. Hausser was one of the most effective of SS combat leaders, rising to command an Army Group in 1945.

won, and any arguments that Huntziger put forward were referred back to Pétain, who tended to agree wholeheartedly with Hitler.

By 1900 on 22 June, the Armistice had been signed. The limits of German occupation were agreed – and the promise made that the French battle fleet would remain under French command. This satisfied Hitler, as one of his main fears had been that the powerful French battleships would join the Royal Navy.

On 25 June Marshal Pétain announced over French radio, 'Honour is saved! We must now turn our efforts to the future. A new order is beginning!' Seventeen days later the French Republic was abolished.

TRIUMPH IN THE WEST

In a few short weeks, Norway, Denmark, Holland, Belgium and France had surrendered to Germany. The *Leibstandarte*'s immediate task was to prepare for the triumphant victory parade through Paris. On 19 July, the Führer rewarded his outstanding SS commanders with the newly created Knight's Cross of the Iron Cross. He presented Sepp Dietrich and Paul Hausser with the awards at the Kroll Opera House in Berlin. A month later he awarded Knight's Crosses to *Oberführer* Georg Keppler and *Oberführer* Felix

Steiner for their leadership of the *Der Führer* and *Deutschland* regiments. Other more junior officers received awards for heroism. Many were to go on to senior rank in the *Waffen-SS.*

In August 1940, the oversize *Leibstandarte* Regiment was expanded to become a full brigade. Hitler sent a message to his bodyguard: 'It will be an honour for you, who bear my name, to lead every German attack.' And that next attack would be Operation Sea Lion, the invasion of the British Isles, whose people now stood alone to oppose Hitler as master of Europe.

Hitler made the decision to invade Britain on 5 June, just as the final German offensive in France was getting underway. Göring supported his Führer, assuring Hitler that the *Luftwaffe* could win control of the air. Naval commanders like Admiral Raeder were not so sanguine: the

German surface fleet was far too small to challenge the might of the Royal Navy, and the *Kriegsmarine* had serious doubts about Göring's claims that he could wipe the RAF from the skies.

Nevertheless, Hitler insisted on going ahead, and troops began to concentrate on possible embarkation points, with the SS preparing to take the lead in the assault. The navy began scouring the ports and river systems of Europe for suitable flat-bottomed craft and barges, and

Below: The SS-VT Division advanced the length of the country during the Battle of France, reaching the Spanish border on the Bay of Biscay by the time Pétain's government sued for a humiliating armistice. Although nominally a motorized division, some of its troops had to march the whole way on foot, relying on horse-drawn transport to carry their supplies.

Above: The *SS-VT* Division was posted to the Biscay coast where they were ordered to prepare for Operation Sea Lion, the planned invasion of Britain. Here, divisional artillerymen practise loading their equipment onto one of the flat-bottomed barges which were to be used to mount the invasion. The loss of the Battle of Britain led to the cancellation of Sea Lion.

troops began practising loading and unloading from such craft as could be collected.

In retrospect, the whole idea was wildly ambitious – Allied experience later in the war showed that it took years of meticulous planning to mount a successful amphibious invasion on such a scale. How serious Hitler was can be judged by the fact that he held the *Leibstandarte*, his favoured spearhead unit, in France for less than a month before moving them to Metz to refit.

In July 1940 both the *SS-VT* and the *Totenkopf* divisions were sent down to the Bordeaux area, where they formed part of the German occupation forces. The *SS-VT* was assigned to Operation Sea Lion, and began to practise amphibious operations in the Bay of Biscay. However, in October and November, following the cancellation of the assault on England, the division was moved to Vesol to continue its occupation duties.

EXPANSION

A fifth SS division was now created, based on the *Germania* Regiment. Originally called the *Germania* Division, it was later renamed SS-Division *Wiking*. Numbers were made up in part by other units detached from the *SS-VT*, but most of its strength was to be recruited from Germanic and Nordic volunteers. This was a sop to the army, who had been complaining about the SS poaching the best German recruits. *SS-Infanterie* Regiment 11, one of the *SS-Totenkopfstandarte*, replaced *Germania* in the *SS-VT* Division.

For a short time, the *SS-VT* was given the new title SS Division *Deutschland*, but this was too close to the name of the Army's showpiece *Grossdeutschland* Division, so in January 1941 it was again renamed, becoming the SS Division *Reich*. It would take its final and most famous name of *Das Reich* in Russia, early in 1942.

The *Totenkopf* were not expected to take part in Sea Lion, and in August members of the division were sent to help with the harvest in the region. In September 1940 the division was transferred to Biarritz as Germany occupied the whole of the Biscay coast.

For the next six months the *Totenkopf* remained in the southwest, but it was far from idle. At the outset of the French campaign, the *Totenkopf* had been 20,000 strong, at least 50 per cent larger than a comparable army infantry division. However, well over half that strength was made up from older reservists. Himmler and *Gruppenführer* Gottlob Berger wanted to replace the over-age men with new blood, but the Army's control over conscription meant that he could not draft selected men into the *Waffen-SS*. Himmler did have one further source of manpower, however. There were 17 independent *Totenkopf Standarten* all over Germany, totalling some 20,000 men. The *Reichsführer* simply transferred them into the *Waffen-SS*, which gave him an instant source of the manpower he needed.

By the summer of 1941 there were at least 40,000 men in *Totenkopf* formations, the younger men serving in the field division while the older men formed the independent regiments. These were used to provide occupation forces in occupied Europe, serving in Norway, Poland and France.

WAFFEN-SS

The successful campaign in the West had changed the status of what was now known officially as the *Waffen-SS*. Initial army dismissal of the SS as political animals, with none of the training, tradition or discipline of regular soldiers, had to be modified. Army commanders admitted grudgingly that the SS could fight with unmatched fanaticism and bravery, and some generals, including von Manstein and Reichenau, were unstinting in their praise.

However, others were less happy. The *Leibstandarte* and the *SS-VT* Division at least had professional leadership, men who had been trained in military realities by the General Staff or whose combat experience in Poland had tempered their aggression with caution. Theodore Eicke's *Totenkopf*, by contrast, was considered to be far too heedless of risk, taking heavy casualties unnecessarily. Even the SS regarded the *Polizei* Division as second-rate.

But Hitler was satisfied. His chosen troops had performed well in the only place that mattered – on the battlefield. They had shown the hardness

---

The German Army reluctantly conceded that the *Waffen-SS* had proved to be a first-class fighting organisation during the campaign in the West.

---

that was one of the qualities most desired by National Socialism. From henceforward, the Führer would ensure that the *Waffen-SS* received only the best of weaponry – its days of fighting the *Wehrmacht* bureaucracy were over.

But the hardness Hitler and Himmler sought to foster had also emerged in a much darker fashion. Eicke's *Totenkopf* Division, whose attitudes to combat had been formed in the brutal classrooms of the concentration camps, had proved its complete disregard for the rules of war. The massacre at Le Paradis demonstrated what prisoners who had hurt the pride of the SS could expect. The countless murders of French colonial troops revealed the evil behind Nazi racial theories. And the massacre of Jews by the *Leibstandarte* in the Polish campaign showed how fanatic fighting ability could readily be perverted into a capacity to murder. It was a foretaste of much worse to come.

STRIKING SOUTH: THE SS IN THE BALKANS

By October 1940, Hitler had been forced to accept that the invasion of England was not going to happen in the foreseeable future. Göring's *Luftwaffe* had been unable to defeat the Royal Air Force, and without air supremacy German troops could never force their way across the Channel in the face of the Royal Navy. Hitler was disappointed, of course, but the British had already been kicked off the Continent and he was confident that they would eventually come to terms.

In any case, operations against the British Isles had never been Hitler's primary concern. The humbling of the French had been personally satisfying, but now his attention was turning eastwards, to the vast expanses of the Soviet

Left: In France, the *Waffen*-SS had shown that they could fight. Now, as the *Wehrmacht* struck south into the Balkans and Greece, they would show that they were a fighting elite to match the best in the world.

Union. The Führer regarded these territories as *Lebensraum* (living space), vital if Germany was to sustain the Thousand Year Reich.

Before planning could fairly get under way, however, Hitler was distracted by the actions of his fellow Fascist dictator, Benito Mussolini. Although allied to Germany through the Pact of Steel, Mussolini had not hurried to get involved in Hitler's war. Italy had remained neutral during the Polish campaign, and Mussolini continued to sit on the fence all winter. Nor did his forces stir when Hitler attacked in the West. Only on 10 June, by which time the British Expeditionary Force had been taken off the beach at Dunkirk, did Italy declare war.

Italian forces attacked French positions in the Alps on 20 June. To Mussolini's embarrassment, his troops could make little progress against the thin French defensive line, and had hardly penetrated into French territory by the time of the armistice four days later. For this belated effort, Hitler awarded Italy a zone of occupation in Provence, much in the way that a master tosses a bone to a dog.

Mussolini was jealous of Hitler's military triumphs, especially since the early years of their relationship had seen the Italian leader being the dominant figure. It was he who could claim to be the founder of modern Fascism. The symbols and pageantry of his regime were deliberately designed to echo the glory of the Roman Empire. Some foreign observers found the bare-chested parading and tub-thumping rhetoric faintly ridiculous, but Adolf Hitler became a devoted admirer of the Italian dictator who styled himself *Il Duce* – The Leader. In conscious imitation, Hitler became *Der Führer*.

By the late 1930s, the roles had been reversed. It was Mussolini's turn to play the admirer. He allied Italy with Germany, the 'Pact of Steel'

Below: The *Leibstandarte* was the spearhead of Germany's invasion of Yugoslavia. Striking southwards into Greece, they commandeered a number of Greek fishing boats, outflanking the Allied defences as they attempted to cut off the retreating British forces at the Gulf of Corinth. The daring plan came very close to success.

welding his fate to Hitler's in the hope of sharing the loot in the event of a second European war. For all his bluster, Mussolini had actually played a cautious hand both domestically and internationally. His foreign adventures were restricted to targets unable to resist and with no friends to intervene. Libya, Abyssinia (Ethiopia) and Albania were incorporated into his latter-day Roman Empire, at the cost of censure from the League of Nations, but with no tangible opposition. It is possible that his support for the Nationalists during the Spanish Civil War (1936–9) had tempered his enthusiasm for war: neither his fascist volunteers nor the regular army divisions he dispatched there performed very well. When Hitler invaded Poland, triggering World War II, Italy stayed neutral.

MUSSOLINI GETS INTO TROUBLE

Depicted by cartoonists as the opportunist jackal to the Nazi lion, Mussolini launched an invasion of his own, deliberately not informing Hitler until his armies were on the move. On 28 October 1940, Italy invaded Greece. War aims can

Above: The SS Division *Reich*, formerly the *SS-VT* Division, was assigned to the northern flank of the invasion of Yugoslavia. Attacking out of Bulgaria, the division raced the army's elite *Grossdeutschland* regiment to be first into the capital, Belgrade. Much to the chagrin of the army, *SS-Hauptstürmführer* Fritz Klingenberg took the surrender of the city with 10 men.

only be surmised: the list of demands given to Athens amounted to military subjugation as a response to 'provocation' on the Albanian border. Unfortunately for Mussolini, the Greek Army was a very different prospect from the ill-equipped African tribesmen his armies had defeated earlier. Not only did the Italian invasion falter that winter, but a Greek counter-offensive in December drove the invaders back into Albania and back a further 80km (50 miles) for good measure.

Hitler had meanwhile already decided to intervene. Indeed, on 4 November he had issued orders for an invasion of Greece, were it to become necessary. Bulgaria was now bullied into allowing German forces free passage and German forces began to assemble opposite the 'Metaxas Line' defences that separated these ancient enemies. German engineers bridged the Danube on 28 February. However, an assault through Bulgaria meant restricting the invasion to a relatively narrow front, from which the Greeks were prepared to resist. More Nazi browbeating secured permission from the Yugoslav Government for German forces to cross their territory to attack Greece: on 25 March, Yugoslavia signed an alliance with Germany and Italy.

The SS were to play a leading part in the campaign that followed. In February 1941 the *Leibstandarte*, which by now had grown from an outsized regiment into a mechanized brigade, was moved from its winter quarters at Metz. It travelled by rail to Sofia in Bulgaria, to join General List's Twelfth Army. At the same time the SS Division *Reich* (formerly *SS-VT*) was ordered to cross Europe from its occupation positions in Southwest France to Romania, to join General Reinhardt's 41st Panzer Corps.

Hitler's plans were soon disrupted. Before Yugoslav Prime Minister Cvetkovic and Foreign Minister Cincar-Markovic returned from Vienna, where they had signed the Alliance with Germany, hardline Serb officers organized a military coup in the name of the young King Peter, overthrowing his uncle, the regent Prince Paul. British troops were already landing in Greece, led by commanders whose doubts were not communicated to the soldiers, the large Commonwealth contingent or Britain's new allies. Bolstered by two infantry divisions, one Australian and one New Zealand, plus an armoured brigade and RAF Hurricanes, the Greeks prepared to meet the German invasion.

To reach the Greeks, Hitler's *Wehrmacht* now had to conquer Yugoslavia, rather than march through it. The plan was to attack Yugoslavia from three directions. General Maximilian von Weichs' hurriedly-formed Second Army, supported by Italian and

Left: The attack on Greece had two main prongs: *Leibstandarte* and 9th Panzer Division would turn south along the Albanian border, while List's Twelfth Army would attack though Macedonia, piercing or bypassing the Greek defensive lines. A smaller force was to make a series of landings on the Greek islands off Asia Minor.

Hungarian armies, would strike south out of Austria and western Hungary. Their aim was to drive through Croatia before turning east towards Belgrade. General Ewald von Kleist's First Panzer Group would attack westwards from southern Romania and northern Bulgaria, directed towards Belgrade. The SS Division *Reich* would be one of his spearhead formations. Finally, part of Field Marshal Wilhelm List's powerful Twelfth Army would attack southwards out of southern Bulgaria into Greece, while the rest of the army, led by the *Leibstandarte* brigade, drove westwards into Kosovo and Macedonia.

INVASION OF YUGOSLAVIA

The German onslaught began on 7 April. Yugoslavia's small air force was swept from the skies and on 10 April the *Luftwaffe* carpet-bombed Belgrade, killing 17,000 people. The country splintered along its pre-1914 boundaries, just as it was to do 50 years later. Two Croatian divisions mutinied, a breakaway Croat republic welcoming the Germans of Weichs' Second Army into Zagreb while Belgrade burned.

Kleist's Panzers drove westwards, the SS Division *Reich* racing the Army's elite *Grossdeutschland* unit for their objectives. The SS men reached the town of Alibunar first, but heavy rains, marshy terrain and muddy roads slowed progress. On 12 April the Germans reached the Tamis River where it joined the Danube (known as the Dunay in Yugoslavia). The delays in reaching their objectives meant that *Reich* and *Grossdeutschland* were halted on the banks of the Danube while new plans were made.

SS-Hauptstürmführer Fritz Klingenberg, commander of *Reich's* motorcycle reconnaissance company, had other ideas, however. Using rubber boats to cross the Danube on 14 May, Klingenberg took 10 men into Belgrade, quickly realizing that the city was very lightly defended. Making contact with staff from the German Embassy, he used an Embassy telephone to contact the Mayor of Belgrade, claiming that he and his men were the forerunner of a powerful assault. He threatened the official with further massive aerial bombardments unless the city was surrendered – neglecting to reveal that his radios were not working and that his 10 men were all the assault force that there was.

The 11th Panzer Division arrived in the city a few hours later. Much to their chagrin, the Army troops found Belgrade already in the possession of one SS officer and 10 of his men. Klingenberg was awarded the Knight's Cross for his bold bluff. He was to go on to command an SS Panzergrenadier division before being killed in 1945.

Relations between the *SS-Reich* and their fellows were not good. Though no-one could deny that the SS men fought vigorously and with great dash, their arrogance rubbed most of the *Wehrmacht* up the wrong way. Relations were not helped by friction in the field: in one incident, a fast-moving Army convoy was about to overtake a column of SS vehicles. Wanting a clear

---

Rivalry between the SS and the Army was intense: so intense, in fact, that some disagreements between the two came close to open warfare.

---

road ahead, and not wanting to eat the Army's dust, the SS commander threatened to open fire if the Army vehicles did try to pass.

The fall of Belgrade signalled the end of the battle – or so the Germans thought when the Yugoslav Government requested an armistice on 14 April. However, two separate groups of Serbs scattered into their barren mountains. Members of one group loyal to the monarchy were known as *Chetniks*. The other fighters were the Communist partisans dominated by Josip Broz, the guerrilla leader known as 'Tito'. The stage was set for an internecine war that continues to the present day.

ATTACK IN THE SOUTH

Further to the south, Field Marshal List's 12th Army was also making rapid progress. On 6 April 1941 the *Leibstandarte* crossed the border as one of the lead elements in the invasion of

Above: The rugged terrain of the Balkans precluded the use of the mechanized forces necessary for *Blitzkrieg*. Fighting men had to fall back on some of the oldest methods of military transport, including mule trains, to get their equipment across the mountains. Physical fitness was at a premium, which may be why the SS performed so well in the campaign.

southern Yugoslavia. Along with the 9th Panzer Division, the *LSSAH* formed General Stumme's 40th Panzer Corps. The *Leibstandarte* and the panzers headed westwards, driving through Macedonia towards Skopje. This force overran southern Yugoslavia to reach the Greek frontier at Monastir on 10 April. Their aim there was to put a barrier in the way of any Greek armies coming to help the Yugoslavs. However, the Greeks were otherwise engaged, since the Germans had already reached Salonika.

Only one corps of List's Twelfth Army had entered Yugoslavia: the other two corps attacked through Macedonia, piercing or bypassing the Greek defensive lines. The XXX and XXXXVIII

Corps drove directly to the Aegean, punching clean through the Greek defences. A British armoured brigade deployed in the north was ordered to fall back along the eastern coast.

Meanwhile, *Leibstandarte* and the 9th Panzer Division were ordered to turn south along the Albanian border. A smaller German force presented a further threat to the Greek defenders, making a series of landings on the Greek islands along the Turkish coast.

The Italians launched a new offensive, timed to coincide with Hitler's intervention. Their forces in Albania had now been resupplied and re-equipped. The Greeks' logistic situation, however, had not improved. Outgunned, outnumbered, and with the Germans pouring into northern Greece, the Greek 'Army of Epirus' started to give way.

Hitler's Directive No. 27 called for the encirclement of the Allied forces by a breakthrough in the direction of Larissa, the key road junction south of Mount Olympus. All north-south traffic east of the Pindus Mountains came through this junction. With 5th Panzer Division charging down the roads and two German mountain divisions outflanking the valley defences, the plan nearly succeeded in trapping the British. The British 1st Armoured Brigade fought a running retreat to the Vale of Tempe, where a New Zealand and an Australian division checked the German advance on 15 April.

The *Leibstandarte* performed outstandingly well. On 11 April, it forced its way through the Monastir Gap after a close-quarter, hand-to-hand battle with the small force of Australian and New Zealand troops who had rushed north. By the 14th, the brigade had engaged the Greek 21st Division defending the Klissura Pass. The Greek resistance was extremely tough, and it was not until a young *Sturmbannführer* named Kurt Mayer infiltrated the *LSSAH* reconnaissance company along goat tracks and over the mountains that the tide turned.

For the next few days the *Leibstandarte* pressed forward, occasionally being held up by stubborn Greek rearguards. They moved down the west flank of the Pindus Mountains while the

British fell back to the ancient battlefield of Thermopylae on 18 April. That they avoided the fate of Leonidas and his Spartans largely thanks to Ultra, provided by British intelligence. A stream of deciphered German signals helped General Wilson keep the British withdrawal one step ahead of the German advance. This itself was no mean trick, given the mobility and tactical initiative of German commanders.

The Greek Government accepted defeat on 19 April, and the British announced that they would withdraw from the mainland, but continue to hold Crete. An orderly evacuation was imperilled on 26 April by a daring *coup de main*: German paratroops attacked the bridge over the Corinth Canal: By this time the *Leibstandarte* had reached the Gulf of Corinth, where Kurt Meyer commandeered two caiques (Greek fishing boats) and organized a ferry across the Gulf. Swinging eastwards, the SS men cleared the southern edge of the gulf before linking with the paratroopers of the 2nd *Fallschirmjäger* Regiment. However, the bridge was blown up and the British retreat continued into the Peloponnese, where a last stand at Kalamata ended with 7000 British and Commonwealth troops laying down their arms after exhausting their ammunition.

German troops entered Athens on 27 April. Elements of the 30th Corps embarked in commandeered local vessels to occupy the Ionian islands of Samothrace, Lesbos and Chios. It should be noted that the Dodecanese islands, including modern holiday favourites like Rhodes and Cos, had been ceded to Italy by the Ottoman Empire in 1912; they were not reunited with Greece until after the war.

The action at Corinth was the last *LSSAH* battle of the campaign. During the previous weeks

Right: After the *Leibstandarte* and *Reich* had been withdrawn from the Balkans, SS representation in the theatre fell to some very different formations. SS Division *Prinz Eugen*, formed in 1942, was far from being an elite fighting division. Nevertheless, its men acquired a fearsome reputation in the vicious, no-quarter war with the partisans.

the *Leibstandarte* won a reputation for being hard but fair – a reputation that was to change dramatically on the Eastern Front.

In keeping with the strict timetable for Operation Barbarossa, the invasion of the Soviet Union, the bulk of the German invasion force began withdrawing in May, leaving Greece to be held by a mixture of German reserve units and Italians. Following a victory parade in Athens, the *Leibstandarte* returned to barracks in Czechoslovakia, where it was to rest and recuperate in preparation for Barbarossa.

Fifty thousand British and Commonwealth soldiers lived to fight another day, plucked from fishing ports and open beaches by the Royal Navy. Many were dropped off on Crete, where something of a holiday atmosphere prevailed on

the scenic island, which was untouched by war. They assumed that their next stop would be Egypt and a temporary break from the war. What they did not know was that General Kurt Student, itching to get his *Fallschirmjäger* division into action, was studying maps intensively, calculating how many Ju-52s he would need to invade the island. The last battle for Greek territory would be fought on the Mediterranean island – and won by history's first great parachute assault.

BALKAN INFIGHTING

The Germans may have thought that they had conquered the Balkans, but nobody had told the locals. The withdrawal of the combat troops to the Russian front was the signal for the start of one of the most brutal, most bitterly fought partisan campaigns the world has ever seen.

Part of the problem was that it was several wars in one. The Croat puppet state was heavily involved, as were large numbers of German troops. At its most simplistic, the Italian, Germans and Fascist Croats were on one side, while Tito's Communist guerrillas were on the other. The Serbian royalist forces, the *Chetniks*, fought

---

The horrors committed in Yugoslavia during the war, where over a million people perished, were not forgotten.

---

either side, depending on circumstances. Croat fought Serb, Communist fought Royalist, and Muslim fought Christian. The Croatian *Ustase* killed hundreds of thousands of Serbs, Romanies and Jews, running a concentration system every bit as harsh as their German mentors.

Following the German victory, Yugoslavia was dismembered and divided among the victors – Germany, Italy, Hungary and Bulgaria. Croatia was granted independence as an axis puppet state under Ante Pavelic, the leader of the Fascist *Ustase*. As a reward for coming over to the Axis, Hitler ceded Bosnia-Herzegovina to Croatia.

Pavelic and the *Ustase* now launched a genocidal campaign against the Serbian and Jewish populations throughout Croatia and Bosnia-Herzegovina. *Ustase* thugs slaughtered tens of thousands of Serbs in Croatia, often forcing them into their Orthodox Churches and burning them alive. Other Serbs were given the choice of conversion to Roman Catholicism or death. Thousands of Jews, Serbs and Gypsies were exterminated in Croatian camps. At Jasenovac, the Croats showed that the German *Einsatzkommandos* had little to teach them about murder, with as many as 100,000 victims being shot or clubbed to death. In Bosnia, Muslims often assisted the *Ustase* killers.

As the war progressed, partisan bands retaliated against the perpetrators of these crimes with massacres of their own. The horrors committed in Yugoslavia during the war, where over a million people perished, were not forgotten. In Croatia, Bosnia or Kosovo, there were few Serbs who had not lost friends or relatives by the end of the war.

Nazi policy towards partisans was severe, as demonstrated by Hitler's 'Partisan Order', issued on 16 December 1942:

The enemy has thrown fanatic, Communist-trained fighters who will not stop at any act of violence…This fight has nothing to do with a soldier's chivalry or the Geneva Conventions. If this fight is not carried out with the most brutal means, our forces may not last long enough to master this plague. Troops are therefore authorized to take any measures without restriction even against women and children if these are needed for success. To show humanitarian consideration of any kind is a crime against the German Nation.

The *Waffen-SS* played a major role in the anti-partisan and pacification campaigns, which were conducted with a medieval level of brutality. This was in part caused by the frustration of not being able to identify the attackers from among the population, and in part by the sadism that exists in many people and to which war often gives licence.

Both sides committed atrocities. Local attacks by partisans were usually answered by German reprisals against the civilian population. These certainly had some effect: the *Chetniks* in particular virtually gave up attacks on German installations for fear of reprisals. This lack of activity did not sit well with the British, who had been clandestinely supplying the Serbian royalists with arms. British support was weakened further when it became clear that *Chetniks* had often fought alongside Germans and Italians against Tito's Communist partisans. However, the *Chetnik* commanders offered to change sides when it became clear that Tito would eventually take over the whole of Yugoslavia. London therefore had no choice but to switch its support to Tito, in spite of the Communist leader's known anti-British sentiments.

THE SS IN OCCUPIED YUGOSLAVIA

Yugoslavia was an important source of raw materials, and also of manpower for the *Wehrmacht*. Moreover, it was strategically located on the Adriatic. The growing partisan threat thus menaced German control of the area, and the war against it was given high priority.

The SS unit most closely associated with the partisan war in Yugoslavia was the *7th SS-*

Freiwilligen-Gebirgs-Division Prinz Eugen. The name commemorates Francois Eugene, Prince of Savoy. Born in Paris in 1663, Eugene fought against the Ottomans at the end of the seventeenth century. He won the campaigns that would secure Habsburg power in central Europe, laying the foundations of the Austro-Hungarian Empire. He also fought against France, as joint commander with the Duke of Marlborough. Prince Eugene captured Belgrade in 1718, making his name appropriate for a division that would spend most of its short life in the Balkans.

Raised on 1 March 1942, the *Prinz Eugen* Division was one of the first fruits of Himmler's recruitment drive among ethnic Germans, or *Volksdeutsche*. Most of the volunteers came from the Balkans, particularly from the Banat (eastern

Below: SS troops return fire after a partisan ambush in Dalmatia. The bitter, multi-sided struggle in the Balkans saw Christian fighting Muslim, Serb fighting Croat, Royalist fighting Communist, and all fighting alongside or against the Germans from day to day. Nobody held much regard for the rules of war: murder, atrocity, reprisal and revenge were commonplace.

Above: One of the more bizarre of Himmler's schemes was to raise a series of SS divisions from the Islamic inhabitants of Bosnia and Albania. The *Reichsführer* felt that Muslims would make good shock troops, even though they were a far cry from the Aryan ideal for which the SS had been created. Here, the Grand Mufti of Jerusalem inspects Bosnian SS volunteers.

Serbia/Croatia) and Siebenbürgen (western Romania/Hungary). The officer cadre was mostly made up from Austrians and Romanians – the Divisional commander, *SS-Obergruppenführer* Artur Phleps, was formerly a Romanian General.

Himmler was disappointed, however, when *Freiwilligen,* or volunteers, did not come forward in sufficient numbers to man the division, and pressure was brought to bear on the German-speaking communities of Croatia and southern Hungary to provide manpower. Conscription was introduced, and a number of other nationalities found their way into the ranks of the *Prinz Eugen* Division.

This was not a front-line formation. Manpower was not the problem: by the autumn of 1942, divisional strength had reached 21,000. However, much of the division's equipment was old, obsolete or captured, with the vehicle parks being filled with outdated French tanks

and Soviet armoured cars, together with an assortment of artillery pieces and small arms from all over Europe – a quartermaster's nightmare.

Employed almost exclusively against Tito's partisans, the *Prinz Eugen* Division quickly gained a reputation for atrocity. In October 1942 the division got its first taste of action on anti-partisan operations on the Serbian-Montenegro border. Then, in March 1943, a major anti-partisan campaign was launched around Slunj, Bihac, Petrovak and Zagreb. Operation White was supposed to seek out and destroy Tito's partisans, but although large numbers of bodies were counted, Tito escaped. Operation Black, launched in April 1943, saw the division again employed against the partisans in western Montenegro. Two months later, part of the division was sent to Sarajevo and later to Mostar.

Next, *Prinz Eugen* was sent to the Dalmatian Coast in September 1943, where its mission was to disarm the Italian soldiers who had been affected by Italy's armistice with the Allies. The 7th SS Division then went on to occupy the Brac, Hvar and Korcula Islands and the Peljesac Peninsula. In December 1943 the *Prinz Eugen* Division was once more in action against Tito's forces, and once more, the actions proved less than rewarding.

In January 1944 the 7th SS Division was transferred to the Split/Dubrovnik area for more training, at which time it was also reorganized. *Prinz Eugen* was transferred back to the Bosnia area in March 1944, and continued its part in anti-partisan operations.

In May 1944 the 7th SS joined forces with the *SS-Fallschirmjäger* Battalion 500, *Brandenburger* special forces units and troops from other German and Croatian formations. Code-named *Rosselsprung* (Knight's Move), the operation was intended to capture Tito once and for all. The 7th SS was assigned the task of securing the area around Drvar, securing key points such as railway stations, bridges and supply dumps. They achieved some success in preventing the escape of partisan groups, but there was no sign of Tito, who had in fact left the area the week before.

The continuing failure to catch the Communist leader proved costly. Over the previous three years, the Yugoslav Army of National Liberation (JANL) had grown from a few scattered bands of guerrillas into a major military force that claimed more than 200,000 men and women under arms – and tied down more than 30 German divisions.

Tito calculated that he would take control of most of the country when the Germans were finally forced to withdraw. However, the royalist *Chetniks* continued to dominate Serbia. In July 1944, Tito therefore asked Stalin to divert one of the Red Army's Fronts to capture Serbia.

WITHDRAWAL FROM THE BALKANS

In August the 7th SS Division encountered the Red Army for the first time, and suffered heavy casualties. Surviving units were part of the force that held open the Vardar Corridor, covering the Axis retreat from Macedonia. Holding the corridor open allowed 350,000 German troops of Army Group Lohr to escape encirclement by the Soviets. In 1945 the Division was engaged against both Soviet and partisan forces in Vukovar, and were in Slovenia when the war finally ended.

Below: SS troops execute men accused of being partisans somewhere in the Balkans. Whether they were partisans or not was incidental: mass executions served as warnings to others not to take up arms against the *Reich*. In the end such actions were self-defeating since they aroused only fury in the local population, and those who died were seen as martyrs.

After the war, apologists for the 7th SS Division claimed that it was no more guilty of atrocity than the partisans. That said, it had been one of the most effective of all German anti-partisan units, its use of terror against the civilian population making it feared by their opponents. Certainly, the Division's methods were usually indistinguishable from mass murder.

The *Prinz Eugen* Division was implicated in *Chetnik* massacres of Muslims at Sandjak in January and February 1943. In July the massacre of the Muslim inhabitants of the village of Kosutica followed the killing of a single *Waffen-SS* soldier. Such massacres were exceptional, however. Much more common were the kinds of reprisal carried out by an army unit at Novo Selo late in 1943. Four partisans were executed after the stabbing of a German NCO. To ram the message home, the local German commander then picked 10 men at random and hanged them, and followed up by razing 10 houses to the ground.

MUSLIM SS UNITS

Though the *Prinz Eugen* Division was the most prominent of the SS units engaged in the partisan war in the Balkans, it was not the only one. Himmler believed that Muslims would make good shock troops, and Bosnia seemed to offer the kind of raw material he needed. Bosnia's Muslim population, which had grown through centuries of Ottoman rule, had suffered terribly from several enemies. Both the *Ustase* from Croatia and the Serbian *Chetniks* attacked and Bosnian Muslims. Some Bosnians appealed to Hitler to make Bosnia a German protectorate, if only to protect them from their bloodthirsty countrymen. *Reichsführer-SS* Heinrich Himmler, always on the lookout for more *Waffen-SS* volunteers, immediately became interested in creating a Bosnian 'SS recruiting zone'.

On the face of it, Slavic Muslims from southern Europe did not fit too well into the Nazi racial ideology of the Master Race. However, as so often happened, Himmler came up with his own crackpot theories to make them acceptable. Bosnian Muslims, according to him, were culturally Turkish but racially Aryan; he also justified their service in the *Waffen-SS* by citing the precedent of Bosnian units being incorporated into the armies of the Austro-Hungarian Empire.

The *13th Waffen-Gebirgs Division Der SS 'Handschar' (Kroatisches Nr 1)* was raised in 1943 from Bosnian Muslims, for use in anti-partisan operations. The word *Handschar* is Turkish for 'scimitar', and the unit symbol included such a sword. Members of the division also wore a red fez. Imams were recruited to serve as chaplains, a pork-free diet was introduced, and the most strident of Nazi political indoctrination was replaced by lectures emphasizing Nazi-Muslim friendship.

The purpose of the division, in Himmler's words, was to, 'restore order to the ridiculous Croatian state', and most of its volunteers joined the division in order to protect their homes and families from *Ustase, Chetnik* and partisan attacks.

The *Handschar* Division had a poor record – some of its Muslim troops mutinied in training, killing several of their German cadre members. It is believed that partisans who had been infiltrated during the recruitment process, fomented the mutiny. The Croatian fascists were particularly hostile to its formation, since Bosnia had

---

Heinrich Himmler convinced himself that Balkan Muslims were neither Slavs nor Turks, but were really Aryans who had adopted Islam.

---

been handed to Croatia after the initial Balkan campaign, and they felt that the SS recruitment drive violated the sovereignty of their state. Nevertheless, Himmler persisted in his attempts to create an Islamic SS unit.

By March 1944, the division was engaged in anti-partisan sweeps around Srem. Initially performing effectively, but only when closely supervised by their German cadre, the Muslim troops became less motivated when the Germans started working with the *Chetniks*, whom they regarded as enemies. After the division was

Above: The problems the Germans faced in Yugoslavia were repeated further south in Macedonia and Greece. The terrain was similar, as were the tough guerrillas who formed the main opposition to the occupying forces. German anti-guerrilla operations had to be fought on partisan terms, by men on foot and mule-back through the harshest of conditions.

posted to Croatia, which was also seen as a natural enemy of all Bosnians, thousands of the division's troops deserted to the partisans. The division was disbanded in November 1944, the *Volksdeutsche* members forming a *kampfgruppe* (battle group) for combat in Hungary.

The *21st Waffen-Gebirgs Division SS Skanderbeg* was authorized in April 1944 and was made up of ethnic Albanians from Kosovo who were mostly of the Muslim faith. The officer cadre came from the *Prinz Eugen* Division, while one largely Albanian regiment was transferred from the *Handschar* Division.

Never an effective unit, it was hampered in its primary security role by the fact that many of its Muslim troops were more interested in settling scores with Serbs than in fighting for Hitler and the *Reich*. Deployed in September 1944 with only 6500 men, it was of brigade rather than division size. Desertions cut rapidly into that number: within a month the 86 officers and 467 NCOs were commanding only 899 men, about half of whom were Albanian.

The high desertion rate resulted in the unit being disbanded and reformed with the German cadre, forming *Kampfgruppe Skanderbeg*, which joined up with the 14th Regiment of the *7th SS Prinz Eugen* in Yugoslavia. This battle group was

in action between December 1944 and January 1945 around Zwornik, Bjellina and Brcko. Only a handful of men survived to be transferred to the 32nd SS Panzergrenadier Division *30 Januar*, a scratch division created in the last six months of the war from shattered units and personnel from recruiting depots and SS training schools.

The *22nd SS-Freiwilligen-Kavallerie-Division Maria Theresa* was raised from two regiments of Hungarian *Volksdeutsche* and *SS-Kavallerie Regiment 17* (formerly *SS-Reiter Regiment 3*) in Hungary during the spring of 1944. Intended for anti-partisan operations in Yugoslavia, the unit was overtaken by events. In October 1944 the division participated in the German overthrow of the Hungarian dictator, Admiral Horthy. Most of the division was annihilated in the battle of Budapest in February 1945.

A second Croatian division, the *23rd Waffen-SS Gebirgs Division Kama (kroatisches nr.2)*, existed from June to October 1944. Raised in Croatia from German officers, *Volksdeutsche* and Bosnian Muslims, the division was never fully formed and trained before it was disbanded and its members transferred to other SS units.

The *24th Waffen-Gebirgs (Karstjäger) Division der SS* was a small unit of mountain troops, formed to fight Italian and Yugoslavian partisans in the mountainous Austrian-Slovakian-Italian border regions. Many of the 24th SS recruits were from south Tyrol or were Yugoslavian *Volksdeutsche*. Its main distinction was that its expansion was overseen by Odilio Globocnik, Higher SS & Police Leader Adriatic Coast and one of the key administrators of the Final Solution in Eastern Europe. By this stage in the war, 6000 men qualified a unit as a *Waffen-SS* division, compared to the 20,000 men or more who made up the SS divisions of 1941.

PARTISANS IN GREECE

The Germans also faced a partisan problem in Greece. Like Yugoslavia, Greece was a rugged, mountainous land, occupied by very tough people with a tradition of fighting against oppressors. There were other similarities: Greek partisans, like their comrades in Yugoslavia, spent as much time fighting each other as they did the Germans. Nevertheless, large-scale Greek resistance managed to tie down equally large numbers of German troops.

Following the Greek surrender in 1941, King George II and Prime Minister Emmanouel Tsouderos established a Greek Government-in-Exile in London, moving to Cairo in 1943. The country they had left was divided into three zones: the Italians occupied Epirus, the Ionian islands, central and southern Greece from the Platona line southward, and Athens; the Germans held central Macedonia, and a strip of the land at the eastern edge of Greek Thrace; and the Bulgarians occupied the rest of Thrace. George Tsolakoglu was made prime minister in a puppet government. Following the fall of the Italian regime in September 1943, the Germans took full control of the Italian zone.

Above: Partisans in the Balkans were more thoroughly organised than resistance fighters anywhere else in Europe. By the last two years of the war, they were tying down more than 30 German divisions who might have been used more profitably elsewhere. Nowhere in the Balkans was safe: German soldiers had to expect partisan attacks any where at any time.

Several resistance organizations were founded. The Greek Communist party formed the *Ethnikon Apeletherotikon Metopon* (National Liberation Front; EAM) in September 1941. Its military arm was the *Ellenikos Laikos Apelethorotikos Stratos* (Popular Greek Liberation Army; ELAS), which was created in December 1941.

From the summer of 1942, guerrilla bands became active in the mountains. Athanasios Klaras, known as Aris Velouchiotis, led the most important of these. The main non-Communist resistance movement was the *Ellenikos Dimokratikos Ethnikos Stratos* (National Republican Greek League; EDES), led by General Napoleon Zervas, which formed in the early summer of 1942.

Greek resistance brought brutal retaliation from the Germans. In October 1941 alone, 488 civilians were shot as suspected guerrillas, while nearly 200 citizens were imprisoned in Salonika as hostages against partisan attacks. German units that had spent time on the Eastern Front were particularly prone to atrocity: in August 1943, troops from the German 1st Mountain Division entered the village of Komeno after a partisan attack and murdered all 317 residents in reprisal. The victims included 74 children under the age of ten.

In a 1985 interview quoted by historian Colin Heaton, Balkan campaign veteran Hans Hossfelder explained:

Those of us who fought in Greece in 1941 simply would not have credited killing innocents simply because we had been given orders. That was not a soldier's job. It was different in Russia: we had been brainwashed into believing that they were a sub-human culture, little more than animals. Now, when those troops returned from Russia and the brutal anti-partisan war in Yugoslavia, it was a different matter. Men had seen and done so much killing, it almost seemed to be part of the job.

Although the *Waffen-SS* played a major part in the conquest of Greece, it had little to do with the occupation forces for the first two years. However, in 1943 the *4th SS Polizei Division* arrived in the theatre, tasked with anti-partisan operations.

The *Polizei* Division had performed indifferently in France and on the Eastern Front. In April 1943 it was withdrawn to Poland, where it was used for security while being upgraded into a *Panzergrenadier* division.

In March 1944, the *SS-Polizei Division* became part of the Salonika-Aegean Administrative Area, alongside the Bulgarian 7th Infantry

Division and under the German 91st Army Corps. It continued operations against ELAS guerillas, and committed a number of atrocities at Larissa in response to a partisan convoy ambush at Klissura.

On 10 June 1944, men of the *SS-Panzergrenadier Regiment 7* massacred as many as 300 Greek civilians in the village of Distomo. According to a member of the Army's *Geheime Feldpolizei*, the *Polizei* troops walked through the village without incident, but were later ambushed by Greek guerrillas outside it. The guerrillas escaped, and the SS troops actually doubled back into the village and began a vicious 'atonement action'. This included rape and looting as well as shooting civilians.

Ten days later a Red Cross delegation inspected the town, finding corpses hanging from every available tree.

Right: From August 1943, the SS Division *Polizei* was on anti-partisan duty in Serbia. In October 1943 the division was attached to the XXII Army Corps for Operation Panther, a large anti-partisan sweep from the Yugoslav border towards Larissa. Three months later the division was posted to Salonika, where it would continue to be used on anti-partisan operations.

EXPANSION AND RECRUITMENT

During the course of World War II, the *Waffen-SS* grew from an elite force of four regiments composed solely of Germans meeting Heinrich Himmler's exacting physical and racial standards, to a polyglot force of 900,000 men in 39 divisions, with over half of its troops being either foreign volunteers or conscripts. Even so, at its peak the *Waffen-SS* represented only one-tenth of the strength of the *Wehrmacht* – although it provided a quarter of German Panzer strength.

Its explosive wartime growth reflected *Reichsführer-SS* Heinrich Himmler's desire to create an instrument of political power that would safeguard the Nazi revolution inside Germany, and also provide a counterweight to the influence of the Army. Although a number of former SS officers claimed after the war that the *Waffen-SS* was no more than a fighting force, in truth the organization was never completely free of its political origins. As late as 1943, the preface to an SS panzer training manual emphasized that the SS

Left: The *Waffen-SS* evolved dramatically during the war. Formerly the 'Aryan' standard bearer of the new Germanic order in Europe, it became a kind of Foreign Legion manned by volunteers from over 20 countries.

ARRUOLATEVI NELLA LEGIONE Italia
SS ITALIANA
si riscatta solo con
le armi in pugn

Left: A recruiting poster calling for Italian volunteers for the SS. With the overthrow of Mussolini and the establishment of a puppet state in Northern Italy in 1943, more and more Fascist volunteers elected to serve under the Swastika. By 1945, more than 20,000 Italians had become members of the SS, many serving with the 29th *Waffen-Grenadier Division der SS* in anti-partisan operations.

(*Oberkommando des Wehrmacht*, or Military High Command) laid down the proportion of men to be conscripted to each arm or service. All men of recruitable age were registered with the local *Wehrbezirkskommando* – WBK, or Military District Headquarters. No volunteer could join a military unit until he had been released by his local WBK, and the Army made sure that as few men as possible were released to join the SS.

Conditions for the SS improved slightly with the outbreak of war. In spite of the rigorous selection process, German volunteers were plentiful. Many were attracted to Himmler's romantic dream of a race of blue-eyed, blond heroes, an elite formed according to 'laws of selection' based on criteria of physiognomy, mental and physical tests, character and spirit.

'fulfils a requirement to provide an unflinching force at the disposal of the leadership of the *Reich* in any situation. This includes the maintenance of order at home by the use of any and all methods.'

SHORTAGE OF MANPOWER

To provide the Nazi leadership with a security force, the SS needed to be much bigger than it had been before the war. However, growth did not come easily. The main stumbling block was the Army. Before the war, the General Staff had blocked SS acquisition of artillery, and had forbidden the formation of an SS field division. Above all, the Army controlled the number of men the SS could recruit. Each year, OKW

The SS also played on its status as an elite force by using its Nazi connections to recruit the cream of the *Hitlerjugend* (Hitler Youth) and the *Reichsarbeitsdienst* (RAD, or Reich Labour Service) before they could be snatched up by the *Wehrmacht*.

Early public approval of the *Waffen-SS*, however, began to diminish, and the Armed SS began to acquire some of the sinister reputation of other branches of the organization. Heinz Höhne, in his seminal work *The Order of the Death's Head*, quoted a *Sicherheitsdienst* (SS Security Service) report, written in March of 1942:

...it may be stated that by its achievements the Waffen-SS *has won its place in the popular esteem. Particular reference is made to the good comradeship and excellent relations between officers, NCOs and men...Unfortunately voices are also to be heard saying that the* Waffen-SS *possesses no trained officers and that therefore SS men are 'recklessly sacrificed'...Critical voices are to be heard saying that the* Waffen-SS *is a sort of military watchdog. SS men are trained to be brutal and ruthless, apparently so that they can be used against other German formations if necessary...The* Waffen-SS *is a most ruthless force.*

Such public discomfort did not, however, thwart Himmler's plans. Indeed, they received a major boost when an energetic Swabian *SS-Brigadeführer* named Gottlob Berger was given responsibility for SS recruitment. Blocked by the Army, Berger suggested to Himmler that he should make use of his control of the Police and the Concentration camp guards to form two new formations, the *Totenkopf* and *Polizei* Divisions. As the SS expanded, these were eventually to become became the 3rd SS Panzer Division *Totenkopf* and the 4th SS Panzergrenadier Division *SS-Polizei*.

Continually looking for fresh sources of manpower that the Army could not block, Berger now began looking outside Germany's borders for troops. After May 1940 and *Sieg im Westen*, (Victory in the West), the SS began an active program to recruit suitably 'Nordic' or 'Germanic' volunteers from Northern and Western Europe to join a number of *Waffen-SS Freiwillige* (volunteer) legions. This effort intensified after June 1941, as the SS exhorted volunteers to join the campaign in the Soviet Union.

At first, Nazi racial doctrine determined the acceptance level of volunteers. Flemish volunteers – Dutch-speaking Belgians – were considered Aryan, and could volunteer for the *Waffen-SS*. Yet Walloons – French-speaking Belgian – were not considered racially suitable, and any Walloon volunteers for the great anti-Bolshevik crusade could only join a volunteer legion in the German Army.

As the war progressed and manpower grew scarcer to find, the SS lowered its racial standards.

NORDIC VOLUNTEERS

However, this lay in the future, and standards were still high in September 1940 when Hitler consented to the raising of a new *Waffen-SS* division. Originally to be named *SS-Division Germania*, the backbone of the unit was to be provided by the experienced and combat-tested *Germania* Regiment of the *SS-VT* Division. However, the bulk of its strength was to be provided by Dutch, Flemish, Danish and Norwegian volunteers serving in the volunteer SS regiment, *Westland*. Further strength was supplied by the transfer of the *SS-Standarte Nordland*. Early 1941 saw the addition of a volunteer unit of Finns, the *Finnisches Freiwilligen-Batallion der*

Forbidden by the Army to recruit from within Germany, *Reichsführer-SS* Heinrich Himmler was forced to look outside the Reich for volunteers.

Waffen-SS Nordost, which had been raised in February 1941. On 20 December Hitler ordered that the division should be known as the SS Division *Wiking*.

Commanded by Felix Steiner, one of the most influential officers in the *Waffen-SS*, *Wiking* was the first 'international' *Waffen-SS* division. It proved to be an excellent fighting unit, and as the 5th SS Panzer Division *Wiking*, it gained a combat reputation second to none. In the process, it served as the progenitor of a number of other SS divisions. *Wiking* operated exclusively on the eastern front, serving as a spearhead unit for Operation Barbarossa in 1941, the drive on the Caucasus in 1942, and for the Citadel offensive at Kursk in 1943. The division served in the Cherkassy pocket and in Hungary as the war turned against Germany. Despite at least one allegation of war crimes, *Wiking* earned a tough but fair reputation – or as fair a reputation as any unit on the Eastern Front could have.

Soon after the formation of *Wiking*, a sixth SS formation was authorized. Formed from members of the *Totenkopfstandarten* of the *Allgemeine-SS*, *SS-Kampfgruppe Nord* was transferred to Norway for garrison duty. The *Kampfgruppe* participated in Operation Silver Fox, the liberation of part of Soviet-occupied Finland, and the invasion of the Soviet Karelia. Routed by the Soviets at Salla in the summer of 1941, it was retrained by the Finns, and operated with the

Below: Norwegian volunteer members of the SS watch German artillery in action on the Eastern Front. The Nordic blood of these first foreign members of the SS was considered by Himmler and his ideological disciples to be entirely acceptable within the Aryan framework of the SS. Later, as manpower needs became pressing, standards changed dramatically.

German Army's 7th Mountain Division, performing well for the rest of the war.

As the 6th *SS-Gebirgs Division Nord*, the formation fought in the Arctic for 1214 consecutive days from 1 July 1941. One of its most effective units was the *SS-Freiwilligen-Schusskompanie Norwegen* – expert skiers from Norway, Sweden and Denmark, who were used on long-range reconnaissance patrols.

Following the armistice between Finland and the USSR in September 1944, the *6th SS-Gebirgs Division* provided the rearguard for the German withdrawal from Finland, eventually marching 1600km (994 miles) through the high arctic to Norway. The division refitted in Denmark before moving south to France, where it took part in Operation Nordwind in the Vosges Mountains of northeast France.

Few people realize that the Nazi forces in World War II were truly international. It is estimated that nearly two million foreign nationals served under the swastika. Many were volunteers, but a large number were more or less willing conscripts. Foreign volunteers found a home in the SS, until parts of it were more like a German 'Foreign Legion' than the elite of the German race. *Waffen-SS* equipment and organization were the same as those of the Army; SS units were interchangeable with Army units; and senior SS officers adopted Army ranks.

NORDIC VOLUNTEERS

The first Danish unit to carry the national flag as an arm patch was the *Freikorps Danmark*, formed in 1940 and disbanded after hard service in 1943. Survivors formed the nucleus of the *SS-Panzergrenadier Regiment 24 Danmark*, part of the 11th SS Panzergrenadier Division *Nordland*.

Early Dutch volunteers served in the *Freiwilligen Legion Niederland*, formed in 1941. The Legion was disbanded in 1943, and the *SS-Freiwilligen Brigade Nederland* was established. This was later given Panzergrenadier division status. The collar patch carried what was known as a 'Wolf's Hook' device, while the arm shield was in the colours of the Dutch national flag.

Volunteers from Flanders originally served in the *Freiwilligen Legion Flandern*, whose collar patch was the three-legged swastika known as a *Trifos*. The unit was disbanded in 1943, some members being assigned to the *Das Reich* infantry regiment *Langemarck*. This was combined with a Finnish regiment to form a brigade, later expanded into a division. It was all but wiped out by the end of 1944.

There were also hundreds of thousands of volunteers from non-Nordic countries. They too were keen to join the crusade against Bolshevism, but the young men from countries such as Holland, France and Spain joined the fight out of conviction, right-wing idealists determined to halt the seemingly inexorable advance of Marxism.

Western European volunteers who joined the *Waffen-SS* were not treated the same as their German counterparts. They did not take the oath of allegiance to Hitler, most being motivated by their own idealistic belief in the fight against Communism; they were certainly exposed to less political and racial indoctrination. In fact, in the early days they were treated with some disdain by their German counterparts. Further problems were caused by communication difficulties, for units from several different countries were often brigaded together for combat.

In the later stages of the war, the Western and Nordic *Freiwillige* divisions were among the most disciplined and fanatical of all SS units. This was possibly because as the war turned against Germany, they realized that their countrymen back home would look on them as traitors, and that their only hope would be to fight as hard as possible for an unlikely Nazi victory.

Although more than 125,000 West Europeans volunteered for the *Waffen-SS*, this was still not enough to satisfy the organization's ever growing need for manpower. Once again, the solution came from Gottlob Berger, by now an *Obergruppenführer* in charge of the SS-*Hauptamt* (SS Main Office). He proposed expanding SS recruitment to include the *Volksdeutsche* – ethnic Germans scattered in communities all over Central and Eastern Europe.

ETHNIC GERMANS

The origins of many of the German-speaking communities dated back to the Middle Ages. Others were remnants of the former Austro-Hungarian Empire and of the Kaiser's Empire. As well as the loss of her colonial empire, Germany was forced by the terms of the Versailles Treaty of 1919 to cede German border territory to Denmark, Poland and Belgium. Closer to home, Germany also lost the important coalfields of Alsace-Lorraine, which went back to France after having been captured by Prussia in 1871.

The desire to undo the perceived iniquities of Versailles and to bring the Germanic territories of Europe from their current foreign control into a greater German state was an article of faith for Hitler and the Nazis.

In Europe there were several countries with large populations for whom German was their first language. Poland, Hungary, Transylvanian Romania, and the Sudeten area of Czechoslovakia had German-speaking communities of between one and five million, while in Yugoslavia there were up to one million German speakers. Within Europe the Nazis were actively engaged in political and propaganda activities in Hungary and Yugoslavia, while pro-Nazi political movements of varying size existed in almost every other country.

For Hitler and his Pan-German mentors, a long-term goal was the creation of Greater Germany, a country that united those people who were ethnically German, or *Volksdeutsche*, into one nation. In November 1937 Hitler explained his plans: 'The aim of German policy is to secure and preserve the racial community – and to enlarge it.' For many Germans or German com-

munities living abroad, Hitler's Third Reich seemed to be a dynamic and vigorous nation that had miraculously grown out of defeat and the decadence of the Weimar Republic. It was exciting to be involved as *Auslandsdeutsche*, whether at a distance or as close neighbours. When the SS began recruiting *Volksdeutsche*, that attitude led to a flood of new recruits.

However, there were problems. Despite their ethnic background, many of the *Volksdeutsche* recruits had only a rudimentary command of German, and the hard discipline typical of SS training

Below: Nearly 40,000 Belgians joined the *Waffen-SS* during World War II, initially from the Dutch-speaking Flemish segment of the population, but later including many from the French-speaking Walloons. Many of the volunteers were ultra right-wing nationalists, who saw service in the SS as being part of a great anti-Communist crusade.

meant that their motivation and commitment to the cause sometimes flagged. Some *Volksdeutsche* units fought well, but as a whole the ethnic Germans had a mixed reputation. Many of the *Reichsdeutsche* members of the SS felt that the *Volksdeutsche* were cowardly and untrustworthy. The flood of volunteers also began to dry up fairly quickly, and Germany leaned heavily on the governments of puppet states to allow conscription of men of the right age straight into the SS.

The next two SS divisions to be formed made extensive use of *Volksdeutsche* volunteers to fill out their respective orders of battle.

POOR EQUIPMENT

The *Waffen-SS* started the war as the most poorly equipped troops in the German armed forces. Most SS formations went into battle on foot, with horse-drawn supplies. SS equipment was procured through the Army, and as long as the Army saw the SS as a potential rival, it refused to supply the latest weapons. Even though the big-name units like the *Leibstandarte* and *Das Reich* were grudgingly supplied with the latest weaponry, less favoured SS units were much less well equipped.

Above: Hitler greets Vidkun Quisling, leader of the Nazi-style *Nasjional Samling* (National Unity) Party of Norway. Following the German invasion in 1940 he declared himself Prime Minister, but his regime had no support, and was replaced by a German administration. Even so, his organization provided more than 6000 vounteers for the SS.

The *7th SS-Freiwilligen-Gebirgs Division Prinz Eugen* was one such unit. Formed for partisan operations in the Balkans, the bulk of its strength consisted of *Volksdeutsche* volunteers and conscripts from Rumania, Hungary and Yugoslavia. Formed as a mountain division, *Prinz Eugen* was equipped with obsolete and captured equipment such as Czech machine guns and French light tanks.

Despite the poor equipment, it was one of the most effective counter-insurgency units the Germans fielded in Yugoslavia during the war, and was greatly feared by the partisans. However, that reputation was gained primarily by brutality and utter ruthlessness. The war in Yugoslavia combined guerrilla war with civil and tribal warfare, and neither side was prepared to give quarter.

The *8th SS-Kavallerie Division Florian Geyer* was also used on anti-partisan operations, and quickly gained an equally unsavoury reputation. The origins of the unit dated back to the formation of cavalry units within the *Allgemeine-SS Totenkopf Standarten* late in 1939. These cavalry units were then consolidated under the command of the *Kommandostab-RFSS* for Operation Barbarossa. Their primary function was security, being used behind the front lines to mop up bypassed Soviet Army units. Gradually, their main function became the waging of an extremely ruthless anti-partisan campaign.

The initial success of his troops in Russia prompted Himmler to expand the *Waffen-SS* still further. Four new divisions were authorized, three of them armoured. These were the 9th SS Panzer Division *Hohenstaufen*, the 10th SS Panzer Division *Frundsberg*, the *11th SS-Freiwilligen-Panzergrenadier Division Nordland* and the 12th SS Panzer Division *Hitlerjugend*. All began forming in 1943, but none were ready to take part in the summer offensive that year.

By the spring of 1944 the SS Panzer Corps was a shadow of the powerful force that had spearheaded Operation Citadel just months earlier. Most units were withdrawn to Western Europe to rest and refit, becoming fully-fledged Panzer divisions in the process. However, the 9th and 10th Divisions had now completed their training, and went into action at Tarnopol in April 1944. At this point, the SS could no longer sustain itself on volunteers alone, and conscripts manned the two divisions. Given full SS-style training, they fought at least as well as the original divisions.

CONSCRIPTION IS INTRODUCED

Amid a dwindling supply of manpower, the SS had no choice but to accept conscripts. In these circumstances, it was impossible to ignore the existence of an entire generation of ideologically pure boys, raised as Nazis, eager to fight for the Fatherland and even die for the Führer.

The first thousand-bomber raid hit Cologne in May 1942. In that month, Reich Youth Leader Artur Axmann persuaded Hitler to set up pre-military training camps that all boys between the ages of 16 and 18 were obliged to attend. In turn, the SS persuaded the *Hitlerjugend* to reserve to them exclusively one-fifth of the product of these camps. During the three weeks of mandatory war training, the boys learned how to handle German infantry weapons, including various pistols, machine guns, hand grenades and *Panzerfaust* anti-tank weapons.

Having exhausted most forms of recruitment inside Germany, Himmler turned to youth, actively persuading members of the *Hitlerjugend* to join the SS.

In this preparation for combat, especially in the camps run by the SS, German adolescents received a training that was heavily laced with psychological brain-washing. War was described as a struggle of competing ideologies, culminating in victory or annihilation. The type of soldier produced under this 'fight or die' indoctrination largely explains the continuing Nazi war effort, even when most outsiders and an increasing number of insiders knew Germany's cause was lost.

The Army High Command and the SS were in constant competition for the best recruits. Both organizations assigned veterans to *Hitlerjugend* administrative posts, primarily as a means of recruitment. The veterans regaled their wide-eyed audiences with the perils and thrills of combat. They reinforced the will to fight the 'Bolshevik hordes' and the 'Jew-backed Western powers'. These Pied Pipers did all they could to produce cannon fodder for the Reich's war machine.

The results were impressive. Army leaders were the first to acknowledge the achievements of the *Hitlerjugend* in preparing recruits for the battlefield. Departing from traditional methods, the *Hitlerjugend* tailored paramilitary training to the particular needs and potential of 16- and 17-year-olds. With the exception of a few coarse SS veterans, there were no hard-bitten drill sergeant types in the training camps. Most cadre members were sensitive young soldiers, most of whom had

Above: Norwegians relax in winter quarters during the siege of Leningrad in 1942. Norwegian volunteers served in some of the most effective *Waffen-SS* units, including the 5th SS Panzer Division *Wiking*, the 6th SS Mountain Division *Nord*, and the 11th SS Volunteer Division *Nordland* – the latter being amongst the last fanatical defenders of Hitler's bunker in 1945.

been in the *Hitlerjugend* itself not too many years before. German youth was in effect training itself.

The camps also served to eliminate class distinctions. Boys from town and city, volunteer and conscript were thrown in together, to become soldiers who fought with greater professional skill, resourcefulness and independent initiative than their enemy counterparts. Between the spring of 1942 and 1945 every German volunteer and draftee filtered through the *Hitlerjugend* training schemes before he donned field grey or SS camouflage. But although he was better trained than his opponent, he was also more prone to embrace the barbarity of battle.

From these training schemes, it was a natural progression to form the 12th SS Panzer Division *Hitlerjugend*. A recruitment drive began, drawing principally on 17-year-old volunteers. However, boys of 16 and under eagerly joined. During July and August 1943, 10,000 recruits arrived at the training camp in Beverloo, Belgium.

HITLERJUGEND, THE 'BABY' DIVISION

To fill out the division with enough experienced soldiers and officers, *Waffen-SS* veterans were drafted from the Russian Front. Many were from the elite *Leibstandarte-SS Adolf Hitler.* The *Wehrmacht* assigned 50 former *Hitlerjugend* leaders as officers for the division. The remaining shortfall of squad and section leaders was filled with *Hitlerjugend* members who had demonstrated leadership aptitude during paramilitary training.

By the spring of 1944, training was complete. The division, now fully trained and equipped, conducted divisional manoeuvres observed by

General Heinz Guderian and Field Marshal Gerd von Rundstedt. Both senior officers admired the enthusiasm and expressed their approval of the proficiency achieved by the young troops in such a short time. The division was transferred to Hasselt, Belgium, in anticipation of the Allied invasion of northern France, where it subsequently fought with fanaticism and bravery against the numerically superior Allies.

Even *Volksdeutsche* volunteers could not solve the manpower needs of the SS, so Himmler began looking for volunteers from beyond the German 'race'. The bulk of the early non-Germanic volunteers fighting for Hitler served with the German Army. Those from Eastern Europe were used initially in secondary roles, serving in police battalions or as prison camp guards, working as labourers or moving supplies on the long lines of communication. But gradually, as the pressure on German manpower increased, they were used more and more often as combat troops. Some fought extremely well, while others were worthless in battle. Some of the auxiliary units, particularly those employed by the *Einsatzgruppen* and as camp and ghetto guards, were among the worst perpetrators of war crimes. Later, by 1943, as manpower demands grew apace with Himmler's ambitions, SS racial standards were relaxed still further and units were formed from Muslims, Slavs, Indians and other Asiatics.

BALKAN MUSLIMS

Raised in 1943, the *13th Waffen-Gebirgs Division der SS Handschar* was a *Waffen-SS* division of Bosnian Muslim volunteers. Most had joined the division in order to protect their homes and families from *Ustase*, *Chetnik* and partisan attacks. The Fascist Croat puppet government disapproved of the formation, since they felt that the SS recruitment in Bosnia violated their sovereignty.

Below: Dutch volunteers in the summer of 1941 apply to join the Netherlands Volunteer Legion soon after the German invasion of Russia. Unlike many of the other volunteer legions, who often started as units of the German Army, the Dutch Legion was a part of the SS from its very beginnings. The unit became a brigade in 1943, being given divisional status in February 1945.

Right: Dutch Nazi leader Anton Mussert founded the *Nationaal-Socialistische Beweging* in 1931 as a direct imitation of the German movement. Following the German invasion in 1940, he and his organization collaborated with the occupiers, though Mussert had little influence on his masters. He is seen here (at left) with Himmler and Nazi Party treasurer Franz Xavier Schwartz.

A small-scale mutiny during training in France was instigated by partisans who had infiltrated the ranks.

The *23rd Waffen-SS Gebirgs Division Kama* was the third *Waffen-SS* mountain division raised in Croatia. Manpower included German officers, leading *Volksdeutsche* troops and some Bosnian Muslims. The division was never fully formed or trained and it was disbanded in October 1944 after only five months.

Although nominally a division, the *24th Waffen-Gebirgs (Karstjäger) Division der SS* was in fact a below-strength brigade-sized formation of *Waffen-SS* mountain troops, originally formed to fight Italian and Yugoslavian partisans in the Alpine terrain where the borders of Austria, Slovakia, and Italy meet. Many of its members were from south Tyrol (now part of Italy) or were Yugoslavian *Volksdeutsche*.

HIMMLER ACCEPTS SLAVS IN THE SS

Also in 1943, and following the defeats at Stalingrad and Kursk, *Reichsführer-SS* Heinrich Himmler began to reappraise the SS attitude towards the 'subhuman' Slavs of Eastern Europe. The *14th Waffen-Grenadier Division der SS* was formed in Galicia, a region that covered southeastern Poland and western Ukraine and which had been colonized by German settlers in the fourteenth century. By the 1770s it had become a province of Maria-Theresa's Austro-Hungarian Empire, with the provincial capital at Lemberg (L'vov). Although considered Germanic by the Nazis, the main cultural influence in the region was in fact Ukrainian, as were most of the troops in the division. The 14th SS was smashed in its only major battle in the Brody-Tarnow pocket. Remnants of the division mounted ineffective anti-partisan operations in Slovakia and Slovenia at the end of the war.

Further volunteers came from Estonia, Latvia and Lithuania, the Baltic republics annexed by the Soviet Union in June 1940. Though Stalin claimed his takeover had been at the instigation of the three countries themselves, it was in effect a military conquest. The Communists moved large forces into the area, and immediately enacted repressive measures against opposition and liberations groups. As a result, the Balts welcomed the 1941 German invaders as liberators, and when the SS formed a Latvian unit there was

Above: One of the most committed of all the right-wing nationalist groups inspired by the Nazis was the Belgian Rexist Party, seen here on parade in Brussels in 1942. Initial recruitment into the *Légion Wallonie* was almost exclusively drawn from the members of the party, who followed their charismatic leader Léon Degrelle into German military service.

no problem with recruitment. Early in 1943, the *Lettische SS-Freiwilligen Legion* was formed from several SS-linked Latvian internal security units, known as *Schutzmannschaft* Battalions. The *15th Waffen-Grenadier Division der SS* was based on these units, to which were added some troops from the *Totenkopf Standarten*. By 1945 the division had been destroyed in combat with the Red Army.

The *19th Waffen-Grenadier-Division der SS* was the second division of Latvian volunteers raised by the *Waffen-SS*. Like its sister unit, the *15th Waffen-Grenadier Division der SS*, German troops from the *SS-Brigade (mot) 2*, part of the *Totenkopf Standarte*, formed the division cadre. It was rounded out with a large proportion of Schuma personnel.

The *20th Waffen-Grenadier-Division der SS* began as the *Estnische Legion*, one of the first eastern volunteer units in the *Waffen-SS*. Formed in August 1942, its troops were later transferred to *5th SS-Panzer Division Wiking* and earned a fighting reputation. The unit continued to attract Estonian volunteers almost to the end of its existence. Other reinforcements included transfers from German Army units, *SS-Freiwiligen Brigade*

3, elements of the *1. SS Infantry Brigade*, former Estonian Army soldiers and police auxiliaries. By January 1944 the Brigade had become a volunteer division. Thrown out of their country by the advancing Red Army, the few survivors who surrendered in Prussia in May 1945 faced the gulag or the firing squad.

The 16th SS Panzergrenadier Division *Reichsführer-SS* began its war service as the *Begliet-Bataillon RFSS*, Himmler's personal escort battalion. In February 1943 it was expanded to an assault brigade and was stationed on Corsica. In October 1943 *Sturmbrigade Reichführer-SS* was expanded still further to divisional size, incorporating a number of Hungarian and Romanian *Volksdeutsche*. *Reichsführer-SS* was the only major SS unit to spend long periods in combat in Italy. During the hard-fought retreat up the Italian peninsula, its members committed a number of atrocities during anti-partisan operations. In 1945 the division transferred to Hungary for Operation Spring Awakening, where it was all but destroyed.

STORMTROOPERS BECOME SS MEN

In January 1944, Adolf Hitler ordered *Reichsführer-SS* Heinrich Himmler to raise a *Waffen-SS* division from a cadre of SA reservists. In fact, the *18th SS Freiwilligen-Panzergrenadier Division Horst Wessel* was cobbled together from a *Totenkopf Standarte* motorized brigade together with elements from the *6th SS-Gebirgs Division Nord* and Hungarian *Volksdeutsche*. Fighting on the Eastern Front, it was primarily used as a repressive threat to keep wavering allies like Hungary and Slovakia in line.

The *21st Waffen-Gebirgs-Division der SS Skanderbeg* was a short-lived unit of Kosovo Albanian *Waffen-SS* volunteers of minimal combat value. The *22nd SS-Freiwilligen-Kavallerie-Division Maria Theresa* was raised from two regiments of Hungarian *Volksdeutsche* brigaded with SS Cavalry Regiment 17 (formerly *SS-Reiter* Regiment 3) during the spring of 1944. In October 1944 the Division provided security forces in the German operation to overthrow Admiral Horthy, the Hungarian dictator. *Maria Theresa* was wiped out during the battle of Budapest in February 1945.

The *25th Waffen-Grenadier-Division der SS Hunyadi* was the first Hungarian division in the *Waffen-SS*. It was formed in October and November of 1944 at the request of the senior police and SS commander in the region – though the 'request' to the puppet government, which had replaced the ousted Admiral Horthy, was much more in the nature of an order. Although at full strength numerically, the 25th SS Division was hardly a fighting division. When it received its weaponry on 18 December 1944, it was supplied with 50 machine guns, 2000 rifles and 27 trucks – for 22,000 men! At the end of the month, mobility was increased by the arrival of 1000 bicycles. Fleeing from the Russians at the end of the war, many of the troops simply abandoned their uniforms and returned to the civilian population.

The *26th Waffen-Grenadier-Division der SS Hungaria (ungarische Nr. 2)* was the second Hungarian *Waffen-SS* division. Again formed at the insistence of the Germans, it was even less capable than the first. Orders for its formation were issued in October/November 1944, and by March 1945 it had a nominal strength of between 13,000 and 17,000 men. However, it was largely an untrained mix of 3000 *Waffen-SS* men, 2600 in Hungarian Fascist uniform, and more than 10,000 still wearing their civilian clothes. Although issued with mortars and anti-tank guns, these were seized by the German 9th Army, and the *Hungaria* had to fight against overwhelming Soviet forces with little more than hand weapons.

The *30th Waffen-Grenadier-Division der SS (russische Nr 2)* was a polyglot force of Russians, Belorussians, Poles, Ukrainians, Tartars and Armenians, plus German *Polizei-Gebiets* (police commands) from Lida, Wileika and Minsk. Formed in 1944 by Wilhelm Kube, the Higher SS and Police Führer for White Russia, the division never attained full strength and performed poorly in battle. It suffered from language and communications problems, was poorly equipped, and very few of its troops were willing recruits. The 30th SS was the only *Waffen-SS* unit of Slavic volunteers to serve in France, being posted to cover the regions of Belfort/Mühlhausen, Venarey and Auxonne in September 1944. However, rather than taking part in antipartisan operations against the Maquis, large numbers of the division's troops preferred desertion, many joining the French Resistance. By December 1944 divisional strength was down to 4400, and it had been withdrawn to the German/Swiss border.

The *31st SS-Freiwilligen-Grenadier-Division* was a late-war scratch unit formed from remnants of the *23rd Waffen-SS Gebirgs Division Kama*, police troops, *Allgemeine-SS* battalions and other stragglers. Half the size of a normal division, its scattered *Kampfgruppen* (battle groups) operated against the Soviets in Austria.

Created in January 1945, the *32nd SS-Frei-willigen-Grenadier-Division 30 Januar* was another ad hoc division. Personnel came from recruiting depots and SS training schools, with a sprinkling of survivors from other shattered units. Named after the date Hitler assumed power in 1933, the 32nd SS Division fought the Soviet Army along the Oder front. A few units managed to break out of the Soviet encirclement of Berlin in April 1945.

The *35th SS-Polizei-Grenadier-Division* was a pick-up formation comprised of former police and cadet units and the 59th and 60th *Volksturm* Battalions. The under strength grenadier division fought briefly against Soviets in and around Berlin in the last six weeks of the war.

Below: Léon Degrelle, the leader of the French-speaking Belgians serving the Third Reich, is awarded the Oakleaves to the Knight's Cross of the Iron Cross. Hitler had a soft spot for Degrelle, who had distinguished himself in the break out from the Cherkassy pocket. 'If I had a son', the Führer said, 'I would like him to be just like you.'

The *37th SS-Freiwilligen-Kavallerie-Division Lützow* was formed from survivors of the *Florian Geyer* and *Maria Theresa* SS Cavalry Divisions, plus additional Hungarian division remnants and stragglers. The division's strength never reached much more than a regiment.

The *38th SS-Grenadier-Division Nibelungen* was the last *Waffen-SS* unit to be called a division. It was formed on 27 March 1945 from personnel at the SS officer training school *Bad Tölz*, plus detachments from the 30th SS Division, *6.SS-Gebirgs-Division Nord*, and 12th SS Division *Hitlerjugend*. The *Nibelungen* division fought a few rearguard actions in Austria and in Landshut, Alpen and Donau in Upper Bavaria before surrendering to US troops on 8 May 1945.

Although most of the late war SS divisions were of questionable combat capability, those which were formed around the western volunteer legions often fought well. The *27th SS-Freiwilligen-Grenadier-Division Langemarck* was one such formation.

Flanders (*Vlaanderen* in Flemish, *Flandern* in German) is the name for the region spanning

Above: By 1943, when this photo was taken, most French anti-communist volunteers serving with the German army had been swept up by the *Waffen-SS Französische SS-Freiwilligen-Grenadier-Regiment.* As members of the *Charlemagne* Division at the end of the war, these right-wing nationalists were to be among the most stubborn defenders of Berlin.

northern France and western Belgium on the North Sea. The people of Flanders, or Flemings, are descended from the Germanic tribes that settled the region. After the German triumphs of 1940, this acceptably 'Aryan' background meant that the SS saw them as a potential source of recruits, and numerous Flemings served with the first three regiments of western European volunteers – *Nordland*, *Westland* and *Nordwest*.

After the invasion of the Soviet Union, the *Waffen-SS* moved the Fleming volunteers into a single *SS-Freiwilligen Legion Flandern*. As usual, the bulk of the strength was made up from from new recruits and a cadre from the previously mentioned three volunteer regiments. In May 1943 the unit was renamed 6. *SS-Sturmbrigade Langemarck*. In October 1944 *Langemarck* was made into a division, although it was only the size of a large regiment, having no more 3000 survivors from the heavy fighting on the Eastern Front. It was reinforced with 3000 troops from the *Vlaamse Wach*, the Flemish National Militia, together with 2000 men transferred from the Flemish *Allegemine-SS*. Further strength was provided by men from the *Luftwaffe*, the *Kriegsmarine*, the NSKK and the Todt Organization.

In December 1944 the 'division' was moved west to serve as a battle group during the Ardennes campaign. Transferred back to the East, *Langemarck* saw heavy fighting on the Oder front. By the time it surrendered to the British, the 27th SS Division was down to less than 200 men.

28th SS-Freiwilligen-Grenadier Division Wallonien was a volunteer unit from Wallonia – French-speaking Belgium. The unit drew its recruits from the right-wing, nationalist, Catholic

---

The original French volunteers for the German army formed the *Légion des Voluntaires Français*, a rabidly anti-bolshevik group.

---

and rabidly anti-communist Rexist Party led by Léon Degrelle. Originally the unit fought as part of the Army, as Walloons were not considered 'Aryan' enough for the SS. In June 1943 the battalion-sized Walloon unit was enlarged and attached to the *Waffen-SS* as *SS-Sturmbrigade Wallonien*. It was commanded by Degrelle, who had risen through the ranks after joining up as a private soldier in 1941. Over 8000 Walloon volunteers served with the unit during the war, and they had a good fighting reputation. Thanks to the presence of Degrelle, a Knight's Cross holder and one of the most famous non-Germans in the German armed forces, the Walloons received a great deal of media and propaganda attention.

FRENCHMEN IN THE SS

France provided a large number of collaborationist volunteer units that fought against the Communists on the Eastern Front. Initially they served in the German Army, but as 'Aryan' requirements began to slide later in the war, most were transferred to the *Waffen-SS*. The first unit was the *Légion des Voluntaires Français*, followed by *La Legion Tricolore*. Both units took part in anti-partisan operations. By late 1943, surviving French volunteers were inducted into the *Waffen-SS Französische SS-Freiwilligen-Grenadier-Regiment*, later upgraded to an Assault brigade.

In February 1945 the brigade became the *33rd Waffen-Grenadier-Division der SS Charlemagne (französische Nr. 1)*, though it was less than half the size of a standard SS division. *Charlemagne* fought against the Soviets in Poland and some remnants of the division were among the last defenders of Berlin in April and May 1945. Even by the standards of the late-war SS, *Charlemagne*'s troops were a particularly wide ethnic mix. Its numbers included French Indochinese, Japanese and Swedes. It is even rumoured that a number of French Jews fought in the unit.

The *Charlemagne* Division took its divisional number from the *33rd Waffen-Kavallerie-Division der SS (ungarische Nr 3)*. Ordered to be raised late in 1944, this formation may never have existed except on paper. Any units destined to be assigned to it were destroyed by the Russians during the capture of Budapest.

The 17th SS Panzergrenadier Division *Götz von Berlichingen* was raised in Southern France in October 1943. Its complement was found in various SS training and replacement units, being brought up to strength by Balkan *Volksdeutche* conscripts and volunteers. The 17th SS fought hard in the 1944 Normandy campaign. Over the last winter of the war the division bled itself to death in the Saar, fighting a vicious battle of attrition with units of the US First Army.

Dutch collaborators joined the *Waffen-SS* and formed the *SS-Freiwilligen-Legion Niederlande* in 1941. Anton Mussert, the leader of the *Nationaal Socialistische Beweging* (the Dutch fascist party) insisted that Dutch volunteers in the SS should serve only with fellow Dutchmen. Recruited primarily to fight the 'anti-bolshevik crusade', the members of the Dutch SS displayed the organization's most characteristic behaviour in fighting extremely hard while suffering from cripplingly high casualty rates. The Dutch volunteer unit was reformed several times, eventually becoming the *23rd SS-Freiwilligen-Panzer-Grenadier-Division Nederland*.

Dutch stormtroopers, the *Landwacht Nederland* and other Dutch collaborationist organizations together formed the *34th SS-Freiwilligen-*

Above: Following the invasion of the USSR in June 1941, Danes were encouraged to volunteer for the SS to take part in the fight against Communism. Initially, they were formed into the *Freikorps Danemark*, which was involved in some of the fiercest fighting on the Eastern Front. Disbanded in 1943, its members were absorbed by the *11th SS Division Nordland*.

Grenadier-Division Landstorm Nederland, a division in name only. It saw little action. *Landwacht Nederland* troops fought against the Dutch Resistance members in northwest Holland. Divisional troops played a small part in the battle against British Paratroopers at Arnhem in September 1944. After that, *Landstorm Nederland* troops saw combat against fellow Dutchmen in an encounter with the *Princess Irene* Brigade, a unit of Dutch volunteers serving with the Allies.

ITALIANS RELUCTANTLY ACCEPTED

A number of Italian Fascists resolved to continue the war after the Italian surrender in 1943. The *Legion Italia* fought in Italy, distinguishing itself in the fighting around Anzio. Until that time Himmler refused to allow them to join the SS proper, and the unit insignia had a red background. After

Anzio, however, some regiments were accepted into the *Waffen-SS* and were allowed to wear black SS patches. The Italian fascists occasionally took part in the German defensive operations against the Allied armies moving north, but for most of the time they were employed against Italian *Red Star* and *Garibaldi* partisan units in what was rapidly becoming an Italian civil war. By the end of the war the unit had become the *29th Waffen-Grenadier Division der SS (Italienische Nr. 1)*, taking over the unit number no longer needed by the bandits of the Kaminsky Division.

The *29th Waffen-Grenadier-Division der SS (russische Nr 1)* was one of the most evil of all *Waffen-SS* units. It was formed in Bryansk in 1941 as an anti-Communist civilian militia. Commanded by Bronislav Kaminski, known as the 'Warlord of the Bryansk Forest', the unit was employed on anti-partisan operations in Belorussia and the Ukraine. For the next three years the trail of the Kaminski Brigade could be followed by the atrocities it committed. Kaminski ruled his territory like a despotic chieftain from the Dark Ages, but since he kept the Soviet partisans at bay and foodstuffs flowing into *Wehrmacht* supply depots, the Germans were willing to accept his bloodthirsty actions.

Heinrich Himmler integrated the unit into the *Waffen-SS* in July 1944. By this time the Kaminski Brigade had a fighting strength in excess of 10,500 men, though it also had more than 15,000 civilian camp followers and nearly 2000 cattle in its train. The division is perhaps most infamous for its barbarity and drunkenness during the suppression of the Warsaw Uprising in 1944. On 19 August, its men killed 10,000 Polish civilians in a single day. This was too much even for Himmler, and Kaminski was summoned

Right: SS recruiting posters varied widely in subject matter and sophistication. Many referred to the 'Germanic' past, while others, such as this anti-Communist work, were out and out propaganda pieces. By presenting the Soviets as a kind of barbaric, ravening horde, the Nazis hoped to kindle an anti-Communist crusading spirit in the young men of Europe.

to the headquarters of *SS-Obergruppenführer* von dem Bach-Zelewski. There he was shot, probably on Himmler's direct orders. His men were sent to be absorbed into the 600th Infantry Division of the *Russkaya Ovsoboditelnaya Narodnaya Armija*, the Russian Army of National Liberation.

MOST EVIL MAN IN THE SS

With an even worse reputation than the Kaminsky brigade, the *36th Waffen-Grenadier-Division der SS* was the most notorious of *Waffen-SS* units, serving under perhaps the most sadistic of all commanders of World War II. *Oberführer* Dr Oskar Dirlewanger was a soldier who had been decorated in World War I, but he was also a drunk and a sadist, imprisoned in the 1920s for sexual assaults on children. A protégé of Gottlob Berger, Dirlewanger suggested the creation of a special punishment unit that would allow SS men convicted of crimes to atone for their deeds.

Dirlewanger formed his brigade in 1940 from former concentration camp inmates convicted of poaching. On the Eastern Front, casualties were replaced with Soviet turncoats and criminals. *Sonderkommando* (Special Command) Dirlewanger went into action behind the front lines during Operation Barbarossa, the Nazi invasion of the Soviet Union. The unit quickly earned a reputation for atrocity in counter-insurgency operations, with a speciality of 'pacifying' an area by slaughtering every man, woman and child. The unit, never large, spent almost all of its career raping, looting and killing in the Soviet Union, but cemented its reputation for barbarity in its brutal suppression of the Warsaw uprising.

Reclassified as a 'paper' division in February 1945, the unit was still only the size of an under-

strength brigade. Soviet troops annihilated the 36th Division in April. Dirlewanger escaped to surrender in the West, but did not live long. Recognized in June 1945 by Polish troops serving with the French, he was beaten to death.

Not all of the foreign volunteers in the SS served in the SS divisions. One of the most interesting units, given Himmler's racial obsessions, was the *Indische Freiwilligen Legion der Waffen-SS*. It was founded by the Indian nationalist leader Subhas Chandra Bose, whose dream it was to raise a German-sponsored Indian Legion that would be in the vanguard of the German advances in the Caucasus. The Indian Legion would then push on through Persia, Afghanistan and onward to liberate their homeland. The *Indische Freiwilligen Legion* (transferred to the *Waffen-SS* in 1944) never did fulfil the martial dreams of its founder: the polyglot force of Sikhs, Muslims, and Hindus was relegated to garrison duty.

Less successful was Himmler's attempt to recruit SS members from British prisoners of war. John Amery, son of Conservative minister Leo Amery and a pre-war fascist, suggested the idea of a volunteer legion of British PoWs soon after his capture in 1940. It was not until 1943 that the *Waffen-SS* expressed interest in the project, creating the 'Legion of St. George'. Despite promises of cash bonuses, limited freedom and access to prostitutes, the SS recruitment efforts were essentially a failure, with fewer than 50 men volunteering. This was too few to have any military value, and the men were too unreliable to have any propaganda impact. The British Freecorps (BFC) spent most of its existence in training, but apart from six individuals who volunteered for the front in 1945, it never saw action. After the war, Amery was tried, convicted and hanged for treason.

FOREIGN VOLUNTEERS IN THE *WAFFEN-SS*

(excluding foreigners transferred into the SS from the Army)

Origin	Number	*Waffen-SS* Units
Albania	3000	21st SS Div
Belgium: Flemish	23,000	5th SS Div, 27th SS Div
Belgium: Walloon	15,000	5th SS Div, 28th SS Div
British	50	British *Freikorps*
Bulgaria	200-1000?	*Bulgarisches* Reg
Croatia (incl Bosnian Muslims)	30,000	7th SS Div, 13th SS Div, 23rd SS Div
Denmark	10,000	*Freikorps Danemark*, 11th SS Div
Estonia	20,000	20th SS Div
Finland	1000	Volunteer Battalion
France	8000	33rd SS Div
Hungary	More than 20,000	25th SS Div, 26th SS Div, 33rd SS Div
India	3500	Volunteer Legion
Italy	20,000	29th SS (Italian)
Latvia	39,000	15th SS Div, 19th SS Div
Netherlands	50,000	23rd SS Div, 34th SS Div
Norway	6000	5th SS Div, 6th SS Div, 11th SS Div Volunteer Legion
Poland/Ukraine	25,000	14th SS Div
Russia (Belorussia)	12,000	29th SS Div, 30th SS Div
Russia (Cossack)	40,000	XV *SS Kosaken-Kavallerie-Korps*
Russia (Turkic)	8000	*Ostürkische* SS, *Tatarishe* SS
Rumania	3000?	*Waffen-Grenadierregiment der SS* (*rumänisches* 1)
Serbia	15,000	Volunteer Corps
Spain	200–1,000?	*Spanische-Freiwilligen-Kompanie der SS* 101
Sweden, Switzerland & Luxembourg	3,000?	5th SS Div, 11th SS Div

OCCUPATION AND ATROCITY

I n the four years between the fall of France in June 1940 and the Allied invasion of Normandy in 1944, most of the *Waffen-SS* was engaged in the fierce battle for survival on the Eastern Front. Hot in summer, ice-cold in winter, and up to his neck in mud through spring and autumn, the average German soldier looked on the idea of a posting to France as a glimpse of heaven. However, few got the chance to enjoy the experience, which was reserved for Hitler's favourites, the premier divisions of the *Waffen-SS*. France was where they went to recuperate and refit in the pauses between periods of murderous fighting in Russia.

In the immediate aftermath of the fall of France, the Germans tasted the sweetness of victory. The average soldier treated the French with some respect. In other countries they despoiled, a trooper had no compunction in taking the personal possessions of a passer-by. But the French people were treated with a caring, if somewhat

Left: Luftwaffe and SS personnel talk peacefully with a Frenchwoman in 1940. In the early days of the occupation things were relatively peaceful, but as resistance grew so too did German oppression.

patronizing attitude. Posters urged the population to put their trust in the German soldier. It was as though the French were abandoned children who had enjoyed the good fortune of being swept up by the big-hearted, nurturing Germans.

To many troops Paris became the ideal place to spend leave. Its delights were obvious: the architecture; the food, to those who could afford it; and the women, who could always be afforded. Café society as portrayed in German propaganda films showed invader and occupied relaxing with each other in the ever-present sun.

Below: To SS front-line units, France was a place to rest and relax after the rigours of combat on the Eastern Front. The *Leibstandarte* spent much of the second half of 1942 being expanded to divisional size in France after sustaining heavy casualties in the Donetz region of Russia. The new Panzergrenadier division was later used on occupation duties in Vichy France.

The French found it difficult to know how to react to the invader. Was ignoring them enough? Was giving them misinformation a sufficient act of defiance? Should you sell to them from your shops? Should you respond to any displays of affability on their part? When did you become a collaborator? Many chose to regard the German as invisible, as encouraged in Vercours' famous book, *Le silence de la mer.*

In fact, the Germans were considered to be an alien presence by the average Frenchman throughout the occupation. The French initially referred to them as *Les Boches* or *Les Autres* after Sartre's oft-quoted maxim: '*L'enfer, c'est les autres*', Hell is other people. Later, when spirits seemed crushed by resignation, the Germans were simply referred to as '*ils*' – the French for 'they'.

That quiescent attitude meant that for three years France was a safe haven for SS units to

withdraw and lick their wounds, after incurring staggering losses in the campaigns in the East.

In June 1942, the *Leibstandarte Adolf Hitler* was withdrawn from its positions on the Mius River in Russia. It was pulled back to France. During this period of refitting, the *LAH* brigade was enlarged and upgraded to become the *SS-Division (mot) Leibstandarte SS Adolf Hitler*. The division's ceremonial function was not forgotten and its men took part in a ceremonial parade through Paris where the *Oberbefehlshaber West*, *Generalfeldmarschall* Gerd von Rundstedt, took the salute.

Over the next two months the division continued to be expanded in the Evreux region, west of Paris. In the process, the division's panzer regiment was one of the first in the German armed forces to receive the powerful new PzKpfw VI Tiger tank, bigger and heavier than any other operational tank in the world. Also, in a change from the formation's earlier history – caused by the general shortage of manpower affecting the SS – membership was thrown open to non-native Germans, and *Volksdeutsche* were allowed to volunteer for the Führer's bodyguard.

LEIBSTANDARTE ENLARGED

In October 1942 the *Leibstandarte* was renamed as the SS Panzergrenadier Division *Leibstandarte SS Adolf Hitler*. It was moved south into Vichy France after the German takeover, where it performed occupation duties for the next four months. By the end of the year, the *Leibstandarte* was at its full strength of 678 officers and 20,166 NCOs and men. However, a powerful Soviet winter offensive early in 1943 saw the *LSSAH* moved rapidly to the Ukraine.

On 5 July 1943 the *Leibstandarte* formed part of II SS Panzer Corps, which formed the southern spearhead of Operation Citadel – the Battle of Kursk. After two weeks the *LSSAH* had lost 2753 men killed and wounded, and over 30 per cent of its armour had been destroyed. Battered and bruised as it was, the *Leibstandarte* was the first unit Hitler turned to when unsettling news arrived from Italy.

Below: Headquarters of the *Sonderkommando RF-SS* Paris, or 'Special Command of the Reichsführer-SS'. The word *Sonderkommando* described many things, including units involved in the final solution in the East, or, as here, a co-ordinating body under the local SS police chief tasked with overseeing SS, SD, Gestapo and police organization in occupied territories.

Allied landings on Sicily had been followed by an attack on the Italian mainland. On 25 July, the Italian government deposed Benito Mussolini and began negotiating for an armistice. Hitler resolved to take over the whole of Italy, and ordered II SS Panzer Corps to be transferred from Russia, though only the *Leibstandarte* eventually made the trip. Leaving its tanks and heavy equipment for the *Das Reich* and *Totenkopf* divisions, the *LSSAH* entrained for Italy. Picking up new armour, the division occupied Milan and helped to disarm Italian troops in the Po Valley.

Although the *Leibstandarte* was in Italy for only three months, it was enough time for the division to commit a number of atrocities. A typical atrocity, similar to numberless such events on the Eastern Front, occurred on 19 September. Reacting to a report that renegade Italian troops had captured a pair of SS officers, *SS-Standartenführer* Joachim Peiper used his self-propelled artillery to shell the town of Boves, killing 34 innocent civilians. It has also been alleged that divisional troops were used to round up Jews for deportation to the death camps of Eastern Europe. Until the German occupation, Italian Jews had been relatively safe, since Mussolini and the Italian Fascists had to some degree protected them.

In October 1943 the *LSSAH* was transferred to the Balkans, where it was again upgraded, becoming the 1st SS Panzer Division *Leibstandarte SS Adolf Hitler* on the 22nd of that month. From the Balkans it was again sent east, where for the next three months it was engaged in heavy fighting with the Red Army. By March 1944, the *Leibstandarte* had been all but wiped out, its strength having fallen to under 1200 men. Pulled out of the line, it was again sent west to be rebuilt.

By 25 April, the *Leibstandarte* was stationed around Turnhout in Belgium. In two months, large numbers of young troops arrived to be trained by the surviving veterans. On Hitler's direct orders, the *Leibstandarte* was re-equipped with brand new equipment. At the beginning of June, the division was again more than 20,000 strong, and as part of the I SS Panzer Corps was part of the armoured reserve being amassed to fight the imminent Allied invasion.

OCCUPATION DUTY FOR *DAS REICH*

After the fall of France in 1940, the *SS-VT* division was retained for occupation duty in the south of France. Renamed the SS Division *Reich (mot)* in January 1941, the division left in March 1941, initially for operations in the Balkans and then to take part in the invasion of the USSR.

Between January and March 1942 the division suffered more than 4000 casualties in fighting off the Soviet winter offensive around Istra, Rusa and Rzhev.

In April 1942, *Reich* was withdrawn to rest and refit in Germany and France. Part of the refit involved upgrading the unit's capability to panz-

---

Many of the most powerful of the SS divisions were based in France to rest and refit after intense combat on the Eastern Front.

---

ergrenadier division standard. From August, the fully restored division was used for occupation duty in northwest France. In October, the division was renamed, becoming the SS Panzergrenadier Division *Das Reich*.

Apart from a period at the end of November, when part of the division was sent to Toulon in an attempt to prevent the scuttling of the French fleet, *Das Reich* remained an occupation force until February. It was then sent east to join the SS Panzer Corps in the fighting around Kharkov. It remained in the East for the next year. After constant hard fighting, it was sent west to refit in February 1944. Hitler personally selected Montaub, 40km (25 miles) from Toulouse, as the divisional headquarters.

By now, southern France was a very different place from what it had been in 1942, much less 1940. The easygoing way of life that had been so attractive to the Germans was gone, and strengthening French resistance meant that the SS troops were getting involved in a partisan war. In May 1944, divisional troops executed 15 civilians at Cahours, seizing 400 cars and 200 trucks as a reprisal for Resistance activity.

On 8 June, two days after the Normandy invasion, *Das Reich* set off on the long march from the south of France to the invasion front. Instead of taking the shorter, safer and much quicker coastal route, its commanders directed the advance through the Massif Central. The idea was to mount a massive anti-partisan sweep, dis-

Above: In most of Occupied Europe, the SS provided the 'hands-on' thugs used to maintain German oppression. In Vichy-controlled portions of France, however, the SS were mainly used to provide guidance to the locally produced breed of Fascist, the *Milice*. Formed to fight the resistance, the *Milice* were also involved in rounding up Jews for deportation to the death camps.

rupting the prospect of a general Maquis rebellion timed to coincide with the Allied landings. The division was expected to take all possible measure to suppress the Resistance. An order from the Commander-in-Chief West, *General-feldmarschall* von Rundstedt, laid down the rules of engagement: 'Limited success in such operations is useless...the most energetic measures must be taken in order to frighten the inhabitants of this infested region.'

Almost immediately, *Das Reich* began encountering Maquis ambushes. In the first such action 23 Frenchmen were killed, at a cost of seven German lives. This was not an isolated occurrence: en route to Normandy, *Das Reich* was attacked time and time again. The Resistance raids did not have much destructive effect, but they did cost the SS men considerable delays, which they could

ill afford, and which aroused a considerable amount of anger. The easiest outlet for that anger was brutality.

The first major atrocity occurred at Tulle on 10 June. The *Der Führer* Regiment was sent to relieve the German garrison, which had been besieged by a Resistance rising. On entering the town, the SS men discovered 40 mutilated German corpses, the work apparently of Communists. As a punishment for the attack, divisional troops hanged 99 civilians at Tulle. A further 148 citizens were deported to Dachau, where 111 were to die.

Given that the slaughter was in reprisal for the murder of Germans, such an action was at least understandable, if not justifiable. A second incident was atrocity, pure and simple.

On 10 June, *Das Reich* officers *Sturmbannführer* Kampfe and *Obersturmführer* Gerlach were captured by the Resistance. Kampfe was killed, but Gerlach escaped. He told *SS-Stan-*

Below: The last class photo from the school at Oradour-sur-Glane, scene of reprisal massacre by the *Das Reich* division. Not long after this photo was taken, all of these children were crowded into the local church with the women of the village. The Germans then set fire to the church before blowing it up. None of the people inside survived.

dartenführer Stadler, commander of the *Der Führer* regiment, that he had been held in the small village of Oradour-sur-Glane. Stadler sent 3 Company of *Der Führer's* 1st Battalion, under the command of *Sturmbannführer* Dickmann, to investigate. Dickmann, the battalion commander, was a close personal friend of the missing Kampfe.

On arrival at the village, Dickmann rounded up the inhabitants. Even though it was highly unlikely that any of them had anything to do with the Resistance – the nearest Maquis camp was at least 10km (6 miles) away – he ordered the women and children to be herded into the village church and the male inhabitants locked up in several barns and garages. At about 15.30 p.m., the company began to shoot the men of the village. At the church, other SS troopers threw in grenades and then opened fire. At the end of the slaughter, 642 French civilians, including 207

children, were dead. After the massacre the SS men (many of whom were French-speaking Alsatians) looted and burned the village.

On hearing the news of the massacre, *Standartenführer* Stadler requested that Dickmann should be tried before a court martial. Dickmann, to whom such massacres had been commonplace in Russia, did in fact face a trial once the division reached Normandy, but he was killed in action before a decision could be made.

The brutality had its effect: further attacks by the Resistance were limited, and the progress of *Das Reich* was slowed only once it had crossed the Loire and came under Allied air attack. It eventually went into action against the Americans at the end of June.

TOTENKOPF DIVISION IN FRANCE

The only other SS division to spend a significant amount of time in France before the Allied invasion was the *Totenkopf*. After the fall of France in June 1940, the division spent the next year on occupation duty in the southwest, initially around Bordeaux and then on the Spanish border at Biarritz. In August 1940, with so many Frenchmen held in prison camps, the men of the division helped in bringing in the harvest.

In June 1941, *Totenkopf* transferred to East Prussia for Operation Barbarossa. It would serve on the Eastern Front until October 1942, when it suffered badly in the fight for the Demyansk Pocket. Withdrawn from the front line, the *Totenkopf* division was posted to France's Mediterranean coast, where it took part in Operation Attila. This was the German occupation of Vichy France, which until Allied successes in the Mediterranean had been allowed to exist without the presence of German forces. The *Totenkopf's* task was to prevent the French fleet from sailing for Africa.

In December 1942, the division was limited to coastal defence duties while being brought up to its full strength of more than 21,000 men. The rest and refitting would last for another two months, until Soviet pressure in the east strained German defences. *Totenkopf* was transferred

from Bordeaux to the Ukraine over the first two weeks in February. The 3rd SS Panzer Division *Totenkopf* would remain on the Eastern Front for the rest of the war.

The only SS unit to spend most of its career in the West was the 16th SS Panzergrenadier Division *Reichsführer-SS*, which fought in Italy. The origins of the division dated back to May 1941, when a combat unit known as the *Begliet-Bataillon Reichsführer-SS* was formed from a guard unit of Himmler's command staff, the *Kommandostab RFSS*. During Operation Barbarossa, *Begliet-Bataillon RFSS* was involved in anti-partisan sweeps behind the front lines. In February 1943 the unit was expanded to brigade size, and was renamed *Sturmbrigade Reichsführer-SS*.

After four months of anti-partisan service in the East, during which it served alongside the thugs and murderers of the Dirlewanger regiment, the *Sturmbrigade* was sent to Corsica. There it had secret orders to attack the Italian garrison if it tried to resist German occupation.

In September 1943 Hitler ordered the evacuation of German troops from Corsica. In October, the *Sturmbrigade Reichsführer-SS* was expanded to divisional size, forming up in Slovenia and Austria. Divisional strength was about two-thirds that of one of the senior *Waffen-SS* divisions. Two infantry companies and a panzer brigade were detached to serve as a guard force for Mussolini's headquarters on Lake Garda. For the rest of the year the 16th SS Panzergrenadier Division *Reichsführer-SS* trained in Slovenia.

SS IN ITALY AND HUNGARY

On 22 January, the Allies landed at Anzio, and the 16th SS sent several *Kampfgruppen* to reinforce *14. Armee* at the beachhead. The *2nd Battalion, SS-Panzergrenadier Regiment 35* and the *2nd Battalion, SS-Panzergrenadier Regiment 36* reached Terracina by 26 January.

While *Regiment 35* and the division's flak detachment stayed at Anzio until March, the rest of the division took part in Operation Margarethe, the German takeover of Hungary. The division was back in Italy by the end of April, and had assembled at Grossetto by May. From August 1944 the *Reichsführer-SS* Division was used predominantly on anti-partisan operations against the *Stella Rossa* Garibaldi Brigades, though it did see some front line combat on the Arno front. In its anti-partisan role, the division was particularly prone to atrocity: on 12 August the armoured reconnaissance unit massacred 560 civilians at Sant'Anna di Stazzema, with a further massacre at Padule di Fucecchio. In the 10 days from 17 August, divisional units killed more than 360 Italians in anti-partisan operations around Bardene San Terenzo. More atrocities were committed in September, again at Sant'Anna di Stazzema and at Marzabotto.

The division left Italy in January in January 1945, though to prevent the Allies from learning that fact it was described in all communications as the 13th SS Division. It spent the last months of the war in the futile fight against the Red Army in Hungary.

ALLGEMEINE-SS IN EUROPE

Regular *Waffen-SS* units were not the only representatives of Himmler's elite order to be used as occupation troops. Members of the *Totenkopfstandarten* also did duty in the conquered territories of Europe.

Created in the late 1930s, the *Totenkopfstandarten* were armed units of the *Allgemeine-SS*, intended to fulfil a more overtly political or security function within Germany than the *SS-VT*, or Armed SS. Originally raised from Theodore Eicke's concentration camp guards – the *Totenkopfverbände* – the *Totenkopfstandarten* came to include overage *Allgemeine-SS* reservists and teenage volunteers too young for military service, as well as concentration camp guards. Despite their being organized along military lines, the *Totenkopfstandarten* were considered by the German Army to be no more than police units or at best paramilitary units, and duty in the regiments did not count as military service.

With the outbreak of war, the *Totenkopf* regiments were used for police and anti-partisan

duties in the occupied territories, principally in Poland, Czechoslovakia and Norway, though they also served in France and the Low Countries. They also performed tasks of a 'special nature', providing manpower and support for the murderous *Einsatzkommando* death squads.

At the end of 1940, when Himmler was looking for a source of manpower for his expanding private army, he transferred the *Totenkopfstandarten* into the *Waffen-SS*. The older members of the regiments were not suitable as replacements for the field divisions, so the younger SS men were reorganized into new SS infantry regiments and brigades, while the older men were reserved for occupation or guard duties. Overall, the *Standarten* troops were poorly armed and poorly trained. Generally suitable for internal security work, they rarely performed well in front line combat.

THE OCCUPIED COUNTRIES

In many of the countries occupied by the Germans, the police and civil service remained in place and kept the country running for their new masters, who often operated through the SS or its security arm, the SD. Right-wing pro-Nazi political parties existed in most countries and provided

---

Reservists of the *Allgemeine-SS* who were used for occupation duties were poorly trained and badly equipped for the job.

---

puppet national leaders for Berlin. Collaboration ranged from neutrality or tacit support to active assistance and even service in the German armed forces fighting in the USSR. For many young men and women, the rapid military triumph of the German forces made the dynamic energy of their former enemies very attractive. Their own leaders had fled the country and Fascism appeared to be the force of the future.

Equally, however, resistance began almost as soon as the invading forces were in place. This

Above: The Allied invasion of Italy and the overthrow of Mussolini saw the *Leibstandarte* pulled direct from the cauldron of the Battle of Kursk, where they had formed part of the II SS Panzer Corps in the greatest tank battle in history. The division was shipped from Russia to the Italian front, where it was used to occupy Milan and to disarm Germany's erstwhile allies.

included providing food or clothing for British soldiers who had evaded capture in 1940, and later aiding Allied aircrew who had escaped from PoW camps or parachuted from burning aircraft. A few resistants were more active, attacking military and industrial targets. These were precision attacks, sometimes against a single critical machine in a production line, and were often more effective than massive air raids. Such attacks often brought about cruel and arbitrary revenge on the population by the Germans. However, their conduct in Western Europe was generally more humane than in the East.

In the early days of the war, the British were in no position to offer assistance to those prepared to resist, though over the following years a network of special operations and intelligence organizations came into being. These made extensive use of Free French personnel who had escaped to Britain in 1940.

But not all of the resistance looked to London. Following the invasion of the USSR, Communist parties in the occupied countries mobilized their cells to form resistance groups. In some areas, differences between London-based resistance groups and those that looked to Moscow for their lead produced a tension and hostility that undermined their efficiency in the field.

In the first year of their occupation of Western Europe, the Germans were confident of victory and conducted themselves arrogantly, but correctly. As the fortunes of war swung against them and resistance, both active and passive, increased, so their conduct and relations deteriorated.

BELGIUM

Belgium was overrun by the Germans in two weeks in May 1940 and the King negotiated a surrender with the Germans on 28 May. He had hoped that surrender would allow the country to remain neutral and enjoy a degree of independence.

However, along with the coalfields of northern France as far south as the Somme, the country was run as a military administration by General von Falkenhausen, who was based in Brussels. The frontier cantons of Eupen, Malmédy and St Vith, which had been transferred from Germany to Belgium in 1919, were reincorporated into the *Reich* by a special Führer decree on 18 May 1940. The Flemish nationalist VNV and the Francophone quasi-Fascist Rexist movement under Léon Degrelle collaborated with the Germans. The Belgians and Walloons formed the *Waffen-SS* divisions *Langemarck* and *Wallonien* that fought on the Eastern Front.

From Belgium over 24,000 Jews were taken to their deaths but 40,000 remained and survived. The total war-related civilian losses in Belgium during World War II (excluding Jews) were 10,000.

LUXEMBOURG

The Grand Duchy of Luxembourg, with a population of 293,000 and a defence force of 87, resisted the German invasion on 10 May 1940 and suffered seven casualties. The population were declared German nationals, but there was a general strike in August 1942, when 13,000 men were conscripted for military service. It was broken when 21 strikers were executed and hundreds sent to concentration camps. Altogether, 2848 Luxembourgers died in German uniform and 5259 Luxembourgers lost their lives.

THE NETHERLANDS

The Netherlands, which had been neutral in World War I, had a small but poorly equipped army and was quickly overrun by the Germans in 1940. The Queen and Government escaped to the United Kingdom. Under two Austrians, Artur Seyss-Inquart and H. A. Rauter, the *Reichskom-*

misiriat administered the country as a dependent province of the Third Reich. It was a brutal rule, in which the two men aimed to exploit all the resources of the Netherlands. Despite this, 54,000 Dutchmen were members of various Nazi organizations and 5000 joined the *Waffen-SS*, serving in the *SS Freiwilligen-Panzergrenadier Division Nederland* and in the *Landstorm Nederland*. Holland was occupied for most of the war, and by the winter of 1944–5 starvation in the population was a major problem. During this period, 16,000 people died from malnutrition.

The Jewish population of the Netherlands suffered cruelly. Only 20,000 survived the war. Some 106,000 were deported and murdered. Total war-related civilian losses in the Netherlands during World War II were 204,000.

DENMARK

In 1940 Denmark was the victim of the world's first operational parachute attack. The country was quickly occupied, but until 29 August 1943 the King and country attempted to maintain an illusion of neutrality. The Germans brought increasing pressure on Denmark and while this produced 100,000 workers for German industry, Danes also served in the *Waffen-SS Division Nordland* on the Eastern Front. However, after 1943, following increased resistance that included strikes and demonstrations, rule of the country was assumed by the Germans, through an unofficial board composed of the heads of the civil service under Niels Svenningsen.

In 1943 all sections of the population of Denmark collaborated in a daring operation in which 5500 Danish Jews were smuggled to Sweden in one night just before the Germans began rounding them up. Only 472 were caught and deported to Theresienstadt; of these, 52 eventually died.

NORWAY

Norway was attacked on 9 April 1940 and the fighting dragged on until 8 June, by which time the invasion of France and the Low Countries obliged the French and British forces to withdraw. King Haakon VII escaped to Britain and formed the basis for a Government-in-exile. The leader of the Norwegian Fascist National Union Party was Vidkun Quisling. Josef Terboven, the Reich Commissioner for Norway, made him Minister President on 1 February 1942. Norwegian volunteers joined the *Waffen-SS* and contributed large numbers to the 5th SS Panzer Division *Wiking* and the *Waffen-SS Division Nordland*, which fought on the Eastern Front.

About 40,000 Norwegians were imprisoned or sent to concentration camps, of whom about 2000, including 700 Jews, died. A further 500 Norwegians were killed or executed for resistance activities. Total war-related civilian losses in Norway during World War II were 8000.

ITALY

Italy entered the war as an Axis Pact ally of Germany, but in September 1943 surrendered to the Allies and became a co-belligerent against Germany. The Allies had liberated Sicily and southern Italy by October 1943; however, the north remained under Fascist and German control until 1945. As in other countries in Western Europe, there were collaborators and resistors within the community throughout the war. German reaction to resistance was often savage, especially in March 1944, when an attack in Rome led to one of the worst atrocities of the Italian campaign.

Below: Benito Mussolini was one of the few men respected by Adolf Hitler, so when *Il Duce* was imprisoned atop the Gran Sasso mountain in the Apennines, the Führer ordered his rescue. Under the command of SS commando Otto Skorzeny, a mixed force of SS and Luftwaffe *Fallschirmjäger* landed on the hilltop by glider, released Mussolini and flew him to Germany.

Above: Assault guns of the *Sturmbrigade Reichsführer-SS* move through northern Italy towards Hungary late in 1943. Formed from Heinrich Himmler's bodyguard battalion, the unit was about to be expanded to become the 16th SS-Panzergrenadier Division *Reichsführer-SS*. The division was to spend much of 1944 in action against Italian partisans.

The idea of Rome as an 'open city' was dear to the heart of Pope Pius XII, and he devoted most of his energy during 1944 to making that ideal a reality. The Holy Father's sentiments were shared by most Romans and even by the leaders of the Resistance. Accordingly, most members of the Resistance avoided provocative acts that might evoke drastic reactions which might jeopardize the existing uneasy equilibrium. Nevertheless, a few members of the Resistance thought it dishonourable that in Rome alone, of all Italian cities, there should be no rising, no open sign of anti-Fascist resistance.

The most active of such groups was the communist-directed *Gruppi Azione Patriotica* (GAP). After a series of attacks, it decided that the time had come for a major gesture. On March 23 1944, in the Via Rasella, a bomb exploded as a German unit was marching by. It killed 33 soldiers.

Regarding the action as a direct challenge to its authority, the German High Command in Berlin ordered the immediate execution of 10 Italians for every soldier who had been killed. Moreover, the order, issued in Hitler's name, insisted that the reprisal be completed within 24 hours. Under the direction of *SS-Obersturmbannführer* Herbert Kappler, 335 Italians who had no connection with the Rasella affair were taken from various prisons. By noon the next day, a convoy bearing the victims of the reprisal, who were yet unaware of their impending fate, was directed to the Ardeatine caves on the outskirts of Rome. There they were shot to death in groups of five, and buried in the caves. The executions were carried out in secrecy, but on the next day German authorities briefly announced that 10 Italians had been executed for every soldier who had been killed in the Via Rasella. Months passed, however, before the identities of all the victims became known.

FRANCE

The largest country to be occupied was France. Following the Armistice of June 1940, Germany and Italy took large areas of the country under direct control. In addition to occupying most of the north and west, the Germans annexed outright Alsace-Lorraine. Future plans included extending the German border westwards to include an area with a north-south line from Mezières, through St-Dizier to Chaumont. The ultimate aim was to remove the French population and replace them with Germans.

The Occupied Zone in France resembled an inverted letter L. It included Paris, the industrial north with its coalmines, and the coast from the Channel down to the Bay of Biscay. Control of French naval and air bases gave the Germans much better opportunities to wage sea and air attacks on Britain. They declared a *zone interdite* (forbidden zone) 10km (6 mile) deep inland from the coast, designed to prevent French citizens from observing the Atlantic Wall defences under construction.

The SS, in the shape of the *Sicherheitsdienst* and the Gestapo, was the executive arm of Germany's brutal struggle against the Resistance.

Part of France remained unoccupied – for a while. Marshal Pétain's right-wing collaborationist government administered the *zone libre*, or free zone. Based in the spa town of Vichy, it included the cities of Limoges, Toulouse and Lyons. This area was finally occupied by the Germans in November 1942.

The Vichy Government at least had some measure of independence. However, in the occupied zone of Paris, the collaborationist groups run by

Jacques Doriot of the *Parti Populair Française* and Marcel Déat of the *Rassemblement National Populaire* were opposed by the Vichy Government. The 3000 Frenchmen who fought with the Germans on the Eastern Front in the *Legion des Voluntaires Française contre le Bolchevism* were later transferred into the *Waffen-SS* as part of the *Charlemagne* Division.

Eighty-three thousand Jews were deported from France and murdered, but in 1944 200,000 were still alive, many sheltered by fellow French citizens. The total war-related civilian losses in France during World War II were 250,000.

On 18 June 1940 Charles de Gaulle called upon the French to resist the German occupation of France. From disparate beginnings the Resistance developed into a regionally organized underground movement, which transcended party politics. It countered the occupation army in the Northern Occupied Zone, in Vichy France and in Algeria.

The Resistance was originally established by intellectuals, politicians and military men. Later on, people from all spheres of society became united in the struggle.

RESISTANCE TO OCCUPATION

De Gaulle's call-to-arms in 1940 initially attracted only a handful of citizens. The Resistance received a vital boost in June 1941, when the attack on the Soviet Union brought the French Communist Party into active co-operation. It was further helped by the German decision to conscript French workers, many of whom took to the hills and joined guerrilla bands that adopted the name *Maquis*, or undergrowth.

Resistance operations included passive and more militant opposition. Some collected military intelligence for transmission to London; some organized escape routes for British airmen; others circulated anti-German leaflets; still others engaged in sabotage of railways and German installations. All of these actions assisted in tying down large German formations.

On 27 May 1943, through his emissary, Jean Moulin, de Gaulle achieved a merger of most

Above: SS troops in action against the *Stella Rossa* Garibaldi Brigades in the Carrara region. The partisan war in Italy followed much the same pattern as it had in the Balkans and Greece. Fighting against a lightweight, fast-moving enemy with intimate knowledge of the local terrain, the SS used savage, no-quarter tactics as well as hostage-taking and reprisal actions.

the age of 22, and was transferred to the SD soon afterwards, where he specialized in clandestine investigations in the Berlin underworld. In May 1941 Barbie was posted to the Bureau of Jewish affairs, as an intelligence officer. He was then attached to the Gestapo in Amsterdam, where he earned a reputation for excessive brutality, even by the Gestapo's standards. He was awarded his first Iron Cross for bludgeoning to death an 'enemy of the Reich' in full public view; The 'enemy', a German-Jewish ice cream peddler, had refused to salute him properly. In November 1942 Barbie was posted to Lyon.

When the Germans occupied Lyon in 1943, the city was a stronghold of the French Resistance and a hiding place for many fleeing the Nazis. The SS wanted to 'cleanse' Lyon as quickly as possible. Barbie's Section IV (Gestapo) deported thousands of Jews to the death camps and killed hundreds of French civilians suspected of aiding the Resistance. A true sadist, Barbie would often pluck random civilians off the street and whisk them away to his headquarters at the Hotel Terminus. There he would torture them until they said something interesting – or until he got bored. Barbie was responsible for many individual atrocities, including the capture and deportation to Auschwitz of 44 Jewish children hidden in the village of Izieu.

Jean Moulin was tortured mercilessly by Klaus Barbie and his men. Hot needles where shoved under his fingernails. His fingers were forced through the narrow space between the hinges of a door and a wall and then the door was repeatedly slammed until the knuckles broke. A fellow prisoner, Christian Pineau, later described the

Resistance fighters in the *Conseil National de Resistance* (CNR). Moulin was tortured to death two months later by *SS-Obersturmführer* Klaus Barbie, Butcher of Lyons.

Klaus Barbie was a typical, if extreme case of the kind of men used by the SS and Gestapo in the occupied territories. He joined the SS in 1935 at

Resistance leader as 'unconscious, his eyes dug in as though they had been punched through his head. An ugly blue wound scarred his temple. A mute rattle came out of his swollen lips'. Jean Moulin was in a coma when he was shown to other Resistance leaders being interrogated at Gestapo headquarters. It was the last time Moulin was seen alive. For the capture and elimination of Moulin, Hitler awarded Barbie the Iron Cross First Class.

In every Gestapo prison in the cities of Occupied Europe, similar forms of torture were committed. Breaking the body was turned into a science of creating the maximum pain for the least effort. Graffiti etched into cell walls testified to the agony of the sufferers. Means of torture were progressively refined. But in the absence of psychoactive drugs traditional methods served the Gestapo well: hanging a victim by his thumbs so that only his toes could scrape the ground for additional support caused dislocation and intense pain.

Estimates of the number of Resistance members who died vary from 20,000 to 30,000. Some 75,000 others were also deported and did not survive the concentration camp system. Besides

Below: An SS panzergrenadier jumps over a puddle in an Italian town. In Italy, unlike in the Balkans, SS troops were often switched between irregular anti-guerrilla operations in the mountains and conventional operations against the advancing American Fifth and British Eighth Armies. However, Italy was never more than a sideshow for the SS.

Left: Klaus Barbie, the 'Butcher of Lyon' was a typical if somewhat extreme example of the kind of SS men used to oppress Occupied Europe. A rabid homophobe who had been used by the SD to investigate brothels and gay bars in Berlin before the war, Barbie ran the Gestapo in Lyon where he found plenty of chances to gratify his taste for physical torture.

February 1943 the Germans deported about 2200 islanders who were not native-born. Of these, 46 died in internment camps or in transit and four women who were Jewish perished in extermination camps.

SS: INSTRUMENT OF TERROR

In Germany and in occupied Europe, it was the SS that provided the terror tactics which allowed the Nazis to rule. The police was under the control of the SS, as were the Gestapo and *Sicherheitspolizei* (SIPO, or Security Police). The SS maintained its control through the *Sicherheitsdienst* (SD), the Security Service that grew from a small party security group into a body which was the overall controller of the Nazi Police State.

The *SD* followed hard on the heels of the German Army. In the wake of the occupation of Austria in 1938, it co-ordinated the arrest of some 67,000 people. Adolf Eichmann, interrogated after the war, described how the *SD* cast its net: several months before the *Anschluss*, the staff at *SD* headquarters compiled an index of every potential enemy in the country. Three shifts worked around the clock, feeding a gigantic rotating card file several metres across. Punch holes indicated whether an individual was a Jew, freemason, Communist, Protestant or Catholic activist. The intention was to crush any anti-Nazi opposition at the outset, and it was fully realized: every potentially hostile group was crushed within weeks of the takeover.

As the Nazi conquests gathered pace, the *SD*'s work increased. It drew up plans for the elimination of racial and political enemies in the East. There were several dozen *SD* officers in each of the *Einsatzgruppen* in Poland and Russia, and in occupied Western Europe. It was the *SD* that

the German forces, police and French collaborators assisted in the executions.

THE CHANNEL ISLANDS

Off the northwest coast of France, the British-administered Channel Islands were occupied by the Germans from June 1940 to May 1945. The islands became fortresses: the residents of Alderney were removed and the island became the site of an SS-administered concentration camp where 1000 French Jews worked on the defences. There were sporadic acts of defiance, but no organized resistance. One of the reasons was the huge garrison – there were higher numbers of armed troops per square mile on the islands than in Nazi Germany itself. Between September 1942 and

abducted suspected resistance fighters under the *Nacht und Nebel* (Night and Fog) decree.

The *Nacht und Nebel* decree was issued at Hitler's order on 17 December 1941 by Keitel, chief of the *Wehrmacht* High Command (*OKW*). It directed that in the Occupied Territories, persons who were charged with 'punishable offences against the German Reich' were to be brought through 'night and fog' to Germany, unless they had already received death sentences from military courts. The so-called *NN* prisoners were then tried by special courts. Upon acquittal or after serving time for their offences, they would invariably be sent into the camp system – the favoured concentration camps were Natzweiler and Gross-Rosen. The prisoners were denied any contact with their families. Some 7000 people were transported under the terms of the decree.

The victims were mostly from France, Belgium and Holland. In Occupied France, many of the 'disappeared' were executed soon after interrogation, their bodies disposed of in secret graves. Relatives did not discover the fate of their loved ones until after the war, when the *SD* files were captured. In the East, record-keeping was not so rigorous and the fate of many victims remains unknown.

SD offices also led the hunt for escaped prisoners-of-war, implementing the 'bullet decree' of March 1944, which ordered the execution of escapees other than British or American servicemen. Recaptured Russians were taken by the *SD* to Mauthausen concentration camp for execution.

Below: A member of the French resistance is about to be shot by an SS firing squad. As many as 30,000 resistance members died in the struggle with the Germans, out of a total of approximately 250,000 French civilian deaths during the war. Approximately 7000 were arrested and deported without trial under the terms of the *Nacht und Nebel* decree.

Above: French Jews being deported from the Gare d'Austerlitz in Paris in 1941. Most were to be sent to the infamous transit camp at Drancy, near Le Bourget. The SS had less to do with such round-ups in France than elsewhere, being more concerned with implementing the *Nacht und Nebel* decree under which Nazi opponents were simply 'disappeared' into the night.

The *SD* administered the infamous 'commando order' too, murdering members of the British special forces who, as soldiers fighting openly in their own uniform, were entitled to prisoner-of-war status.

THE FINAL SOLUTION

The SS and the *SD* also had a great part to play in implementing the Final Solution in Occupied Europe. The first task for the authorities was to identify and locate Jews. As in Germany, civil

---

The Nazi aim in implementing the Final Solution was to create a Europe totally free of all Jews.

---

liberties were restricted, Jews were ousted from public service employment, anti-Semitic laws were passed, property was confiscated, businesses were taken over, and Jews were restricted to specific areas of cities. From September 1941 all Jews in the *Reich* were required to wear a prominent Star of David, and those in other countries soon followed suit.

By this time, the Gestapo and the *Sicherheitsdienst* had access to extensive records of European Jewry. Using data from the German census of 1939, the SS used advanced card-sorting machines to perform the relatively easy, if time-consuming, process of identifying and locating all of the Jews living in Germany. The 'Reich catalogue of Jews and part-Jews' was finally completed in December 1942. There was less data on Jews in other parts of Europe: while the governments of some countries, such as Vichy France, co-operated enthusiastically in the cataloguing, others – most notably Mussolini's Italy – refused to co-operate.

The Nazi aim was not just a Jew-free Germany, but a Jew-free Europe. Early in the process, the SS started moving Western Jews into transit camps – concentration camps in all but name. From there, they were told, they would be resettled in the East. This may have been true at an early stage in the Nazi plan. However, by early 1942, when the first transports were already being moved across the continent, a meeting in the Berlin suburb of Wannsee had settled on a more permanent solution to the Jewish problem: a Final Solution, in fact. The 'resettlement' in the East would last until only until the extermination camps were up and running.

Europe's extensive rail network was the key to the deportations, and to the Holocaust that followed. In the West, Jews were rounded up by armed police and concentrated at assembly points or in transit camps until there were enough for a transport – usually between 1000 and 2000 people. The Germans went to great efforts to disguise what they were doing: the transported were told they were being moved to labour camps, or to settle new territories in the East. They were told to bring money, warm clothes, food and any household gear that they could carry. To take the deception further, many were charged for their one-way tickets, which went some way to defraying the costs of the transport.

DEPORTATION BY RAIL

In the surreal atmosphere surrounding the whole Final Solution, the SS arranged the transport by booking one-way tickets on the German national railway organization through travel agents. The *Reichsbahn* charged the SS four pfennigs per kilometre for each individual, with children being charged at half rate. Infants and toddlers were carried free. *Reichsbahn* employees used the same forms with the SS as they used to book holidaymakers on *Kraft durch Freude* package tours. They gave discounts for volume: there was a special group rate for more than 400 deportees. The SS even had to buy tickets for the *Totenkopf* guards who rode along with the transport.

Although they were booked as passengers, Jews were transported like cattle. The journey to the Polish ghettos might take two or three days: from Greece or Holland, it could last for a week. The transportees were sealed into unheated freight cars that were stifling in summer and freezing in winter. There was little provision for food or water. If they were lucky, the transportees had a bucket for sanitation, but for most of the trip they had to sit amidst their own excreta.

In 1941 and 1942, most of the transports were used to deliver Jews to the newly established ghettos in the larger cities of what had been Poland. From 1942, however, the transports were increasingly used to take Jews direct to the extermination camps at Chelmno, Belzec, Sobibor, Majdanek, Treblinka and Auschwitz. Between the middle of May and 9 July 1944, at the height of the mass slaughter of Hungary's Jews, the rail system was stretched almost to breaking point as 147 trains took over 430,000 victims to Auschwitz.

German policy in Occupied France was to hold Jews in three camps, all under French administration with SS or *Totenkopf* supervision. These were at Beaune-la-Rolande and Pithiviers in the Loiret, and at Drancy, northeast of Paris. In 1941, the camps held mainly Parisians, who were picked up in *rafles*, or round-ups. Drancy was an unfinished housing estate near Le Bourget airport. It was entirely deficient in electricity, water and toilets. One latrine in the courtyard served the whole population, which amounted to 27,000 by August 1941.

Prisoners slept 50 to a room, on bunk beds or planks and later just straw. Relatives were forbidden to bring in food, and starvation and disease set in by August 1942, at which point the deportations to Auschwitz began. By 17 August 1944 – the eve of liberation – 76,000 Jews had been deported from France. The overwhelming majority had passed through Drancy, of whom only three per cent survived.

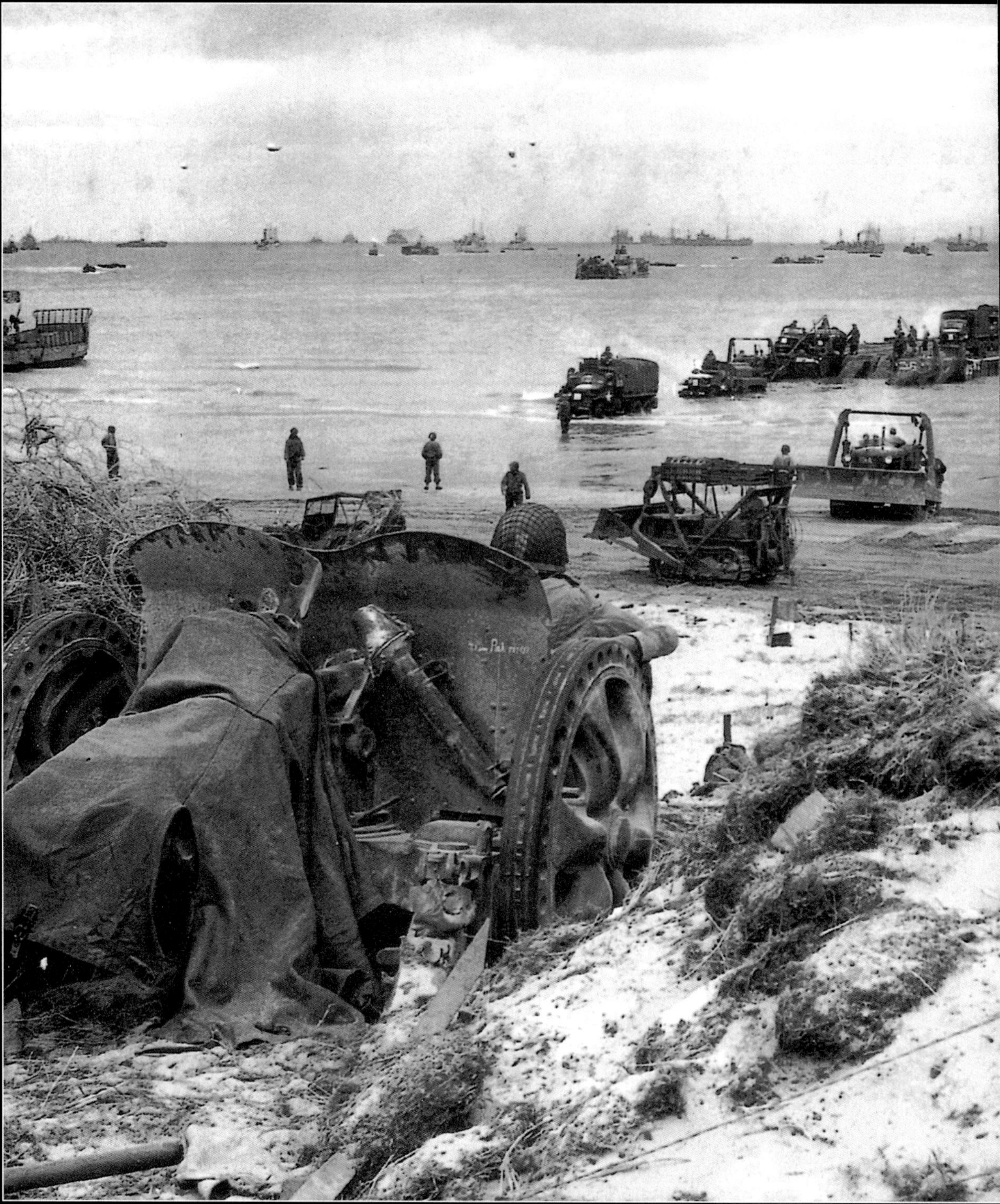

NORMANDY

The *Waffen-SS* played a major part in the German defence of Normandy. The panzer and panzergrenadier divisions of the two SS armoured corps provided the stiffest resistance to the Allied invaders – but the battle was to cost them dearly. By the end of the campaign, German forces had been shattered and driven from France. Most would be reconstituted in one way or another, but combat losses amongst the most experienced units meant that they would never be what they once were.

Man for man and tank for tank, the SS men were superior to their opponents, but the sheer numbers they faced made their task almost hopeless. The total superiority of Allied air power over the battlefield was the deciding factor, with fighters, fighter-bombers, light bombers, medium bombers and even heavy strategic bombers available to the Allies to destroy anything that moved in daylight. At the beginning of June 1944, Germany still occupied most of Europe. Within five short months, the German Army would be forced back to the borders of the *Reich*. What had gone wrong?

In some ways, the story of the Allied invasion, and its eventual success, began during the previous year on the Eastern Front. By the autumn of 1943, Hitler though undefeated was certainly bowed. He had suffered a serious strategic reverse at Kursk, and had been driven onto the

Left: The long-awaited Allied landings in Northwest Europe came in Normandy on 6 June, 1944. Although expected by the Germans, the location and timing took the High Command by surprise.

defensive by the newly invigorated Soviet Army. Italy been forced out of the conflict, and the Allied bomber offensive was bringing the war home to the German people.

However, the *Wehrmacht* still occupied huge swathes of territory in the East, as well as the Western lands held since 1940. Italy had been occupied by the Germans, and the *Wehrmacht* was contesting the peninsula inch-by-inch. And Hitler still had hopes for 1944, even though the

Below: The defenders of Normandy did everything they could to cause problems for the Allies. The marshy areas at the base of the Cotentin peninsula were flooded, which would hamper both infantry and armour, and carefully emplaced machine guns like this MG42 were prepared to sweep the area with fire.

year would almost certainly see the Western Allies return to the continent in force.

His Generals were less confident. The one thing they had always feared was a two-front war, and now they were faced with the prospect of fighting on three fronts – in Russia, in Italy, and now in the West. But where would the Western attack come? And when?

NEED FOR A SECOND FRONT

Even though the Red Army now held the initiative on the Eastern Front, Joseph Stalin doubted that he could defeat Hitler alone. The Russian dictator had his own agenda to follow: he wanted to expand the Soviet sphere of influence into middle Europe and the Balkans. To achieve this, he needed to weaken the powerful German

armies on the Eastern Front. He therefore demanded that the Western Allies establish a second front in 1944.

The ailing US President, Franklin Delano Roosevelt, was keen to aid Stalin, whose people had suffered so much at German hands. Winston Churchill, suspicious of the Soviet dictator, wanted the main Allied effort to be launched from the Mediterranean, through the 'soft underbelly' of Europe. However, Roosevelt's wishes prevailed. At a conference in Tehran, the 'Big Three' decided upon an invasion of France, to be scheduled for the early summer of 1944.

Churchill's hesitation came from his personal history. His first experience with amphibious landings had been the bloody affair in the Dardanelles in 1915. The slaughter at Gallipoli weighed heavily on the British Prime Minister's mind when planning the liberation of France. And Hitler's 'Atlantic Wall', bristling with concrete bunkers and minefields, was a far more formidable prospect than the Turkish defences had been in World War I. Moreover, the political stakes were higher. Gallipoli may have cost Churchill his job as First Sea Lord in 1915, but if the Allied invasion of France was thrown back, the liberation of Europe would be set back years.

Since his failure to bring Britain to terms in 1940, Hitler had been creating 'Fortress Europe'. Wanting to shield the Western borders of the Reich, he ordered massive defences to be built in depth. Under the efficient leadership of Reich Armaments Minister Fritz Todt, the Germans began to turn the whole Atlantic coast, from Norway to the Pyrenees, into an impregnable barrier. Todt, however, died in a plane crash before the project got seriously under way.

Late in 1943 Hitler appointed Germany's most famous soldier, Field Marshal Erwin Rommel, to take charge of the possible invasion front. Rommel was shocked by the poor state of the defences. Like most ordinary Germans, he had believed in Goebbels' propaganda images of massive concrete redoubts, linked by bombproof shelters and protected by anti-personnel and anti-tank devices of every sort. In reality, the

Above: Field Marshal Erwin Rommel, accompanied by Sepp Dietrich, inspects I SS Panzer Corps before the invasion. Rommel, commander of Army Group B, wanted to stop the Allies on the beaches. For that he needed Dietrich's tanks – but the 'Desert Fox' could not move them without direct permission, which had to be obtained from Hitler personally.

Atlantic Wall was little more than a thin defensive line, punctuated at intervals by strong bastions, which could simply be bypassed.

As commander of Army Group B on the French coast, Rommel threw himself into the task of making the Atlantic Wall a truly effective shield. Slave labour combined 17 million cubic yards of concrete with 1.5 million tons of iron to build a network of bunkers, pillboxes, observation towers and machine-gun nests. Anti-tank ditches were dug inland; steel girders were fixed at low water to impale incoming landing craft.

Rommel worked feverishly through the winter of 1943 and spring of 1944 to make good the neglect. But in the new age of mobile warfare, the Field Marshal knew that relying on static

Above: The newly formed 12th SS Panzer Division *Hitlerjugend* was part of Dietrich's I SS Panzer Corps. Commanded by Fritz Witt (centre), it was led in the field by outstanding fighting leaders like Kurt 'Panzer' Meyer (left) and Max Wünsche (right). Witt was killed by naval gunfire 10 days after the invasion, with Meyer taking his place as divisional commander.

On the first day of the invasion the *Luftwaffe* managed less than 100 sorties. The British and Americans launched a staggering 14,674. They lost only 113 aircraft, mainly to flak.

Even though many of its U-boats had been withdrawn to Norway, the *Kriegsmarine* readied its remaining submarine flotillas at Brest and Lorient to attack the invasion fleet. This was virtually a suicide mission, and 13 boats were sunk in the Channel in June and July 1944. Surface vessels fared little better: S-boats and a handful of destroyers stood no chance of having any impact on an invasion fleet of over 5000 vessels, manned by more than a quarter of a million men. Nine Allied battleships, 23 cruisers and 73 destroyers were assigned to shore bombardment missions alone. The English Channel, which had frustrated Hitler in 1940, was to the Allies little more than an inconvenience. The only place to beat them was ashore.

HIGH-LEVEL DISAGREEMENT

Field Marshal Gerd von Rundstedt, *Oberbefehlshaber* (Commander-in-Chief) of the German Army in the West, believed the invasion would take place in the Pas-de-Calais. Here, where the Channel is at its narrowest, the Germans would have less time to react once the invasion fleet had been detected. Once a beachhead had been secured, Rundstedt feared the enemy could use the good tank country inland to reach the Rhine in four days.

Normandy he ruled out, because the hinterland was dominated by the *bocage*, narrow lanes and high hedgerows that for hundreds of years had developed a root system as tough as chain mail, and which needed a bulldozer to penetrate. With the lanes sunken deep below the

defence lines was doomed to failure. The defeat of any Allied landings would require all the guile and fighting experience of the German Army, combined with an all-out effort by the Navy and the Air Force.

Unfortunately for Rommel, the *Luftwaffe* and the *Kriegsmarine* in the invasion area in 1944 were even more badly off than the Army. By the autumn of 1943, with its strength leeched away by commitments on the Eastern Front, the *Luftwaffe* had lost control of the skies over the Reich itself. *Luftflotte 3* had responsibility for defending France and the Low Countries. It had just 820 aircraft of all types, of which 170 were combat ready. By contrast, the Allies had more than 5000 operational aircraft available in June 1944.

hedgerows, worn down by generations of farm carts and animals being taken to market, the terrain was ideal for defence. Furthermore, there were no major ports in the area, and these were assumed by the Germans to be essential. The Allies' 'Mulberry' artificial harbours would come as a disagreeable surprise.

Runstedt's conclusion was reinforced by German intelligence, which reported a major concentration of Allied troops in the southeast of England. Designated FUSAG (First US Army Group), it was commanded by none other than General George S Patton – the one general in the British and American armies that the Germans really feared.

Hitler agreed with the advice of his Commander-in-Chief, and the Pas-de-Calais sector received the bulk of the new fortifications and the strongest concentration of troops. However, there remained disagreement about how to

tackle the landings. While the Allies prepared for the greatest amphibious invasion in history, Rommel and von Rundstedt each championed his own proposal.

Rommel, who had bitter experience of fighting against superior air power, believed the Allies had to be destroyed on the beaches. Once a beachhead was established, he had little confidence that the German Army could throw the invaders back into the sea. He wanted panzer divisions positioned near enough to the coast to intervene within hours, not days.

Below: The Germans expected the main Allied invasion to take place in the Pas de Calais. Convinced that the Normandy landings were a feint, the *Oberkommando der Wehrmacht* did not realise their error for at least 24 hours. By that time, the end of the first day of operations, the Allies had put 170,000 men ashore, losing fewer than 5000 in the process.

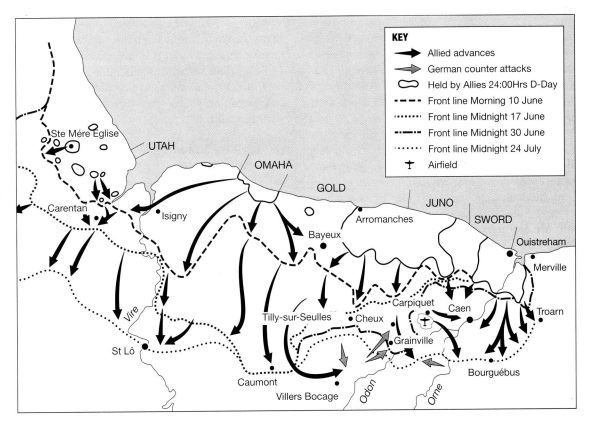

Von Rundstedt, his immediate superior, disagreed. He planned a conventional defence, accepting that the Allies would probably succeed in landing. Once the enemy's main thrust had been identified, the Germans would counterattack with a concentrated blow led by the panzer divisions.

Von Rundstedt accepted that daylight movement behind the lines would be vulnerable to air attack, but most divisions received additional anti-aircraft gun batteries. Since these guns would need to accompany the Army, light and heavy flak pieces were mounted on any chassis that was available. These included half-tracks, obsolete tanks and trucks.

It should be remembered that to many Germans, operations in the West were almost a sideshow. The bulk of the German Army remained on the Russian Front. Facing the Red Army were 164 divisions – and they would all be needed. The Soviet High Command was poised to launch five operations – each of which involved more troops than the Normandy invasion!

No surprise, then, that the 60 divisions deployed on or near the Atlantic Wall seemed to be a formidable force. Surely they were enough to counter the 50 Allied divisions poised to cross the Channel. But their task was not as easy as it looked. Many of the units in the West were second-line infantry divisions. Poorly equipped, their numbers were made up with semi-invalids and older men – a quarter of the German Army was in its mid-30s or older by 1944. Foreign troops of dubious loyalty were also used.

The infantry divisions also had an impossibly long coastline to defend. In northeast France, divisional sectors averaged 80km (50 miles); along the Normandy coast, each division guarded 150km (93 miles); and divisions along the shores of the Atlantic and Mediterranean were expected to cover over 250km (155 miles) of coast.

Yet, if the troops on the coast inspired no confidence, those behind the brittle coastal wall were a very different matter. German hopes rested on 11 armoured and four airborne divisions,

the latter serving as elite ground troops. But Rommel's disagreement with von Rundstedt over how to fight the battle was never resolved. Hitler assigned some panzer divisions to Rommel, others to Rundstedt's reserve, decreeing that none could move without his personal authorization.

Much of the firepower available to the Germans was provided by heavy SS panzer divisions. I SS Panzer Corps, created in Russia in 1943, was deployed in the West as the reserve corps of

---

The delay in releasing the Panzer reserve to contest the invasion beaches directly led to considerable confusion at the front.

---

the *Oberkommando der Wehrmacht* (OKW, or Armed Forces High Command). It could not be moved without Hitler's approval, an arrangement that led to confusion on D-day. Intended as a mobile armoured fire brigade, its mission was to engage any Allied landings on the coast of northwest Europe, from Antwerp to Cherbourg.

Obergruppenführer Josef 'Sepp' Dietrich, the former commander of the 1st SS Panzer Division *Leibstandarte SS Adolf Hitler*, commanded the I SS Panzer Corps. The initial composition of this elite corps included the *Leibstandarte* and 12th SS Panzer Division *Hitlerjugend*, the recently formed 17th SS Panzergrenadier Division *Götz von Berlichingen*, and the Army's *Panzer Lehr Division*.

MASSIVE BOMBING CAMPAIGN

In the months leading up to D-Day, the Allied air forces systematically bombed the French railway system. Bridges, marshalling yards, and key junctions were attacked in a campaign that cost the lives of some 10,000 French civilians. Radar installations were knocked out one by one in the final days. On 6 June, only one survived.

The station at Calais detected a massive radar contact crossing the sea at an apparent speed of eight knots. But this was an Allied spoof. The Calais station had been spared deliberately. RAF

bombers flew low over the sea, dropping patterns of 'window' – strips of foil that appeared as a mass of radar reflections. At the same time, a flotilla of small boats fitted with radar reflectors made for France. At 04:00 the two 'fleets' lay off the coast, broadcasting the sounds of anchors rattling through hawse-pipes from behind a thick smokescreen. Then they turned for home.

This was not the only deception. In the early hours of 6 June, the German High Command received reports of landings from Normandy to Calais. British bombers dropped dummy paratroopers as far west as Caen and Cap d'Antifer. Even after it was known that Allied troops were ashore in Normandy, the Germans believed the real attack would come at Calais; Normandy was assumed to be a feint. Not until many days later did OKW realize its mistake.

FUSAG had never existed: Patton's tours of his 'command' were reported widely, but his army group consisted of dummy vehicles, empty barracks and some very busy radio operators

Above: Wounded SS soldiers are helped to the rear. Even the veterans among them were shocked by the sheer power of the Allied air forces and navies. The air forces flew more than 14,000 sorties on D-Day alone. But to many Germans it was the naval gunfire support from dozens of battleships, cruisers and destroyers which created the most fear.

whose stream of radio traffic was monitored from the other side of the Channel. *Luftwaffe* reconnaissance flights were few and far between; the real invasion forces along the south coast were heavily camouflaged, while FUSAG units exposed huge dummy supply dumps to aerial observation. Moreover, the *Abwehr* spy network in Britain had been eliminated, its agents either executed or 'turned' to transmit bogus intelligence to their controllers.

The landings took place on a 96-km (60-mile) front, with five divisions assaulting from the sea and three by air. The airborne forces were the first into action. The American 82nd and 101st airborne divisions were dropped at the foot of the Cotentin peninsula. They spread confusion behind the lines and blocked any swift movement of German formations heading for the coast. Errors in navigation, and bad marking by pathfinders, together with deliberate German flooding of the drop zones led to significant casualties. Nevertheless the airborne units had the desired effect.

At the Eastern end of the landing area, the British 6th Airborne Division was tasked with seizing a bridgehead between the Orne river and the Caen Canal, halfway between Caen and the coast. This would secure the eastern flank of the invasion force.

The timing of the attack also caught the Germans by surprise. The weather was unfavourable, but the Allies had the advantage in forecasting. German weather ships had been swept from the

Below: If the Germans were shocked at the sheer weight of Allied fire support, the Allies who landed in Normandy found the determination and superb fighting ability of the German troops on the ground equally disturbing. Here, a British officer is taken prisoner by members of the *Hitlerjugend* Division following a failed attack on Hill 112, north of Caen.

Atlantic, so only the Allies knew that a break in the storms was on its way. When the landings began on 6 June, Rommel was in Germany, visiting his wife. Many junior officers were away, ironically on an anti-invasion staff exercise – and Hitler was asleep.

He was still asleep in the middle of the morning, by which time Rommel's staff had badgered von Rundstedt to request the Führer's permission to commit the panzers. But no one at OKW dared wake him. Accordingly, it was not until the late afternoon of 6 June that the nearest armoured unit was given orders to intervene. Rommel's defensive strategy had collapsed before the battle had even begun.

BREAKING THE ATLANTIC WALL

British and Canadian forces landed on the three eastern beaches, code-named Gold, Juno and Sword. The German 716th Division – a second-line formation including an *Ostruppen* battalion – was pounded by naval gunfire, bombed by the RAF, then driven from its defences exactly according to plan.

The Atlantic Wall was pierced by a number of ingenious armoured assault vehicles: flail tanks that beat paths through the minefields, bridgelayers and tanks fitted with bunker-busting howitzers. Only the belated intervention of the 21st Panzer Division prevented a complete disaster for the Germans. Once unleashed, the experienced unit reacted with characteristic aggression and skill. 21st Panzer counter-attacked the Canadians, and was only stopped short of the beach by naval gunfire. The Germans held on to the city of Caen, a key Allied objective for D-Day.

Meanwhile, the US Army divisions landed on Utah and Omaha beaches. At the extreme west of the Allied line, Utah was seized to facilitate a rapid advance into the Cotentin peninsula and the vital port of Cherbourg. Defended by elements of the second-line 709th Infantry Division, it was within reach of several veteran units, notably the 91st infantry division and 6th *Fallschirmjäger* Regiment. However, such was the confusion caused by the American airborne

assaults – scattered across the battlefield to the bewilderment of both sides – that neither German formation reacted in time.

Only at Omaha beach did the Allies face determined resistance. Allied intelligence had not detected the recent arrival of the German 352nd infantry division, a battle-hardened formation fresh from the Russian Front. A last-minute raid by 480 B-24 heavy bombers looked spectacular, but the bombs fell too far inland. Naval bombardment damaged some positions, but several newly built machine-gun nests had not been included in the fire plan. As a result, the first waves of American troops suffered hideous losses.

Small groups eventually found their way up various gullies. They outflanked the pillboxes and one by one, the gun positions fell silent. Follow-

Above: The M4 Sherman medium tank was the mainstay of Allied armoured forces. Although it was mobile and reliable, it was no match for the Tigers and Panthers operated by the SS and by the German Army. It was also vulnerable to German anti-tank units, who had learned their trade in the vicious fighting on the Eastern front against the superb Russian T-34.

on waves of troops came ashore in relative safety. Of the 35,000 US troops landed at Omaha on 6 June, 2200 became casualties. The German 352nd division retreated grudgingly, bitterly contesting every terrain feature and losing a quarter of its strength in a day.

Midnight on D-Day saw the Allies firmly lodged all along the Normandy coast. In just 18 hours, 170,000 men had been landed, with losses

of fewer than 5000. Thanks to the Mulberry harbour system, the Allies were able to feed troops and supplies into the beachhead almost as quickly as if they had captured a port. Moreover, although the 21st Panzer Division's counterattack out of Caen had initially penetrated the area between Juno and Sword beaches, it had been driven back. The British and Canadians had penetrated 8km (5 miles) inland. At Omaha the US Vth Corps were ashore, albeit after a bloody battle, and to the west at Utah the US VII Corps had crossed the flooded area close to the beach. By the end of the day, it had linked up with the men of the 82nd and 101st Airborne Divisions.

VETERAN TANK CREWS

Swiftly getting over their surprise, OKW began to move reserves to block the Allied advance. Among them were the *Waffen-SS* divisions, most with a hard core of troops seasoned in the bitter fighting on the Eastern Front. The *Waffen-SS*

Above: Man for man and tank for tank, the Germans in Normandy were better than their Allied counterparts. This *Panzerjäger* crew has just been decorated in the field for knocking out seven Shermans in one battle. But no matter how good they were, they could not match Allied numbers and air power, and German combat losses were staggeringly high.

panzer divisions that took part in the Normandy battles brought with them a wealth of invaluable and hard-won combat experience gained in years of vicious fighting on the Eastern Front, and many were survivors of the greatest tank battle of all time – Kursk.

Allied tank crews, on the other hand, had nothing like this experience. A high proportion of the armoured units that landed in Normandy were 'green' and inexperienced, and their tanks were no match for the best of the German panzers. That said, not all German units were equipped with the formidable Tiger or Panther;

many were still operating the venerable Panzer Mk IV, with which the Allies could compete on reasonably even terms.

The attack by the 21st Panzer Division was the only major German armoured assault on D-Day. The Allied invasion had come at a time when I SS Panzer Corps had only the *12th SS Panzer Division Hitlerjugend* in the vicinity. *Leibstandarte* was refitting in Belgium, *17th SS* was deployed south of the Loire, and *Panzer Lehr* was at

---

The SS panzer divisions were scattered all over France and Belgium, and it would take weeks to concentrate them in Normandy.

Nogent-le-Rotrou, 140km (87 miles) from the beach. The last was ordered into action, but would take many hours to reach the fighting. *Götz von Berlichingen* was released from OKW reserve and assigned to LXXXIV Corps of the Seventh Army, but it would take even longer to get into action.

Nor was the *Hitlerjugend* as ready for action as had been reported by commander Fritz Witt on 1 June. The divisional units were scattered all across Northern France. From a strength of some 20,500 men, some 18,000 were ready for action, but on 6 June the divisional HQ was at Dreux, near Paris.

When no orders from OKW were forthcoming, Army Group B assumed control of elements of the *Hitlerjugend* in the invasion area, and ordered them to engage the Allies on the beach north of Caen, specifically to intercept the British and Canadian armies advancing on Caen. In the first major SS involvement of the campaign, *SS-Panzergrenadier Regiment 25* counter-attacked advancing Canadian troops near Caen on 7 June. Fiercely defended and cautiously attacked, the city did not finally fall to the Allies until 13 July.

As the battle developed, I SS Panzer Corps, subordinated to Seventh Army, assumed command of 12th *SS* and *Panzer Lehr*, together with the Army's 21st Panzer Division and 716th

Infantry Division. 21st Panzer was engaged in a dual role. First, it was to support the 716th, which was being badly battered by British Second Army on the coast northeast of Caen. Then it was to attempt to join with 12th SS in a drive to the sea east of the Orne River.

However, the Allies had too firm a hold. Over the next 48 hours, the Corps counter-attacked the British on both sides of the Orne River, north and northwest of Caen. They had some success. By 9 June the Corps had established a defensive line north of Caen that would not be cracked for a month.

It was during one of these attacks, on 8 June, that members of the 12th SS shot 45 Canadian prisoners captured at Authie. It was one in a series of atrocities committed by the 12th SS; between 7 and 16 June, the young fanatics of the *Hitlerjugend* murdered more than 60 British and Canadian prisoners. They also lost a lot of men: over the same period the division reported more than 900 casualties.

By 13 June, the *Götz von Berlichingen* Division had reached Normandy from Tours, and was immediately thrown into battle against the Americans at Carentan. By 17 June, the *Leibstandarte* had arrived from Bruges to join the battle for Caen.

Further reinforcements were on their way: the 9th SS Panzer Division *Hohenstaufen* and 10th SS Panzer Division *Frundsberg* were ordered from Poland to Normandy on 14 June, when it dawned on Hitler that there would be no further Allied invasions in northern France. The two divisions, which would form the heart of a second SS panzer corps, arrived at Caen around 25 June. At the same time the 2nd SS Panzer Division *Das Reich* was battling its way north from Toulouse, fighting the resistance and committing atrocities on the way.

HITLER'S HOPES

Curiously, Hitler welcomed the Allied landing, confident that the *Wehrmacht* would inflict the same sort of carnage that the Canadians had suffered at Dieppe in 1942. Hitler believed, probably correctly, that if the Allies were defeated in this major landing, they would not attempt another for some time. This would give the Germans greater strategic flexibility and the opportunity to fight the Soviet Union to a standstill.

The Allies also feared getting stuck in a crowded beachhead. Their first priority was to link up along the coast. This was achieved on June 11. Then came a severe setback. Two Mulberry prefabricated harbours had been constructed at Omaha and at Arromanches, but on June 19 a

Below: Allied tanks had no answer to the armour and gun of the PzKpfw VI Tiger, which equipped Army and SS heavy tank battalions in Normandy. Neither could their crews match the experience of men like *SS-Obersturmführer* Michael Wittmann, seen here in the turret of his Tiger soon after being awarded Swords to add to the Oakleaves of his Knight's Cross.

severe storm in the Channel wrecked the Omaha port. Up to this point, the Allies had been winning the logistics race, for Allied air superiority meant that the Germans found it extremely difficult to reinforce the invasion front. Now, though, the capture of a port became a major priority. General J. Lawton Collins' VII US Corps drove up the Cotentin peninsula. Naval gunfire from three battleships and four cruisers as well as 1100 tons of bombs pounded the German garrison of Cherbourg into submission, the garrison commander, von Schliemann, having no stomach for a fight. However, the harbour and dock facilities had been comprehensively destroyed, and it took six weeks before supplies started flowing through the port in any great quantity.

Tactical air power was the major cause of German difficulties. Although reinforcements were getting through, Allied air superiority was making

Right: Michael Wittmann was the most successful armoured 'ace' of World War II. Credited with more than 130 tank 'kills', he and his crew found an ideal platform in the fighting power of his Tiger tank. Wittmann's Tiger single-handedly stopped an assault by the British 7th Armoured Division at Villers-Bocage on 13 June 1944.

it difficult and costly. Squadrons of Typhoons, Spitfires, Mustangs and Thunderbolts orbited continuously over the battlefield, on call at a moment's notice. These were used to neutralize *Wehrmacht* strong points and to blunt German counter-attacks. The fighter-bombers ranged freely over the lines of communication, making it almost impossible for supplies and reinforcements to be moved towards the front by day.

CAMOUFLAGE AND CONCEALMENT

But air power was never as decisive as the Allied propaganda attempted to portray. The Germans were masters in the art of camouflage, using the dense vegetation to conceal men, vehicles and rocket and conventional artillery. All major troop movements were carried out at night. Such was German success that by July the *Wehrmacht* reached a rough parity with Allied strength in France. That strength stood at a million men and 177,000 vehicles.

In Normandy, the terrain favoured the German defenders. The *bocage* channelled vehicles down narrow lanes, where they were vulnerable to lurking German infantry armed with the ubiquitous and deadly *Panzerfaust*. Allied infantry were compelled to cross exposed fields, where German machine-gun crews were dug in to give overlapping fire, while 8cm (3.15in) mortars were positioned to catch infantry forming up prior to an attack. Right across the field of operations the Allies were faced with the deadly cocktail of German professionalism and determination.

No unit better displayed these qualities than the 12th SS Panzer Division. This brand-new formation had recently been formed with volunteers from the *Hitlerjugend*. It was commanded by veteran *Waffen-SS* men, with experience of the

Eastern Front, and was equipped with the latest and very best equipment from the *Reich*'s factories. It was often said of the *Hitlerjugend* that they were trained to be fighters rather than soldiers. Certainly their training was heavily based towards combat skills and fieldcraft, with less emphasis on drill. The young grenadiers, many of them barely 17 years old, were the first generation to reach maturity under National Socialism. Skilful but fanatical, they lacked all compassion towards their foes, but they paid dearly for their devotion to the Führer: the unit suffered 80 per cent casualties within the first month of battle. Their commander, Fritz Witt, was one of the first to die when his headquarters was hit by naval gunfire.

At the eastern end of the beachhead, British and Canadian divisions fought to reach Caen. In the D-Day plans, the town had optimistically been listed as an objective to be secured within a

day of landing. From there, they would push out into the plain beyond the town. Stretching 30km (19 miles) to Falaise, this ground was ideal tank country, and was perfect for the construction of airfields to provide fighter support.

BATTLE OF ATTRITION AT CAEN

Despite the strong forces ranged against him, Field Marshal Montgomery did find some cause for satisfaction. The Allied ground force commander knew that the defence of Caen was essential to the Germans, and if the British kept up the pressure, the *Wehrmacht* would be committed to feeding more and more of its reserves into the battle. By the end of June, the Germans had indeed concentrated the XXXXVII and the I and II SS Panzer Corps opposite the Allied right flank. In all, 14 German divisions, six of which were armoured, faced the British and Canadians.

This meant that the forces facing the Americans at the other end of the line were weaker.

On 10 June, after careful preparation, British armour attacked the Caen–Villers-Bocage road. The British movement was intended to take the 7th Armoured Division around the flank of the German *Panzer Lehr* and 12th SS Panzer Divisions. As the leading British tanks reached Hill 213 behind the German lines, they and their supporting infantry stopped nose to tail down the road, the men dismounting to brew tea and stretch their legs.

Then a small group of panzers emerged from a small wood to the south of the road. Unfortunately for the British, *SS-Obersturmführer* Michael Wittmann, probably the most lethal tank commander in history, commanded the lead Tiger. As an NCO, Wittmann had commanded armoured cars and assault guns in Poland,

Facing page: Oberführer Fritz Krämer was Chief-of-Staff of 1 SS Panzer Corps in Normandy. When Sepp Dietrich was promoted to *Oberstgruppenführer* in August, he was also awarded the Diamonds to the Knights Cross. Hitler insisted that he returned to Berlin to receive the award, so Krämer briefly took command of the Corps.

France and Greece, serving with the *Leibstandarte-SS* as it evolved from Hitler's bodyguard to a fully-fledged armoured division. Sent to the *SS-Junkerschule* at Bad Tolz in Bavaria, he returned to the division as an officer in 1943. There he was made a section commander in the Tiger-equipped *schwere SS-Panzer Abteilung-13*, heavy SS Panzer Battalion 13. He quickly turned his regular crew – Woll, Berger, Kirschner and Pollmann – into a lethal team that knocked out 30 Soviet tanks, 28 anti-tank guns, and two artillery batteries during the Battle of Kursk.

By 9 January 1944, when he was awarded the Knight's Cross, Wittmann's score stood at 66 tanks. As if to celebrate the award of the decoration, he then shot up 19 T-34s and three heavy assault guns. On the 20th he was promoted to *SS-Obersturmführer* and 10 days later added the Oakleaves to his Knight's Cross. By the time he was transferred to France, Wittmann's score stood at 117 tanks and assault guns.

On the morning of 13 June 1944 he took four Tigers from *sSSPzAbt 101,* the heavy tank unit of the 1st SS Panzer Corps, and a solitary Panzer IV. Spotting the British armour nose to tail in the sunken lane, Wittmann brought his own tank forward. The rear tanks of the leading British unit, A Squadron, 4th County of London Yeomanry (CLY), were destroyed. Wittman then motored down the column at a range of about 80m (262ft), shooting up the half-tracks and Bren-gun carriers of the 1st Battalion, the Rifle Brigade. The British tanks were trapped in the sunken lane, unable to turn or climb the banks on either side of the road. Wittmann's astonishing feat saw the destruction of 25 British tanks, 14 half-tracks and 14 Bren gun carriers.

Wittmann then drove into the village of Villers-Bocage, knocking out 4 CLY's reconnaissance troop and then its headquarters troop. While he was doing this, three more of his Tigers had attacked the British tanks on Hill 213, forcing them to surrender. However, Wittmann was now in trouble, being in a built-up area without infantry support, and coming under increasingly heavy attack. A British anti-tank gun managed to disable the Tiger, and Wittmann and his crew baled out and escaped back to German lines. Nine days later he was awarded Swords to his Knight's Cross.

ONE TIGER AGAINST A DIVISION

The significance of Wittmann's action should not be underestimated. It stopped the entire British 7th Armoured Division as it attempted to fight its way around the German defences of Caen, and may have extended the Normandy campaign by several weeks.

Between 12 and 18 June I SS Panzer Corps absorbed the British Second Army's attacks on Caen, Villers-Bocage, and Tilly-sur-Seulles, skilfully committing its reshuffled elements in local offensive and defensive combined arms actions. Although Allied naval bombardment and air supremacy prevented the corps from launching a decisive counter-attack, the defenders forced the Allies to fight a battle of attrition that was costly to both sides, thwarting Montgomery's plans to capture Caen on 6 June.

It was during one of these offshore naval bombardments that the commander of the 12th SS Panzer Division Fritz Witt was killed. The command of the division was taken over by *SS-Sturmbannführer* Kurt Meyer, who became the youngest divisional commander in the German armed forces.

After Wittmann's action at Villers-Bocage, the British respect for the Tiger became even more profound. A general, if unofficial, rule was formulated by British tankers, which went something like 'If one Tiger is reported, send four Shermans or four Churchills to deal with it – and expect to lose three of them!'

From the middle of June, Montgomery began to marshal his resources for a major assault on Caen. His 21st Army Group launched two major attacks over the next months. Operation Epsom lasted from 26 June to 1 July. It was followed by Operation Goodwood between 18 and 20 July.

BREAKTHROUGH AT CAEN

The British initially broke through the German lines on 27 June and repulsed heavy counter-attacks by the 12th SS to contain them. The Germans were attacked on 4 July by the Canadians, who were attempting to capture the airfield at Carpiquet. Caen eventually fell on 13 July after the Canadians had been reinforced by the British 3rd and 59th Divisions. The *Hitlerjugend* had held the city for 33 days and in doing so had suffered 60 per cent casualties, one in three of whom had been killed. They had also lost half their tanks. Because of their heavy losses they were withdrawn for rest and refitting, but were back in action on 18 July when the British attacked east of Caen.

By now, the *Hitlerjugend* Division was no longer the only SS panzer formation in the field: reinforcements were arriving from all over Europe for the Normandy front. Not the least of these was the senior *Waffen-SS* unit, the 1st SS Panzer Division *Leibstandarte*.

At the beginning of the year, *Leibstandarte* had been fighting in Russia, and had sustained heavy losses. In April, the remnants of the division left Russia for rest and refitting in Belgium. By 25 April it was in place around Turnhout, receiving young replacements who were quickly taken in hand by the 'Old Hares', or veterans. On 3 May, the Führer gave orders that the *Leibstandarte* should be first in line for new equipment. By the beginning of June, *Leibstandarte* was around 20,000 strong, with 50 Panzer IVs, 38 PzKpfw V Panthers, 29 PzKpfw VI Tigers, and around 50 self-propelled and assault guns.

On 6 June, the division was assigned to I SS Panzer Corps. It began the transfer to Normandy on 9 June, with orders to join the 12th SS Division near Caen. On 22 June the division's Panther tanks were unloaded at Rouen. A day later the divisional HQ was established 20km (12 miles) south of Caen. On 28 June *Panzergrenadier Regiment 1* arrived at Caen, immediately seeing combat with the British troops along Highway 175.

On 6 July, one month after the Allied landings, the *LSSAH* was fully committed to the campaign. Over the next three days it would repulse a British assault, and when the 12th SS was pulled out of the line for a rest, the *Leibstandarte* took over the defence of the Caen sector. Between 18 and 21 July, the *1st SS Panzer Division* met the major Allied offensive known as Operation Goodwood, driving back the British 7th and 11th Armoured Divisions and inflicting heavy casualties in the process.

Alongside the *Leibstandarte* were two fresh SS panzer divisions, the 9th and 10th, operating as the II SS Panzer Corps, which was commanded by the experienced and capable *Obergruppenführer* Paul Hausser. (A former General Staff officer, Hausser had been the original inspector of the Armed SS before the war, and had commanded the *SS-VT* Division in France and the *SS-Reich* Division in the invasion of Russia.) Based in Poland when the Allies landed, the *Hohenstaufen* and *Frundsberg* divisions were immediately ordered west, beginning the transfer on 12 June.

The two divisions were experienced units. Formed during the expansion of the *Waffen-SS*

Montgomery's stubborn drive on Caen drew the bulk of German armoured reserves, weakening the forces facing the Americans at St. Lô.

---

in 1943, they were to operate together for much of their existence. Their combat debut came at Tarnopol on the Eastern Front in April 1943, where they punched a hole in the First Soviet Tank Army to relieve the trapped First Panzer Army. Ordered west soon after D-Day, they began their move on 12 June, to attack the Allied beachhead once they arrived.

They were, however, delayed by constant Allied air attacks. The Allied air campaign had succeeded in its main aim: German reinforcements found just getting to the front a major problem. The 9th and 10th SS took longer to cross France than they had taken in getting to France from the Russian border. As a result, the Allies were too firmly established for an attack against the beachhead to be feasible, so they were thrown into the battle for Caen. Nor were matters made easy for the II SS Panzer Corps by the promotion on 29 June of Paul Hausser to the command the Seventh Army – the first time an SS officer had risen to such heights. He was replaced as corps commander by Wilhelm Bittrich, till then the *Hohenstaufen* Division.

Defending Caen, the Corps immediately encountered Montgomery's 'Epsom' offensive, and in a week of heavy fighting stopped the 51st

Above: The *Wehrmacht* relied heavily on landlines for communication in Normandy, since messages sent down the lines were impossible to intercept, unlike wireless communications. However, landlines do not stand up to the rigours of battle very well, and Army and SS communications technicians spent a lot of time tracking down and repairing breaks.

Highland Division in its thrust towards the Orne River. The *Hohenstaufen* suffered over 1200 casualties: by 30 June divisional manpower was down to under 16,000 men. That day the *Frundsberg* Division, already understrength, lost 500 men in combat on Hill 112.

The fighting around Caen continued for the first three weeks in July. By 18 July the *Frundsberg* division had lost more than 2200 men dead or wounded. Yet, in spite of their best efforts, the British were unable to drive back the German

defenders. Montgomery even used heavy bombers to blast the German positions, but despite this, the attack ground to a halt with heavy losses in infantry and armour.

Nevertheless, such intense effort eventually brought results. Most of the city had fallen by 13 July, though some strongpoints continued to fight for a week or more. On 18 July, as Bittrich expressed alarm to OKW about the heavy losses his corps had suffered, British and Canadian forces finally breached the last German defences around the rubble of the old Norman town, over a month behind schedule.

HITLER SURVIVES THE BOMB PLOT

By this time, events elsewhere were having a profound effect on the battle. On 20 July the German opposition just missed killing Hitler. A bomb tore through a meeting room in the Führer's headquarters in East Prussia, where he had been in conference. Shielded from the worst effects of the blast, a shaken Hitler emerged with remarkably light injuries.

Above: Although in open country it generally took five British tanks to deal with one German machine, tanks were vulnerable in urban combat. In the villages of Normandy, SS tank crews relied on accompanying infantry for security. Here a *Hitlerjugend* Panzergrenadier checks that a village is clear of enemy troops before allowing a Panther to move through.

The assassination attempt had serious implications for the embattled German forces in Normandy. Firstly, they were to lose two of their best commanders, who were implicated in the Plot. Secondly, Hitler, the irrational dreamer, believed that his survival was no accident, but rather the result of divine providence willing him to continue as Germany's Head of State. His self-confidence, never absent for long, returned. In the coming weeks it would cause him to intervene disastrously in operations in Normandy.

The constant battering against the German right flank proved costly to the Anglo-Canadian forces, who made little progress. But the Germans had only finite reserves, and were short of fuel and ammunition. Even so, they continued to fight ferociously. By the end of July, the *Leib-standarte* were still holding their positions on the Caen-Falaise highway, standing firm against repeated attacks from Montgomery's 21st Army Group. By this time the formation's panzer strength had fallen to 33 Panthers, 30 Mark IV panzers and 22 *Sturmgeschutz* assault guns. Around 1500 men had been killed, wounded or captured or were missing.

Meanwhile, at the other end of the line, the German defenders were even weaker.

SS AGAINST THE AMERICANS

Rommel had far more respect for the British, as opponents, than the Americans. Accordingly, he and his staff opposed General Omar Bradley's powerful US First Army with 11 seriously under-strength divisions, only two of which were armoured. One of these was a newly raised SS formation, the 17th SS Panzergrenadier Division *Götz von Berlichingen*.

Orders to raise the division in Southern France had been issued on 3 October 1943. *Reichsführer-SS* Heinrich Himmler gave the unit the honorific title *Götz von Berlichingen* after a fifteenth-century German mercenary knight who led the peasants of Franconia during the Peasants' War and served with Holy Roman Emperor Charles V against the Turks and the French. The unit was raised from training, replacement units and some Balkan *Volksdeutsche*. It began forming at Tours at the end of November, and was formally activated on April 10 1944.

At the time of the Allied invasion it was stationed at Thouars. The formation had received

Below: A heavily camouflaged SS anti-tank gun is moved into action in Normandy. Utilising the hard-learned lessons of the Eastern Front, German anti-tank units would often allow advancing Allied tanks to move through their well-concealed positions before opening fire. The effect was devastating, with armour-piercing shells taking the enemy in the flank and rear.

only 22 weeks of training, and was short of officers and experienced NCOs. Although nominally a Panzergrenadier division, its armoured regiment had no tanks, being equipped with assault guns. On 10 June, the division was ordered to Normandy, some troops having to use bicycles to reach the front. First combat came against US Airborne forces at Carentan on 11 June. For the rest of the month, the 17th SS Panzergrenadier Division was in combat with the Americans.

In July it was joined by one of the premier divisions of the *Waffen-SS*, the 2nd SS Panzer Division *Das Reich*. Formed from the original *SS-VT Standarte*, *Das Reich* had fought in most of Germany's campaigns with the exception of Norway and North Africa. Given the best of equipment that was constantly updated, *Das Reich* earned an enviable combat reputation – unfortunately marred by an all too frequent tendency to commit war crimes.

On 6 June it had been on occupation duty around Cahours, near Bordeaux. By 9 June it was on the march through the Massif Central, skirmishing with and being delayed by the Resistance all the way. On 10 June, a company of *Das Reich* men committed the massacre at Oradour-sur-Glane in reprisal for the apparent kidnapping of *Sturmbannführer* Kampfe. The SS men massacred 642 civilians, including 207 children, in one of the worst outrages to have taken place in Western Europe. Such events were far from unusual in Russia, however, and many of the *Das Reich* troopers still had an Eastern Front mind set.

Commanded by *Gruppenführer* Heinz Lammerding, *Das Reich* units began reaching the combat zone early in July, and were immediately engaged in combat with American forces at Coutances, St. Lô, Percy and Mortain.

OPERATION COBRA

The relative weakness of the German units in the western sector of the front was fairly obvious to the Americans, who were far from being the amateur incompetents Rommel imagined. General Omar N. Bradley was not going to pass up this opportunity. At the end of July, in spite of

bad weather, Bradley readied the US 1st Army to punch through the German lines west of St Lô.

Known as Operation Cobra, the breakout began on 24 July 1944 after heavy bombers of the 8th US Air Force carpet-bombed the German forward positions. This, despite the fact that bad

---

Once clear of the deadlock in Normandy, American tank units were free to race through France, cutting German lines of communication.

---

weather led to the cancellation of the attack, by which some bombers had already delivered their payloads. Some missed the target altogether – killing 25 and wounding 131 men of the US 30th Division when their bombs fell short.

On 25 July the full weight of Cobra – 15 American divisions – fell on the men of the *Panzer Lehr* Division. This elite army force had been so ravaged by the intense fighting of the previous month that it could call on only 2200 men and 45 operational armoured vehicles.

At 09:38, 500 fighter bombers, unaware that their operation had been cancelled, attacked the German positions for 20 minutes, concentrating on the forward defences in a belt 250m (820ft) wide. These were followed by 1800 medium and heavy bombers. After the bombers came the artillery, and 1000 guns saturated with their fire a front that was 7km (4 miles) wide.

Yellow panels and smoke markers had been prepared to indicate the US front line, and the road from St Lô to Lessay provided a clear east-west reference point. Under a barrage of high explosives, German bunkers were caved in, barbed wire ripped up, ammunition dumps exploded and tanks were thrown into the air.

But even though the squadrons had been instructed by Bradley to attack on an east-west axis, the aircraft approached the target area from the north. In the prevailing wind, dust and smoke from the attack obscured the target and the reference points, and the bomb-aimers started to release their loads short of the targets. By the time the air attack was over, 111 soldiers of the hapless 30th Division had been killed and 490 wounded. It required considerable courage and leadership to put the 30th on its feet and send it into the attack after two such catastrophes.

The Sherman tanks began to roll forward. They now sported a new attachment, which eliminated the problems caused by hedgerows. A sharp-edged plough, made from Czech hedgehog anti-tank obstacles recovered from the Normandy beaches, was welded to the front of each tank. The ploughs cut through the *bocage* hedgerows, and the tanks were no longer trapped in the narrow country lanes.

To their amazement, given the sheer scale of the bombardment, the Americans encountered resistance. However, it was only a thin grey line.

By July 28 the Seventh Corps, under the dynamic General L. J. (Lightning Joe) Collins, and General Troy Middleton's Eighth Corps had pushed the Germans back over 20km (12 miles).

The tough *Fallschirmjäger* of General Meindl's Second Parachute Corps counterattacked the left flank of the salient, but were brushed aside by the Americans. Crossing the river Sienne near Coutances, Middleton troops

Below: The primary weapon of German infantry was the machine gun, the rifles of the infantry squad simply being there to support the MG42 gunners. Each member of the squad carried extra ammunition, since with its rapid rate of fire the weapon went through bullets at an enormous rate. That rate of fire made the MG42 one of the weapons most feared by Allied infantrymen.

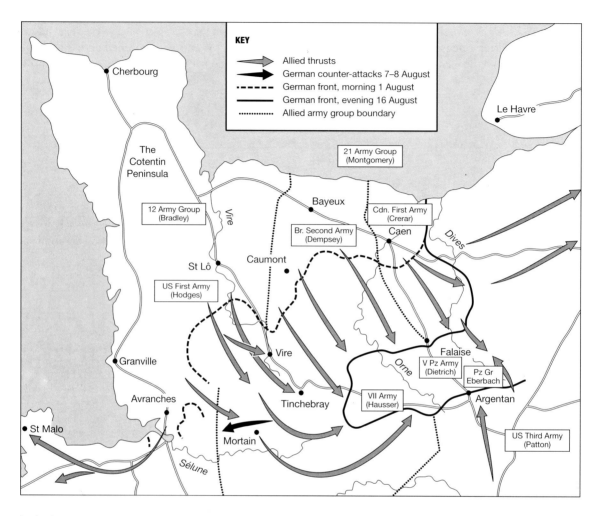

KEY

→ Allied thrusts
→ German counter-attacks 7–8 August
--- German front, morning 1 August
— German front, evening 16 August
······ Allied army group boundary

Cherbourg

Le Havre

The Cotentin Peninsula

21 Army Group (Montgomery)

12 Army Group (Bradley)

Bayeux

Cdn. First Army (Crerar)

Vire

Br. Second Army (Dempsey)

Caen

Dives

St Lô

Caumont

US First Army (Hodges)

Granville

Vire

Falaise

Orne

V Pz Army (Dietrich)

Pz Gr Eberbach

Avranches

Tinchebray

VII Army (Hausser)

Argentan

St Malo

Mortain

US Third Army (Patton)

Sélune

linked up with Collins to trap the Germans in a pocket at Roncey. By July 30, the lead American units had reached Avranches, and a day later were across the Sélun River.

The breakthrough gained the base of the Cotentin south of Cherbourg, where *Das Reich* had pinned down the US First Army. The gap in the German lines allowed two columns of Allied armour to pour through, one column headed for the Seine and the other westwards to Brittany.

Despite this rupture of their left flank, the German forces in Normandy held on, though with new commanders. Following the July Bomb Plot, Field Marshal Günther von Kluge had replaced the veteran Field Marshal von Rundst-

Above: The success of Operation Cobra saw fast moving American tank units flooding out into France from the Normandy beachhead. In a massive wheeling manoeuvre, Bradley's 12th Army Group threatened to join up with Montgomery's 21st Army Group pushiong south from Caen, trapping the German forces in Normandy in a gigantic pocket around Falaise.

edt. Rommel, who had been injured badly by RAF fighters in Normandy on July 17, was recovering in Germany. Both he and von Kluge were implicated in the plot, and both were to take their own lives before August was out.

In the meantime, Hitler ordered von Kluge to launch an all-out effort to cut the Allied supply lines and drive the Americans into the sea. For this attack Hitler released the armoured divisions held in the Pas de Calais, for a counter-attack against the narrow spearhead of the US advance from Avranches to Mortain. The exchange of signals between Hitler and von Kluge was intercepted and decoded by British Intelligence, and General Hodges, who had taken command of the US First Army, was alerted well in advance.

The four panzer divisions of General Paul Hausser's Seventh Army were also assigned to the counter-attack. On 4 August, they struck westwards. The attack covered nearly 20km (12 miles) of ground towards Avranches before being stopped. It was then reinforced on 6 August by the 1st SS Panzer Division.

Meanwhile the *Leibstandarte* were relieved on the Caen sector and had marched across the battlefield to continue the thrust. Bradley, now promoted to command the Seventh Army Group, sensed the danger and threw in two corps from the US First Army. Despite bitter fighting, the *Leibstandarte* could not reach Avranches.

What finally stopped the attacks were artillery fire and a devastating series of attacks by Allied

Below: The Allies were slow to close the pocket at Falaise, partly because the remnants of the SS panzer divisions which had been smashed in Normandy were fighting fiercely to hold it open. In spite of devastating Allied air attacks being launched around the clock, large numbers escaped – but they left their equipment and the bodies of many of their comrades behind.

Left: Normandy had been hard on German Field Marshals. Rundstedt had been sacked, Rommel had been wounded when British Spitfires strafed his car, and his replacement, Field Marshal von Kluge, committed suicide after being implicated in the 20th of July Plot. The final German retreat was eventually led by the 'Führer's Fireman', Field Marshal Walther Model.

The Germans were now in full flight. By 10 August the US 20th Corps had reached Nantes and a day later Angers. Meanwhile, George S. Patton had taken command of the US Third Army, and under his driving personality it raced deep into France. After the liberation of Le Mans on the 8 August, Patton swung north. His troops reached Argentan on 13 August, and the Canadians punched through to Falaise three days later.

On 14 August, Dietrich again asked for permission to pull back, but the Führer would have none of it – even though the Seventh Army, the Fifth Panzer Army and the composite force designated *Panzergruppe Eberbach* were in danger of being cut off in the 'Falaise Pocket', a trap with only one narrow exit to the east.

Now it was time for the Allied fighter-bombers to reap a bloody harvest. Most of the German combat troops in Normandy were penned in a pocket 65km (40 miles) long and 20km (12 miles) wide. As Allied ground forces moved in for the *coup de grâce*, aircraft cannon, machine-gun fire and rockets pulverized vehicles that clogged the roads and river crossings.

The 12th SS held one of the lower jaws of the Allied pincer movement open and the 9th SS held the other. Although tens of thousands of Germans were captured or killed in the pocket, far more escaped, albeit without weapons or equipment. Paul Hausser, commander of the Seventh Army, was wounded in the face, but managed to escape. So did Kurt Meyer, though the comman-

fighter bombers. On 7 August the *LSSAH* attack was shattered by Hawker Typhoons of the RAF's 245th Squadron. By 10 August, the *Leibstandarte* was on the defensive at St. Barthelemy, and Sepp Dietrich was asking the Führer for permission to pull back. He was refused.

FULL RETREAT FROM NORMANDY

Field Marshal Walther Model, 'The Führer's Fireman', had by now replaced von Kluge. This tough, monocled general had earned the reputation of being able to save crises on the Eastern Front. On this occasion, though, all he could do was to call a halt to the attack at Mortain.

Even as the Americans continued pushing southeast, an attack by the Canadian 1st Army now threatened Falaise. It needed no great imagination to see what would happen if the pincers were to meet. Montgomery was playing it cool when he said '...if we can close the gap on the enemy, we shall put him in the most awkward predicament'.

der of the *Hitlerjugend* division was captured later in Belgium.

The tough Polish tank crews serving with the British 4th Armoured Division closed the steadily shrinking Falaise Pocket. On 19 August they fought through to an isolated position at the village of St Lambert, and held it against desperate German attacks from both east and west. When the Canadians and Americans linked up with the Poles at the town of Chambois, there was nowhere to run.

Some Germans did manage to slip through the Allied lines at night, in bad weather, but up to 50,000 were taken prisoner, leaving another 10,000 dead behind them in the killing ground. Indeed, in the campaign for Normandy the Germans had lost 1500 tanks, 3500 guns and 20,000 assorted vehicles. These were losses that could never be made good.

Waffen-SS losses, in particular, were appalling. Divisions that had entered the fray with hundreds of tanks and thousands of men were reduced to little more than battalion strength. The *Leibstandarte* and *Frundsberg* lost all their tanks and artillery; *Das Reich* was left with 450 men and 15 tanks; *Hohenstaufen* had 450 men and 25 tanks. The *Hitlerjugend* had shrunk to 300 men, 10 tanks and no artillery. All but annihilated in France, the 12th SS Panzer Division was reconstituted with an even younger core of volunteers, though it needed a further hodgepodge of conscripts to bring it up to strength. This division participated in the Battle of the Bulge in Belgium, and in 1945 played its part in the abortive attempt to recapture Budapest. Finally, on 8 May 1945, the 12th SS Panzer Division *Hitlerjugend* surrendered to the American 7th Army. It numbered just 455 soldiers and one tank.

The battle in Normandy ended on 21 August with the remaining divisional remnants fleeing eastwards towards the Seine. Many German survivors said they had never experienced anything like the destruction brought to bear on them from Allied air strikes, naval guns and artillery – not even on the Eastern Front, a fact that many of its SS veterans would not have believed possible. It gave the Germans a lesson in the importance of air superiority – a lesson that would sound the death knell for the *Waffen-SS* armoured divisions employed in the West.

Many of the divisions were sent back to Germany for rest and refit, with the exception of II SS Panzer Korps under Wilhelm Bittrich. This was sent to Holland for refitting, ready to take on General Patton's forces, whom the Germans thought would launch a new offensive. However the next confrontation would come sooner than the *Hohenstaufen* and *Frundsberg* divisions expected – right on their very doorstep, at Arnhem.

CATASTROPHE FOR THE *REICH*

The Normandy campaign had been a stunning success for the Allies. They shattered the ring of steel that had surrounded the Normandy beachhead for more than two months. The Germans had no other prepared defence lines inside France upon which to fall back, and throughout the summer and early autumn, they fought a well-organized but inevitable retreat back to the very borders of the Reich. By early September 1944 all but a fraction of France had been liberated. The American and British/Canadian forces had occupied Belgium and part of the Netherlands and had reached the German frontier. Though they had now outrun their logistic support and lacked the strength to launch a culminating offensive, Allied commanders dared to think that they would be in Berlin by Christmas.

The final chapter of the War in the West was opening. But Germany was not ready to surrender. The huge loss of armour at Falaise, and the equally large losses to the Soviets following the Red Army's devastating summer offensive on the Eastern Front, was made good in a surprisingly short time. This was thanks to a remarkable feat of emergency industrial manufacture supervised by Armaments Minister Albert Speer: round-the-clock bombing of the Reich could not prevent tank factories exceeding all previous production figures to produce the advanced tanks, guns and other armaments used in the Ardennes Offensive in December 1944.

ARNHEM

Late summer 1944: having broken their opponents in Normandy, the Allied armies were racing across France. The Germans were in full retreat, with no prepared defences to the west of the Rhine and no reserves left to fill the breeches in their lines. The tide of liberation was as dramatic as the German Blitzkrieg four years before, and even the most cautious of commanders were talking of a final German defeat by Christmas. Surely nothing could save Hitler now?

NO RETREAT

Hitler insisted that the German Army cling to its positions in Normandy until it was too late for an orderly withdrawal. The result was catastrophic: instead of the fighting retreat across France envisaged by his generals, the German Army collapsed in rout. US armoured columns fanned out in pursuit, Allied aircraft strafed and bombed every road east. Between D-Day, 6 June and the end of August 1944 the German Army lost 221,000 men killed, missing or captured in France. Another 67,000 were wounded. The *Westheer*, or Army of the West, began the campaign with 50 infantry divisions and 12 panzer divisions. By the time Field Marshal Model gathered up the wreckage, there were only 24 infantry divisions and 11 panzer divisions – divisions in name only, since all had been reduced to a fraction of their

Left: In an astonishing feat of reconstruction, the German armies in the West were able to defeat a major Allied drive on Arnhem – less than a month after the catastrophic defeat in Normandy.

Left: Although many of the formations shattered in France retreated to Germany to regroup, the survivors of two veteran SS panzer divisions were sent to a quiet backwater in Holland. The presence of the 9th SS Panzer Division *Hohenstaufen* and the 10th SS Panzer Division *Frundsberg* was to have a far-reaching effect on the conduct of the war in the West.

authorized strength. The 11 panzer divisions existed in theory, but none was larger than a regimental *Kampfgruppe*, or battle group, and their average number of operational tanks was between five and ten.

The SS had fought harder than any to defeat the invasion, but by the end of the Battle of Normandy, they had been virtually wiped out. The *Leibstandarte* had been reduced to less than 30 serviceable vehicles and no tanks; *Hohenstaufen* had 25 tanks; *Das Reich* had only 15 tanks and 450 unwounded troops; *Frundsberg* had no vehicles or artillery, and *Hitlerjugend* had only 300 men and 10 tanks. Most of the divisions were pulled back to Germany to refit. *Hohenstaufen* and *Frundsberg* were sent to Arnhem in Holland, a quiet backwater well behind the lines, where it was assumed they would be undisturbed.

The Allied armies reached the Seine 11 days before they had expected to do so, and liberated Paris a full 55 days ahead of schedule. The American Seventh Army, which landed on the French Riviera on 15 August, broke German opposition in the south and linked up with Patton's forces by mid-September. At the same time, the American First Army closed on the German city of Aachen, a full eight months ahead of schedule.

The Germans were driven back towards the borders of the *Reich*. The British Army crossed into Belgium. Antwerp was liberated on 4 September. *Generaloberst* Kurt Student was ordered to establish a defensive line to hold the Low Countries, although his grandly titled 1st *Fallschirmjäger* Army consisted of rear echelon troops, returning wounded and raw recruits.

At last, the subjugated peoples of Europe could smile again. Even the most pessimistic allowed themselves to think again of peace, and everywhere British and American troops were embraced as conquering heroes.

However, the Allies headlong rush was at its zenith. Tenacious resistance by German garrisons in French ports was restricting Allied supplies. The armies of liberation were short of front-line infantry replacements. Men were exhausted and vehicles were in desperate need of overhaul. The advance slowed, then stopped.

MONTGOMERY'S GAMBLE

To retain the initiative, Field Marshal Sir Bernard Montgomery, the British commander, planned to break open the German defences in the north before they had the chance to solidify. His idea was to land the British 1st Airborne Brigade and the Polish Parachute Brigade near the Dutch town of Arnhem, a strategically located city on the lower Rhine, far behind the German lines. The attack was planned for 6–7 September, but cancelled when fierce German resistance slowed the advance of the British ground troops. However, after a meeting with Allied Supreme Commander General Dwight Eisenhower, the British scheme evolved into a far more ambitious plan. Eisenhower expanded Montgomery's plan to include the entire 1st Airborne Divison, as well as the US 82nd and 101st Airborne Divisions would also be committed.

Given the code name Operation Market Garden, the plan called for the US 82nd and 101st Airborne divisions to seize the bridges from Eindhoven to Arnhem, ahead of an armoured drive by the British XXX Corps. If the bridges fell intact into Allied hands, tanks could race through Holland and into Germany's industrial heartland before winter.

The strategy of Operation Market Garden was simple. Three-and-a-half airborne divisions would land along a 100-km (62-mile) corridor and the ground forces would race along it to link up with them within three days. If all went to plan, British tanks could reach the Ruhr before Christmas. Given the parallel collapse of German forces on the eastern front, following the Red Army's spectacular summer offensive, the operation held out the prospect of an end to the war in 1944.

The problem was that the road from Eindhoven to Arnhem, while a good one, was elevated on a bank for much of the way. The surrounding terrain was waterlogged and largely unsuitable for armoured vehicles. The Germans were well aware of this: their 1940 invasion plans had taken the terrain into account and had been rerouted.

German defence rested on a succession of rivers running parallel to the front line. The first obstacles faced by the Allies were the Meuse-Escaut and Zuid-Willems Canals. Some 25km (16 miles) to the northeast lay the Maas River, with a bridge at Grave. A further 15km (9 miles) northeast of Grave, there was a major bridge over the Waal River at Nijmegen. A further 15km (9 miles) north of Nijmegen was the biggest obstacle of all: the lower Rhine. There was a modern road bridge at Arnhem, plus a railway bridge and a ferry crossing just upstream.

Field Marshal Model anticipated an Allied airborne assault, but expected the blow to fall further to the east. Although he gave orders to prepare the target bridges for demolition, he withheld permission for their immediate destruction. Whether under Hitler's direct instructions or not, he seems to have intended some sort of operational level counterstroke for which he

---

The elite British paratroopers taking part in Operation Market Garden did not expect to encounter veteran SS panzer units.

---

would need the bridges intact. Some of his subordinate commanders criticized this strategy after the war. They argued, correctly, that if all these bridges had been dynamited, the campagin at Arnhem need never have happened. Furthermore, the demoralized German Army did not have the ability to launch a sustained counter-attack at that time.

INTELLIGENCE FAILURE

The British were confident of success. Military intelligence convinced them that the opposition to the elite Allied airborne formations would come only from second-rate German units consisting of old men, teenage conscripts and Dutch SS troops who could not wait to change sides.

But the Germans had received timely reinforcements. The 9th and 10th SS Panzer Divisions were being sent to the Arnhem area to refit and re-organize. Curiously, British intelligence lost track of both divisions and their presence so near to the airborne landing zones upset the Allied plan from the very beginning.

It could have been very different, had British Intelligence taken heed of, or reacted faster to, the warnings of the Dutch Resistance. Resistance groups in the Arnhem area were well organized. They sent detailed reports about growing German strength in the area. Alarmingly,

Above: Promoted to the rank of Field Marshal on 1 September 1944, Bernard Law Montgomery was a methodical general, willing to accept a battle of attrition when the odds were in his favour but usually sparing with the lives of his men. His daring plan to seize the Rhine crossings went against type, but had it worked it could have shortened the war by months.

they reported the presence of SS troops, armoured cars and tanks in the woods around Arnhem. After spotting SS staff cars carrying high-ranking *Waffen-SS* officers, Resistance members located and identified the headquarters of the 9th and 10th SS divisions together with a corps level headquarters. None of these reports reached the planners of Operation Market Garden, and the airborne forces were given the go-ahead.

On Sunday 17 September, the peoples of Britain and Holland looked skyward to an airborne armada heading east. A total of 1545

transports and 478 gliders were assigned to the operation, escorted by 1131 fighters: the formation was 16km (10 miles) across and 150km (93 miles) deep. Gliders offered the advantage of putting down a platoon of men in one spot; paratroops could be more scattered and take longer to prove an effective force.

Fewer than 50 *Luftwaffe* interceptors were available to attack the huge aircraft fleet, and they made little impression. Flak caught some of the lumbering transports as they neared the landing zones, but within 80 minutes there were 20,000 paratroopers on the ground across a great swathe of Holland. The most exposed of the forces was the British at Arnhem.

The task of the pathfinding Airlanding Brigade was to secure the drop and landing zones for the second lift on the next day. The supporting troops consisted of part of the divisional artillery and some of its 6-pdr anti-tank guns, engineers and the divisional reconnaissance regiment. To lift the First Parachute Brigade and this force, 161 parachute aircraft of the US 9th Troop Carrier Command and 297 gliders and tug aircraft of 38 and 46 Groups RAF were required.

In the second lift on the second day would come the 4th Parachute Brigade, intended to be landed on a drop zone between Planken Wambuis and the railway, and the remainder of the Airlanding Brigade. They were to be carried in 126 parachute aircraft and 305 gliders. A further 35 aircraft would drop supplies at the same time.

On the third day the 1st Polish Parachute Brigade Group was to land south of the main bridge, the assumption being that enemy flak in Arnhem would no longer be operative at that point. The troops would be carried in 114 parachute aircraft and 45 gliders. At the same time 163 aircraft would drop supplies for the 1st Airborne Division.

After securing the landing and drop zones, the Airlanding Brigade was to operate in concert with the 4th Parachute Brigade and the 1st Polish Parachute Brigade Group to form a perimeter round Arnhem, leaving the 1st Parachute Brigade holding the bridges and in reserve. That was the plan – unfortunately, the Germans were not working to the same script.

UNPLEASANT SURPRISE FOR THE ALLIES

The Dutch Resistance had been right: SS units were around Arnhem in some strength. The first reports of the airborne armada had prompted Field Marshal Model to alert all of his forces in the area, and those forces included II SS Panzer Corps under the command of *SS-Obergruppen-führer* Wilhelm 'Willi' Bittrich.

Willi Bittrich was one of the most capable and experienced commanders in the *Waffen-SS*. An army officer in World War I, he joined the *SS-Ver-fügungstruppe* in 1934. In 1939 he joined the *Leibstandarte* before quickly being moved to command the *Deutschland* Regiment of the *SS-VT* during the campaigns in Poland and France. He was promoted to command the 2nd SS Division *Reich* during the invasion of the USSR, before being given the responsibility of working up the newly formed 9th SS Division *Hohenstaufen*. In Normandy he replaced Paul Hausser in command of the II SS Panzer Corps after Hausser had been promoted to command the Seventh Army.

On paper, two SS panzer divisions should have been enough to annihilate the lightly armed airborne forces in very short order. However, this was less than a month since a large chunk of the German Army had been annihilated in the Falaise pocket, from which the *Hohenstaufen* and *Frundsberg* divisions had escaped by the skin of their teeth. *Hohenstaufen* had been in continuous action for more than two months from 29 June. During the collapse in Normandy, it had retreated westwards for two weeks, barely escaping encirclement at Falaise. Harassed by fighter-bombers and the French Resistance, it reached the Nether-

Right: Operation Market Garden called for British and American airborne troops to sieze key river crossings in Holland. The British XXX Corps would then create a land corridor through which Allied ground forces could be funnelled right into the industrial heart of Germany. Unfortunately, the plan did not take into account the ferocity of German resistance.

lands with only 3500 of the 18,000 men who had arrived in Normandy in June. It had only a handful of armoured vehicles. *Frundsberg* was in a similar situation.

The plan to reorganize the two divisions called for *Hohenstaufen* to return to Germany for refit.

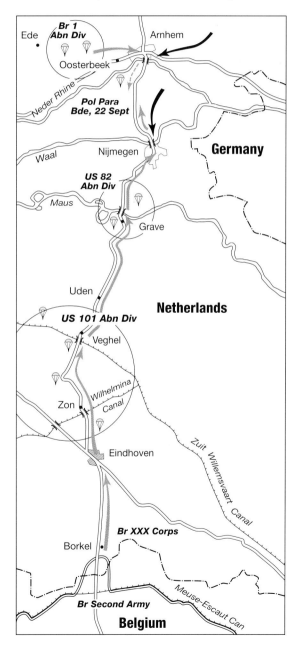

Early in September, it was due to hand over its vehicles to *Frundsberg* before being moved by train into Germany. From September 12, technical and support personnel began to leave. By 17 September, *Hohenstaufen* was reduced to the size of a weak brigade of around 2500 men.

Vastly understrength, with their equipment replacement programme barely under way, the two divisions nevertheless provided a solid core on which the Germans could base their defence of the Rhine bridges. Partly this was due to their immense combat experience, but their particular

Below: Members of an SS *Kampfgruppe* await the arrival of British paratroopers soon after the first airborne landings around Arnhem. Built around a solid core of experienced veterans and trained to repel parachute attacks, the German battle groups were tactically very flexible, operating mostly on their own initiative with minimal interference from higher commanders.

training also gave them a major advantage. Back in 1943, while they were first working up to operational status and awaiting the delivery of their panzers and mobile artillery, both divisions had been trained to counter airborne operations. Aggression was already a characteristic of SS training: now it was applied to dealing with unannounced attack by parachute forces. Commanders were instructed not to wait for orders but to make their own decisions, and make them fast.

Since airborne forces seemed likely to be the only threat facing German troops in what appeared to be a backwater of the war, the SS men around Arnhem were deployed to deal with an airborne threat. The two divisions were divided into 19 or 20 small *Kampfgruppen*, or battle groups, trained for quick-reaction operations. They were located at 12 sites along good roads in smaller villages around the city. Few

were in Arnhem itself: experience in Russia and Normandy had shown the *Waffen-SS* that urban fighting could be very costly.

The presence of these two battle-hardened units was decisive in defeating Montgomery's drive on the Rhine. Neither division acted as a unit: the *Kampfgruppen* operated independently with only the lightest of direction from Bittrich's II Panzer Corps. As a result, when the British paratroops landed at Arnhem, they immediately found themselves in combat with one of the *Kampfgruppen* made up from the tough panzergrenadiers of the *Hohenstaufen* division.

Meanwhile, Bittrich had sent another *Kampfgruppe*, centred on the remnants of the *Frundsberg* division, south towards Nijmegen. These were expected to block the Allied ground advance, which was supposed to link up with the paratroopers. Other *Kampfgruppen* were formed from whatever material was available: they included one centred on the staff of an SS junior officer's school, the *SS-Unterführerschule* at Wolfheze, to which was added some 400 troops, cooks and clerks from the 16th SS *Stammbatallion*, a replacement battalion.

FIRST PARATROOPERS LAND

On Sunday 17th September, 1944, the weather was fine and the flight from England to Arnhem was uneventful. Landings began soon after noon. Initially, they were successful, being completed with very little opposition and to the great delight of the local residents, who received the paratroopers enthusiastically. By about 15:30, the lead battalions of the 1st Parachute Brigade had started their advance to capture the bridges. Moreover, Field Marshal Model, who had his field headquarters of Army Group B at Oosterbeek, had been forced to flee when paratroopers of the British 1st Airborne Division began dropping almost in his

Above: German soldiers open fire on British paratroopers from a wood near Oosterbeek. Airborne operations succeed through speed and surprise: at Arnhem, the British had both. However, paratroopers are very lightly equipped, and against a well-armed, well-trained enemy able to react with speed, they can find themselves in serious trouble.

lap. Arriving at General Bittrich's II SS Panzer Corps headquarters, Model exclaimed, 'They almost got me! They were after my headquarters!'

At the same time, the British XXX Corps attacked along the road to Eindhoven. The advance of the tanks was preceded by a rolling artillery barrage that knocked out many, but not all of the German anti-tank guns that lay in wait in nearby woods. The US 101st Airborne Division captured the bridge over the canal at Veghel. The US 82nd Airborne took the bridge at Grave. But the SS held the bridge at Nijmegen, and there looked to be trouble at Arnhem.

The main target for the British was the road bridge at Arnhem. A secondary target, the rail bridge, was 3km (2 miles) further down the

Rhine, and some 8km (5 miles) further west was a ferry, which was scuttled during the course of the battle. By 20:30, after a small amount of fighting, the 2nd Parachute Battalion (2 Para), under the command of 34-year-old Major John Frost, had captured the north end of the main road bridge. Buildings on either side offered excellent observation points, overlooking the bridge itself and its approaches.

However, one company of Frost's battalion was detached to capture the railway bridge, only to

Below: **A British paratrooper watches over two SS soldiers taken captive. Generally, although the battles were fought fiercely and there were reports from both sides of atrocities committed in the heat of battle, the two sides at Arnhem treated prisoners honourably, with British and German medical officers working side by side to treat the wounded.**

have it blown up in their faces as they arrived. Surrounded by unknown but larger German forces, they were forced to break out and were never able to rejoin their fellows at the main bridge.

FATAL FLAWS

There were further problems. Despite the apparent success of the initial landings, the early stages of the operation were fatally flawed. Firstly, the drop zones were too far from the objective. Multiple lifts also caused problems, especially since only the first lift arrived on schedule; the rest were delayed due to bad weather, and when they did arrive, were often dropped at the wrong location. Later in the battle, supplies were dropped perfectly as arranged – except for the unfortunate fact that the pre-arranged drop-zones were now in the hands of the Germans. Without adequate supplies, the paratroopers were doomed. Air-

Above: Members of the British 1st Airborne prowl through the village of Oosterbeek, where most of the division had concentrated. Oosterbeek had been the location where *Generalfeldmarschal* Walther Model had set up his tactical headquarters: the commander of Army Group B had been forced to flee when the British landed almost on top of his head.

borne forces are lightly armed, with light scales of equipment. They are not designed to fight over long periods without relief or re-supply.

Initial resistance by the local Dutch SS battalions was light, but the experienced veterans of the 9th and 10th SS Panzer Divisions soon stiffened opposition, and the forces were more numerous and better trained than the British paratroopers had been led to expect. Though General Bittrich's II SS Corps was in urgent need of rest and replen-

ishment, but it reacted with blistering speed. As one post-war British Army study commented, 'The 2nd SS Corps reaction to the crisis read like a staff command and control exercise.'

One thing that the Allies could not have known was that German commanders knew every detail of Operation Market Garden before it happened: the entire battle plan had been recovered by the Germans from a crashed glider.

2 PARA ISOLATED AT ARNHEM

One end of the bridge at Arnhem was held by 2 Para, which unfortunately was isolated from the rest of the force. Nor did it help that the Allied division with the toughest mission had to be landed in two waves – there were not enough aircraft to carry them in one lift. When the second lift arrived, its delivery was not accurate. And until these scattered paratroopers could concentrate themselves for an effective attack, Frost's battalion would be on its own.

Frost came under attack from a unit of *Waffen-SS* armoured reconnaissance troops who had been on exercise to the south of the bridge. More ominously *Kampfgruppe Hohenstaufen*, commanded by *SS-Obersturmbannführer* Walter Harzer, was moving in from the south.

Early attempts to dislodge the paratroopers soon convinced the Germans that they had a real battle on their hands: in a series of vicious hand-to-hand fights, 2 Para fought off their German attackers and maintained a firm hold on the northern end of the bridge. The SS then attempted to rush 2 Para: *SS-Hauptsturmführer* Viktor-Eberhard Graebner, commander of *SS-Panzeraufklarungsabteilung 9*, a reconnaissance

battalion, led the charge, straight over the bridge. Graebner commanded the highest concentration of armoured vehicles at Arnhem, a mixture of 22 armoured cars and half-tracks, mounting a variety of armament from machine guns through 2cm (0.78in) cannon to 7.5cm (2.95in) guns. The charge was the sort of bold manoeuvre that had often worked on the Russian front, although it had not been as successful in Normandy. (Even so, Graebner had been awarded the *Ritterkreuz*

Below: Landing the bulk of the airborne force around Oosterbeek, six miles from Arnhem, was a major mistake by the British. Field Marshal Model and *Obergruppenführer* Willi Bittrich, commander of II SS Panzer Corps, ordered troops into the gap between the Paras and their objective, and the tough SS troopers quickly blocked any progress towards the bridges.

(Knight's Cross) for gallantry for his actions in Normandy, and had been presented with the medal just 24 hours before.)

The attack was a total failure: the paras greeted the armoured cavalcade with PIAT bombs and 6-pdr anti-tank guns. Graebner was killed and the wreckage of 20 of his 25 vehicles lay on the bridge for the rest of the battle. As one paratroop officer-turned historian wrote, 'it was a typical armoured commander's approach to an infantry problem'. The SS now called for reinforcements, and fresh supplies of artillery and several panzer units were already on their way.

KAMPFGRUPPEN IN DEFENCE

The rest of the British 1st Airborne Division was unable to reach Arnhem. Its way was blocked by determined German forces, who had quickly formed ad hoc battle groups to blunt the British thrusts towards the bridge. Among these was *SS-Kampfgruppe Spindler*, which lay between the city of Arnhem and the outlying village of Oosterbeek, where the bulk of the British paras had concentrated. The *Kampfgruppe* was initially located near the railway bridge downstream of Arnhem, but to block the advance of the 1st Parachute Brigade it moved rapidly.

Indeed, the story of *Kampfgruppe Spindler* during the Arnhem battle is a remarkable example of just how quickly the size, composition and mission of a *Kampfgruppe* could vary. *SS-Obersturmbannführer* Ludwig Spindler commanded the self-propelled artillery regiment of 9th SS Panzer Division *Hohenstaufen*. Aged 34, he had already won the Iron Cross in Russia and the German Cross in Gold for his bravery in Normandy. Spindler's regiment existed only in name: he had 120 men but no artillery pieces of any kind. On the afternoon of 17 September, he was ordered to take command of several infantry companies as part of a 'quick reaction' force. Before the battle was over, he would have 16 different units in his *Kampfgruppe*.

Driving around in his staff car to assemble his *Kampfgruppe*, Spindler nearly ran into disaster when a building he stopped at turned out to be occupied by British paratroops. By evening, he had several rifle companies together and was attacking from Arnhem town centre towards Oosterbeek. He added some personnel from anti-aircraft batteries and some *Reicharbeitdienst* (labourers), whom he equipped with captured British weapons. On 18 September he added some tank crews who were still waiting for new vehicles, plus two understrength companies of panzergrenadiers. The next day he obtained 10 *Sturmgeschütz* assault guns. Over the next week, *Kampfgruppe Spindler* swelled to include the survivors of the reconnaissance battalion's charge over Arnhem bridge, assault pioneers and – a mighty reinforcement indeed – 15 Tiger IIs from SS Heavy Tank Battalion 506.

A nearby *Kampfgruppe* was made up from *Hohenstaufen*'s pioneer battalion, which was commanded by *SS-Oberstürmführer* Hans Möller. Möller was familiar with the area: as a

---

By forming a series of ad hoc *Kampfgruppen* or Battle Groups, the Germans managed simultaneously to contain the British airborne troops at Arnhem, while blocking the northward drive of General Horrocks' XXX Army Corps

---

platoon sergeant in the engineer platoon of *SS Regiment Der Führer*, he had fought through Arnhem and Oosterbeek in May 1940. Advancing east from the railway station, Möller's unit made contact with *Kampfgruppe Gropp*, and the two units set up a defensive line to the east of Den Brink park, which extended to the positions held by *Kampfgruppe Spindler*. The three *Kampfgruppen* managed to contain the advance of the 1st Parachute Brigade, preventing it from reaching 2 Para.

SS-Hauptsturmführer Klaus von Allworden commanded another *Kampfgruppe*. Made up from dismounted tank destroyer crews of *Panzerjäger Abteilung 9* of the *Hohenstaufen* division, together with a few *Kriegsmarine* personnel left ashore after their river craft had been sunk,

Kampfgruppe von Allworden had a strength of 120 men, and was equipped with two SP guns and a handful of 7.5cm (2.95in) towed PAK anti-tank guns. The *Kampfgruppe* was formed at Apeldoorn, and was sent down to Arnhem from the north. Although far from being the most powerful SS unit, the *Kampfgruppe* set up an ambush on the Dreyenseweg, 6km (4 miles) from Arnhem, where their surprise attack prevented two battalions of British paratroopers from making any further progress towards 2 Para and the bridge.

EINDHOVEN AND NIJMEGEN

By the afternoon of 18 September, tanks from the British Guards Armoured Division had linked up with the Americans at Eindhoven. A day later the ground troops were in Nijmegen, an advance of nearly 80km (50 miles) in 48 hours. But the same day saw the British Airborne at Arnhem in increasing difficulty – German attacks meant that 4 Para had been forced to establish a defensive perimeter around Oosterbeek.

On the 19th, the 1st Parachute Brigade made a determined attempt to close the gap between Oosterbeek and the isolated 2 Para on the bridge at Arnhem, but the attack ran straight into the prepared defences of *SS-Kampfgruppe Spindler*, and was beaten back with heavy losses. An attempted reinforcement, the landing of Polish glider-borne troops to the west of the city, ended in disaster. Elements of Major-General Sosabowski's Polish Parachute Brigade landed in the middle of a battle between between the the 4th Parachute Brigade and Krafft's 16th SS *Sturmbatallion*, and were virtually wiped out. This was followed by a disastrous aerial supply operation in which only 30 tons out of a total of 400 tons fell into Allied hands. The Germans, who had overrun the drop zones, captured the rest. Relief was not to come to the embattled 2 Para at the bridge, who were enduring a series of increasingly heavy assaults.

A unit from the 10th SS Panzer Division, part of *Kampfgruppe Frundsberg*, was experiencing the same thing at Nijmegen. They clung to the bridge in the teeth of intense artillery barrages fir-ing across the river and so denied the vital bridge to the British armour. Nijmegen was finally taken by a desperate effort. At 15:30 on the 20th, the 3/504 Parachute Infantry of the 20th US Infantry Brigade paddled over the Waal in assault boats. The American infantrymen crossed the Waal downstream of Nijmegen; the German defenders were thinly stretched here and the Americans assumed they would escape observation. However, it was not to be: within a few minutes alert German observers directed artillery and mortar fire onto the river. Even so, the Americans gained a toehold on the east bank.

The bridge itself was taken by a British tank platoon acting with astonishing bravery. Through a smokescreen thickened by the smoke from nearby buildings burning down, four Sherman tanks charged the bridge at the same time that German engineers were working among the bridge girders, secured by harnesses, to check the demolition charges. The tanks shot the engineers down with their machine guns as their drivers worked up to top speed. British artillery silenced the 8.8cm (3.45in) guns guarding the bridge exit. When a frantic defender pressed the plunger to detonate the charges, nothing happened. Finally the road to Arnhem lay open, but the XXX Corps was far behind schedule: the British in Arnhem had been expected to hold the bridge for just two days. So far, they had resisted for four.

The route to reach them, the road from Eindhoven to Arnhem, was christened 'Hell's Highway' by the Americans, who had to hold it against repeated German counter-attacks. Having captured an intact set of operational orders from a crashed glider, the Germans had full details of where the 82nd and 101st were deployed and what they were trying to achieve.

German airborne commander Kurt Student later wrote, 'I knew more than anybody else that an airborne landing is at its weakest in the first few hours, and must be sorted out quickly and determinedly.' However, Student began the fight with very few units he could rely on, whereas the Americans were veteran airborne troops, the toughest and most experienced in the US Army.

Horrocks' armour raced along the raised main road that linked up the target bridges. The road, although a good one, was elevated on a bank for much of the way. The high silhouette of the advancing vehicles presented an irresistible target for surviving German anti-tank crews, firing from

Below: The bridge at Arnhem was the ultimate aim of Operation Market Garden. Between four and six hours elapsed before British troops reached it, progress having been slowed by enthusiastic Dutch civilians welcoming their liberators. 2 Para reached the bridge, but were then cut off from further support by the rapid German reaction to the landings.

well-camouflaged positions off the road. Nor was there a way round the knocked-out vehicles; the surrounding terrain was waterlogged and could not support armoured vehicles.

AN UNUSUAL BATTLE

To the SS soldiers who had been hardened to slaughter on the Eastern Front, the battle for the bridge at Arnhem had some strange characteristics. Bittrich, the corps commander, tried a piece of psychological warfare by bringing forward loudspeakers. He played jazz records to get the British attention, then urged them to surrender. Appeals for them to remember their wives and

sweethearts, together with the threat of an assault by a fresh, fully equipped panzer division were greeted with jeers and a burst of machine-gun fire.

Even stranger to the Eastern Front veterans were the occasional ceasefires to allow wounded to be collected from the battlefield for medical care – which more often than not meant German doctors working alongside captured British medical officers, assisted by SS men as they treated both British and German wounded.

GERMAN ATTACKS REPELLED

By this time Frost's troops on the northern end of the bridge at Arnhem were under attack from *SS-Kampfgruppe Knaust*. Though largely made up from SS men, this was led by an Army officer, *Oberst* Hans-Peter Knaust, an experienced panzer battalion commander. *SS-Kampfgruppe Brinkmann* was also hitting them from the west, yet the tough British paras repelled all that the SS could throw at them, having at this time only about 250 unwounded men. Urged by the Germans to surrender, Frost and his men refused. Expecting relief at any moment, they were unaware that XXX Corps had in fact met stiff resistance from the Germans.

On 20 September the situation had reached a stalemate. The British were exhausted and low on both ammunition and food rations, especially water since the Germans had turned off the city's water supply. Frost himself had been wounded quite badly. Nonetheless, the paras put up a desperate resistance against the relentless attacks by the SS, who were themselves too weak to completely overrun the British positions. However, the British perimeter was shrinking, and first aid stations could not be sited out of range of German guns. An agreement was reached in which the British were allowed to withdraw from the aid stations, leaving their wounded behind in the vacated buildings to be cared for by the *Waffen-SS* medics.

At about 18:00 on 20 September, four King Tiger tanks of *SS-Kampfgruppe Knaust* forced their way over the bridge from the north to ren-

Facing page: Following the capture of the complete Allied plans for the operation, German ground units were ideally placed to intercept subsequent parachute drops. As German pressure increased it became obvious that the British forces had to be evacuated. On 25 September General Horrocks ordered General Urquhart's men to fall back.

dezvous with the *Frundsberg* troops on the south side. The tanks crossed successfully – nothing the Paras had in the way of weaponry could challenge the thick armour of a King Tiger – but the British prevented the rest of Knaust's armour from following. That evening a temporary truce was agreed and the British and Germans evacuated their wounded, who numbered about 200 – including Major Frost.

2 Para's last stand ended in surrender on 21 September. *SS-Kampfgruppe Knaust* finally drove the survivors of Frost's battalion off the northern end of the bridge. The remnants of Frost's greatly depleted force, under the command of Major Gough, attempted to break out towards the north through the area held by Knaust's battle group. The British were fragmented into a number of small groups, most of which were eventually captured, although some held out for several days.

SS veterans of the war on the Eastern Front reckoned that the British paratroopers were the toughest opposition they had ever faced.

Further west in the British enclave of Oosterbeek, the Germans had surrounded the area with two battle groups, *SS-Kampfgruppe Hohenstaufen* and *SS-Kampfgruppe Tettau*. Here too the situation was a stalemate, as the Germans simply did not have the strength to bulldoze their way through the British positions.

Officers and men of II SS Panzer Corps were later unanimous in their praise for Frost's men and the rest of the division now pinned against the Rhine. As one German NCO remembered,

'This was a harder battle than any I fought in Russia. It was constant close range hand-to-hand fighting. The English were everywhere... it was absolute Hell.' Another commented, 'The only way to get the British out of the houses was feet first.' The Germans dubbed the Arnhem sector, the 'Witches' Cauldron'. The paras refused to stay in their perimeter and launched frequent counter-attacks.

To counter these, the SS resorted to their usual tricks. On one occasion an ambulance drew up to rescue the wounded, and out came a section of stormtroops, their sub-machine guns blazing. The combatants gave no quarter and there were occasions when prisoners were shot in the heat of battle – by both sides. In general, however, the SS men and their officers were punctilious in their treatment of prisoners.

But, as ever, the SS had two faces. Called to escort the British paratroops to camps in Germany, the *Totenkopf Standarte* refused for two days and nights to provide either food or medical treatment, and any prisoners who fell out of line on the march were beaten mercilessly.

POLISH SACRIFICE

Even as the survivors of 2 Para were fleeing or surrendering, a final effort was made to save the position in Arnhem. On 21 September, the British landed the Polish Parachute Brigade south of the Rhine, the other side of the river from 1st Airborne Division. However, the Germans prevented them from breaking through to Arnhem. Further efforts were made on the night of 22 September to get as many of the Polish Parachute Brigade as possible across the river from south to north. As a

result of enemy action and a shortage of boats or rafts, only about 50 men got over to join the British paratroopers fighting out of Oosterbeek. The following night the Polish Parachute Brigade again tried to cross the river in force. Though managing to ferry a further 200 men to the north bank, they suffered many casualties in the process.

All this time, British armour was pushing its way north along the road from Nijmegen. The next day, two *Kampfgruppen* counter-attacked at Veghel, with German *Fallschirmjäger* and a panzer brigade spearheading the assaults. The attack threatened to cut off the leading elements of the British armoured column, and the advancing XXX Corps was compelled to pull back one of its armoured brigades to keep the road open. On 24 September the road was cut south of Veghel by the *Jungwirth* Battalion. The German battle groups suffered grievous losses, but they

Above: Ordered to hold Arnhem for up to four days, the British clung to their positions for nine. They hoped in vain for the breakthrough of General Horrocks's XXX Corps, lying just a few kilometres outside the town. Once it became clear they would not be relieved, exhausted Paras either tried to break out or surrendered to the Germans.

slowed the northward progress of XXX Corps just long enough for a new German defensive line to be established north of Nijmegen.

At Elst, south-west of Arnhem, *Kampfgruppe Knaust* had arrived after taking the bridge at Arnhem and was now attempting to hold off the British XXX Corps, who had crossed the Waal at Nijmegen and were giving fire support to the British troops commanded by Major-General Robert Urquhart, who were trapped 17km (11 miles) away in the Oosterbeek pocket.

The stalemate was eventually broken by the arrival from Germany of a battalion of the most powerful tanks in the world, the King Tigers of *SchwerePanzer Abteilung 506*. Two companies of 15 tanks each were sent to confront XXX Corps at Elst while the remainder were sent to the eastern flank of the Oosterbeek pocket to eliminate the last pockets of resistance.

WOUNDED ARE EVACUATED

On 24 September, II SS Panzer Corps agreed to a truce with the British at Arnhem to allow 700 wounded airborne troops to be evacuated from the area, and a further 500 were evacuated the next day. Many lives were saved by the efforts of a medical officer of the *Hohenstaufen* Division, *SS-Sturmmbannführer* Egon Skalka, who worked alongside Colonel Warrack, the Chief Medical Officer of the 1st Airborne Division. Later, after the battle, the medical personnel of the British division were evacuated with the casualties to Apeldoorn. The majority became prisoners, but some, including Colonel Warrack and Brigadier John Hackett, who had been seriously wounded during the battle, successfully escaped.

On the night of the 24th, troops from XXX Corps made contact with the paratroopers at Oosterbeek. The ground between Nijmegen and Arnhem is a low-lying 'island' ringed by rivers and is too swampy for armoured vehicles to manoeuvre off-road. The British had pushed forward an infantry division, the 43rd Wessex, whose reconnaissance units had managed to reach the beleaguered paratroops on 22 September. But it was a token effort, achieved with boats. Unless a bridge could be secured, the airborne division was doomed.

Now the 4th Battalion The Dorset Regiment, led by Lieutenant-Colonel Tilly, made a gallant attempt to cross the river. But the crossings were made under heavy German fire, and this, together with the swift river current, ensured that the battalion was to remain scattered on the north bank after their landings.

The failure of the relief assault had a grim effect. By the morning of 25 September, it was clear to General Urquhart that heavy casualties, fatigue, and the lack of ammunition, food and water were increasingly affecting the defenders of the perimeter and that further strong enemy offensive action might cause them to disintegrate. At this point, the British Second Army gave the order for the evacuation of the pocket. At 21:00 on 25

Left: A British officer is captured while trying to slip through German lines disguised as a local Dutch resident. The failure of the Arnhem operation was to cost the Allies more than 13,000 of their finest troops killed, wounded or taken prisoner. German losses were about half that figure.

September, a massed artillery barrage by XXX Corps began, giving covering fire while 37 assault boats from British and Canadian engineer units crossed the Rhine to evacuate the men of 1st Airborne.

It was a difficult and dangerous operation: the paras had to extricate themselves from a small perimeter, which was surrounded by a vigilant enemy who threatened to overrun the positions at any time. Just over 2000 finally escaped. No real attempt was made by the Germans to strike at the retreating British paras, who blew up their ammunition stocks before they left their positions. The evacuation was over by first light on 26 September. However, the British had been forced to leave behind their wounded with volunteer medical staff. The Germans captured 6000 men from 1st Airborne – more than half of them wounded.

REPRISALS AGAINST THE DUTCH

Operation Market Garden was over. Bad planning had resulted in the death and injury of thousands of highly trained British paratroopers and gliderborne infantry as well as thousands of Dutch civilians. There was much suffering to come for the local population, as reprisals were carried out for collaborating with the British. Those members of the Dutch Resistance who were merely suspected of having fought alongside the British were summarily shot.

The astonishing thing about the defeat of the British airborne forces in Operation Market Garden was that it was accomplished by forces that only a month before had been on the point of complete destruction in the Falaise pocket. Since the war, it has been claimed frequently that Montgomery's gamble failed because of the unexpected presence of two first-line SS panzer divisions. But the *Hohenstaufen* and *Frundsberg* Divisions were shadows of their former selves.

In fact, the defeat of some of the toughest troops in all of the Allied armies was largely accomplished by rear echelon personnel hastily assembled into battlegroups. The elite Allied parachute forces were fought to a standstill by teenage recruits, wounded or infirm soldiers, or air force and navy personnel drafted in from training schools. 'It is with personal pride that I regard this German victory,' wrote *SS-Obersturmbannführer* Walther Harzer, commander of *Kampfgruppe Hohenstaufen,* 'because it was achieved not by regular units, but by railway workers, *Arbeitsdienst* and *Luftwaffe* personnel as well, who had never been trained for infantry work and who were actually unsuitable for house-to-house fighting.' The one advantage for the inexperienced soldiers of these ad hoc battlegroups was that they were led by a core of experienced troops, the *Alte Hasen* (Old Hares).

The ability of the Germans to fling their troops into action in such an ad hoc manner was critical in stopping the Allied airborne operation. The defenders reacted so quickly that the Allied plan fell behind schedule from the first day. It came as a disagreeable surprise to an overconfident Allied command, but the British at least should have been cautious; they had the experience of World War I. From the early days of trench warfare, the Germans had established the principle that the commander on the scene of an enemy attack would take charge of any rein-

---

Montgomery refused to admit that the Arnhem debacle had affected his plans, but most people knew that he had gone 'a bridge too far'.

---

forcements he received, even those commanded by an officer who out-ranked him. Even junior officers and NCOs were trained to think 'two levels up', so company commanders anticipated what was happening at battalion and regimental level. Training hammered home the lesson that a platoon in the right place today was worth a battalion there tomorrow.

Within 24 hours of the withdrawal and surrender of 1st Airborne division, Montgomery signalled London that the failure to secure a bridgehead over the Lower Rhine would not affect operations 'eastwards against the Ruhr'.

This was nonsense. Between them, Model and General Student had denied the Allies a strategic victory that could have dramatically foreshortened the war. Many years later Major-General John Frost, the same John Frost who had so heroically commanded 2 Para on the bridge at Arnhem, caustically commented on the British offensive: 'I always knew that Monty was going a bridge too far.'

The battle did not end with the loss of the Allied bridgehead. The forces north of Nijmegen were involved in heavy fighting into October. Total Allied casualties during Market Garden and its aftermath amounted to 13,000 men. German losses are estimated at betwen 6000 and 8000 men.

However, though Montgomery's gamble had failed, the advantage to the exhausted German armies was short-lived. Within a further 10 days, XXX Corps had overcome the resistance put up by II SS Panzer Corps, and Allied bombers closed the Arnhem Bridge to German traffic.

Above: Half-track mounted SS Panzer troops, led by a Jeep captured from the British, withdraw from the fighting zone after the failure of Montgomery's great gamble. The Germans had successfully blocked a plan which, had it succeeded, would have seen Allied troops pushing deep into Germany's industrial heartland before the end of 1944.

The two SS divisions that had done so much to defeat Montgomery remained in the area for another two months before being separated for the first and last time. The 9th SS Panzer Division *Hohenstaufen* was recalled to Germany, where three months later it would form part of the II SS Panzer Corps in the 6th SS Panzer Army's drive into the Ardennes. The 10th SS Panzer Division *Frundsberg,* considered for much of its career the 'twin' of the 9th SS Division, went its own way after Arnhem. Posted south to Aachen, it fought hard in Germany's last line of defence as the Americans flooded into Germany in the early months of 1945.

THE BATTLE OF THE BULGE

Though the battle for Arnhem had been a victory for the *Waffen-SS* and the *Wehrmacht*, Germany was in no position to take any advantage. The Allies, meanwhile, were free to turn their full attention to the problem of Antwerp. This vital objective had been captured early in September, but the port was not operational, and strong German forces guarded its approaches.

Hitler sent strong reinforcements to bolster the defenders of the Scheldt estuary and deny the Allies the use of the port. Two infantry divisions were in position – the 64th on the south bank in the Breskens Pocket between Zeebrugge and the Braakman inlet, and the 70th in South Beveland. Just to the east on the mainland, the 719th Infantry Division and General Student's First Parachute Army stood in reserve. There were also powerful defence batteries at Breskens, Cadzand and on the dunes at Walcheren. These were manned by fresh crews, so far unaffected by

Left: Although the *Wehrmacht* was on the run for much of 1944, it was far from beaten. New weapons like the massive Tiger II tank had been introduced, which would give the Allies an unpleasant surprise.

Above: Defeat in France and Russia had forced Germany back into its own territory for the first time since the beginning of the war. Now the Allies had to face the West Wall, built in the 1930s to protect against a French attack, but now instead of facing a full-strength German Army they would be fighting whatever forces the German High Command could scrape together.

the traumas of the retreat from Normandy. While the battle for Arnhem was in progress during Operation Market Garden, the Canadians of the Algonquin Regiment attempted to break into the Breskens Pocket. They were repulsed by the defenders with heavy losses. By the end of September, the Canadian Army, under General Simmonds, was deploying its infantry and armoured divisions for an all-out attack. The British 1st Corps and the Polish 1st Armoured Division were in support.

All through October, the Allied troops increased the pressure on both the pocket and the area at the neck of the Beveland Isthmus. Operations were assisted by total Allied command in the air, but the weather was now threatening to break. Antwerp had to be secured before the Allied air fleet was grounded. Bombing by Lancasters and Mosquitos destroyed vital dykes, and some of the defence works were flooded. Finally it was decided that a full-scale amphibious landing on Walcheren was necessary.

On 1 November, 4th Special Service Brigade with two Royal Marine Commandos and one Army Commando were landed at Westcappelle. It took them a week to quell all resistance on Walcheren, and they then joined with the Canadians to attack German positions along the Scheldte. By the end of the second week, these were safely in their hands. Even then, however, engineers had enormous problems of mine-clearance and repairs to essential dockyard equipment. All of this could have been achieved before the onset of winter, but Arnhem had cost the Allies vital time.

Now Christmas was only two weeks away, the weather was excessively cold, and most Allied soldiers wanted a break – at least until the New Year.

ALLIED ADVANCES NORTH AND SOUTH

By mid-December 1944 the main bulk of the Allied forces, and the attentions of Allied High Command, were concentrated towards the ends of the battlefront. The Anglo-Canadian armies were in the north around Antwerp, with the US First and Ninth Armies being set to close up to the Neder Rhine, where they threatened the vital Roer dams.

In the south, General Patton's US Third Army, after its spectacular drive across France, was poised to sweep through the equally important Saar region towards the Rhine.

Between the two powerful groupings were strung out some 80,000 American troops along 145km (90 miles) of front. The bulk of these consisted of General Middleton's VIII Corps, which had been brought across from Brittany. It was backed by one armoured division, the 9th, which had not yet seen action. The troops were

---

The reconstructed German army at the end of 1944 might have lacked training, but it was equipped with some of the best weapons in the world.

---

stationed here because this part of the front, the Ardennes section, was quiet. It was covered in front by the sparsely settled German Schnee Eifel, and behind by the steep wooded hills and foaming trout streams, which had always been regarded as unsuitable country for open warfare.

The first winter snows had fallen and heavy clouds overhead kept the Allied and German air forces on the ground. Green and veteran troops

alike crouched in their foxholes, listened thankfully to reports of bitter fighting to north and south and dreamt of Christmas.

But Christmas was to prove a nightmare.

THE *WEHRMACHT*'S LAST GASP

Even as the fighting in the Falaise Gap was ending, Hitler announced that by November a force of some 25 divisions must be prepared to launch a huge counter-offensive against the Anglo-American armies.

To the astonishment of the German High Command, men, weapons and equipment were found to create that force. It had been conjured from every corner of Germany: staff from rear-area administrative echelons, 16-year-old boys, civil servants, small shopkeepers, university students and the scourings of the prisons had been swept into the armed services. They were fashioned into the new so-called *Volksgrenadier* divisions, formed and trained by Himmler and the SS.

Such troops fell far short of Himmler's intended ideological warriors, but they were well equipped. The Reich's factories were still producing surprisingly large quantities of weaponry, despite round-the-clock pounding by the Allied bomber fleets. Infantry had plentiful supplies of *Panzerfaust* anti-tank rockets and new semi-automatic weapons. The Panzer formations were being fitted out with some of the best armour then in service. The new King Tiger, with its thick, sloped armour was virtually impervious to Allied weapons, and could command the battlefield with a new long-barrelled high-velocity 8.8cm (3.45in) gun. There were also large numbers of Panther tanks available, which by now were mostly reliable – combat experience had ironed out early design faults.

Thus, for his final offensive in the West, Hitler had created three German armies. By mid-December, in an operation remarkable for its secrecy, these forces had been marshalled opposite that thinly occupied 145-km (90-mile) strip of line so tenuously held by the US VIII Corps.

In the north were poised the units of the Sixth SS Panzer Army under *SS-Oberstgruppenführer* and *Generaloberst der Waffen-SS* Sepp Dietrich, formerly commander of Hitler's personal body-guard in its street-fighting days and later of the crack 1st SS Panzer Division *Leibstandarte Adolf Hitler.* This new army, the first time a formation of such size bore the SS title, was made up from two heavy armoured corps. I SS Panzer Corps incorporated the *Leibstandarte* and the 12th SS Panzer Division *Hitlerjugend.* These two elite formations, brought up to nearly full strength after being hammered almost into oblivion in Normandy, were supported by three further divisions: the *Wehrmacht*'s 12th and 277th *Volksgrenadier* Divisions and the *Luftwaffe*'s 3rd *Fallschirmjäger* Division.

Below: In an incredible feat of logistics, the Germans managed to amass three new armies in the Ardennes, opposite the weakest point in the Anglo–American lines. Astonishly, this huge collection of men and material had been gathered under the noses of Allies without being spotted by British or American reconnaissance assets.

SS-Obergruppenführer Wilhelm Bittrich, who had masterminded the defeat of Montgomery's airborne offensive at Arnhem, commanded II SS Panzer Corps. Bittrich's corps consisted of the 2nd SS Panzer Division *Das Reich* and the 9th SS Panzer Division *Hohenstaufen.* Other troops assigned to the Sixth SS Panzer Army included the Army's LXVII Corps, commanded by *Generalleutnant* Otto Hizfeld, which comprised the 272nd and 326th *Volksgrenadier* Divisions. The Panzer Army could also call on a number of independent units equipped with assault guns, Tiger tanks and *Jagdpanther* tank-destroyers, as well as combat engineers, artillery and other support troops. As was by now standard German practice, these formations were split up into several all-arms *Kampfgruppen,* each having tanks, infantry, flak units and combat engineers.

The central section of the attack front was the responsibility of the Fifth Panzer Army, which was commanded by the very capable Army Panzer expert Hasso von Manteuffel. One of the

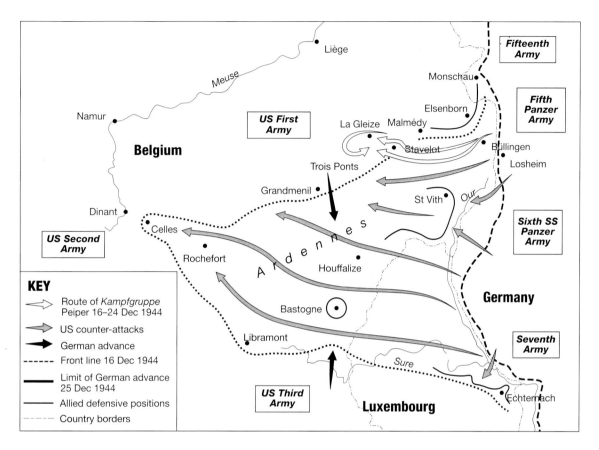

KEY

⇨ Route of *Kampfgruppe* Peiper 16–24 Dec 1944

⬅ US counter-attacks

⬆ German advance

----- Front line 16 Dec 1944

▬ Limit of German advance 25 Dec 1944

——— Allied defensive positions

–·–·– Country borders

Above: The German plan was simple, if any plan involving quarter of a million men can ever be called simple. Attacking through the lightly defended Ardennes, German spearheads would drive a wedge between the British in the north and the Americans in the south. Then, according to Hitler's wildly optimistic hopes, they would capture Antwerp.

Army's top Panzer generals, who had commanded the army's elite *Grossdeutchland* Division in Russia, Manteuffel could call on a number of *Volksgrenadier* Divisions, but as in the north the *Panzêrwaffe* was to provide the real punch of his force. In addition to a number of independent Panzer Corps, the Fifth Panzer Army included the 116th Panzer Division and the veteran and highly skilled *Panzer Lehr* Division.

On the southern flank of the attack, intended to form a 'hard shoulder' against any possible Allied counter-attacks, was the Seventh Army under the dogged but unimaginative General Erich Brandenburger. Some troops were also on call from the Fifteenth Army, but the paucity of German resources can be judged from the fact that the reserve for the operation consisted of just one Panzergrenadier division and two *Volksgrenadier* divisions of dubious quality.

Altogether, some 200,000 men would take part in *Unternehmen Wacht am Rhein* (Operation Watch on the Rhine), equipped with more tanks, more artillery and more ammunition than had been granted to any similarly assembled German force for many months past. In addition to the conventional fighting divisions were 1250 *Luftwaffe* paratroops under Oberst von der Heydte, a veteran of Crete. They were to drop in front of the main assault, seize bridges and crossroads, and attack any headquarter organizations they could find. To help spread panic in the American rear, the famous raiding commander Otto Skorzeny commanded a special force of volunteers. This unique force, designated Panzer Brigade 156, was committed to *Unternehmen Greif* (Operation Griffin). They were tasked with the capture of bridges across the Meuse and with spreading confusion in the rear areas of the US Army. The unit was composed of about 2000 English-speaking German soldiers dressed in US uniforms, driving US vehicles. However, only 150 could speak convincing 'American', and their promised tanks had not been delivered. As a result, the most capable of the English speakers, commanded by *Hauptsturmführer* Steilau, were organized into nine four-man teams in Jeeps. One group penetrated as far as the Meuse on 17

Operation Griffin was incredibly risky, since by the rules of war any man caught wearing false uniforms could be tried and executed as a spy.

December, but the entire team was killed by an anti-tank mine. Eighteen of those who were caught operating in American uniforms were tried as spies and subsequently shot. Nonetheless, their presence behind American lines did cause considerable confusion, and led to a rumour that they were an assassination squad targeting General Eisenhower.

UNREALISTIC AMBITIONS

The German objective of *Wacht am Rhein* was far too ambitious. After the severe mauling the Germans had received during the Normandy Campaign, the *Wehrmacht* received replacement tanks, troops and supplies with astonishing speed, but the replacement soldiers were largely green troops. Nevertheless, Hitler maintained his plans for an ambitious counter-attack that involved driving four armies westwards through the Ardennes region of Belgium.

The primary aim was to split the British and American forces before driving on to capture

their main supply port of Antwerp. Hitler's last strike force could then turn on and annihilate the Anglo-Canadian armies and the US First and Ninth Armies alongside them. Hitler planned on causing the Allies so much panic and confusion that Allied co-operation would then break down and wreck future strategic planning for weeks and possibly months. 'If we succeed,' he enthused, 'we will have knocked out half the enemy front. Then let's see what happens!' His hope was that by taking out the western Allies in one knockout blow, he would be free to transfer powerful tank forces eastwards, and there deliver a similar strike against the Red Army. In short, what Hitler was anticipating was a re-run of May 1940.

Most of Hitler's commanders, including *Generalfeldmarschal* Gerd von Rundstedt, Commander-in-Chief West, and *Generalfeldmarschal* Walther Model, Commander of Army Group B, were horrified at the Führer's totally unrealizable 'Grand Strategy'. Von Rundstedt, whom Hitler had placed in overall command of the front, commented: 'Antwerp? If we reach the Meuse we should go down on our knees and thank God!'

Model, famously dubbed the Führer's fireman, was quoted as saying: 'This plan hasn't got a damned leg to stand on.' Even Sepp Dietrich had by now lost his original admiration for the Führer. As he later remarked: 'All I had to do was cross the river, capture Brussels, and then go on to take the port of Antwerp. The snow was waist deep and there wasn't room to deploy four tanks abreast, let alone six armoured divisions. It didn't get light until eight and was dark again at four, and my tanks can't fight at night. And all this at Christmas time!'

No surprise, then, that the commanders argued for more realistic objectives, suggesting a 'small solution' pincer attack to cut off US forces. Dietrich tried to point out the problems to the Führer on 23 November, at the final briefing conference for senior officers. Lack of fuel meant that the hundreds of new Panzer drivers had so little instruction that they could hardly control their

Above: The two panzer armies providing the spearhead to the Ardennes offensive had better equipment than their enemies, and the poor December weather meant that Allied air power, which had been the deciding factor in Normandy, had a much less important part to play in the battle. However, the Germans had one crucial shortage, and that was petrol.

machines, let alone carry out complex tactical manoeuvres. Five years of war had produced massive losses amongst a generation of men of fighting age, and this meant that the high standards of the SS had been diluted: the *Leib-standarte* itself had to be topped up by conscripts.

Furthermore, Germany's chronic lack of fuel had a more direct effect. Dietrich's Sixth SS Panzer Army had stocks of fuel enough for only 200km (124 miles) of operations. Fuel depots

were located far behind the lines, meaning that fuel would have to be brought to the front along unsuitable roads clogged with follow-up troops. Dietrich told the Führer that if his units got sucked into a serious fight, his tanks would run dry.

As usual, such objections were ignored, the Führer's will prevailed, and the attack went ahead as planned. At 05:30 on 16 December 1944, after a short but intense bombardment, 200,000 men of German Army Group B threw themselves against the unsuspecting Allied positions in the fog-shrouded, snow covered hills of the Belgian Ardennes.

The area chosen for the advance was defended by General Middleton's VIII Corps, just four weak divisions of the US Army. This was supposedly a quiet area, and they were not expected to have any difficulty in covering a front of 135km (84 miles).

NORTHERN FLANK

On the northern flank, the main thrust was to come from Sixth SS Panzer Army, attacking on a narrow front between Monshau and Losheim. After breaking through, the SS tanks would then drive hard for the Meuse River between Liège and Huy. Hitler expected the lead units of the offensive to reach the Meuse in only four days.

Spearheading the advance would be I SS Panzer Corps. The *Hitlerjugend* Division was to launch from start points at Hollerath, Udenbreth and Loshiem, heading for the area between Liège and Huy in the north. The *Leibstandarte* would attack from Loshiem and Manderfield, aiming for the southern part of the target area.

Ahead of all of these were the sabotage troops of Otto Skorzeny's *Panzerbrigade* 156. SS men disguised as US Army Military Police redirected convoys, changed the direction of signposts and

generally tried to cause disruption to any Allied movements. In addition to causing as much confusion, panic and sabotage behind the American lines as was possible, the *Obersturmbannführer's* SS commandos were to seize and hold two of the Meuse bridges from either Amay, Huy or Ardenne. Their bravery should not be underestimated: disguised as American GIs, driving American vehicles and speaking English, they knew that they faced almost certain execution if caught. Nor were their plans made easy: a shortage of captured American vehicles meant they had to disguise German vehicles, painting them olive green and putting white stars on their sides.

Aided by the essential factor of surprise, some of the German units did very well at the beginning of the campaign. They were aided by yet another example of what had come to be known as 'Führer Weather' – helpful weather conditions, in this case cloudy skies, which meant that the Allied air forces could not fly. Under the shock of the attack, some 9000 men from the 106th US Infantry Division were captured on the Schnee Eifel on 19 December.

Other German units were less lucky, things going wrong almost from the start. Indeed, a large proportion of its units saw no action in the battle. Poor weather, poor terrain and poor roads meant that tanks and armoured vehicles spent days trying to reach the combat zone, and many failed to get past the operation's jump-off points before the end of the battle. This in spite of the fact that Allied defences were manned largely by inexperienced GIs, who were not expecting an attack in this sector. Nonetheless, the 1st SS Panzer Corps was stalled. Determined resistance by the out-numbered and outgunned American infantrymen managed to play havoc

Above: Although many of the SS troops in Sepp Dietrich's Sixth SS Panzer Army were raw recruits or reservists, they were formed around a core of some of the most experienced combat soldiers in the world. The men of the *Leibstandarte, Das Reich* and the rest had fought and survived ferocious battles from Normandy to the gates of Moscow.

with the tight schedule that was necessary if the SS tank forces were to achieve their goals.

Problems caused by the defenders were compounded by further delays caused by massive traffic jams on the routes leading to the front, as I SS Panzer Corps, 12 *Volksgrenadier* Division and 3rd *Fallschirmjäger* Division all tried to move on towards Losheim along the same few roads. The US troops stood firm and by the end of the first day I SS Panzer Corps had still not achieved a decisive breakthrough.

KAMPFGRUPPE PEIPER

In the meantime, to the south, a *Kampfgruppe* commanded by 29-year-old *Standartenführer* Joachim 'Jochen' Peiper was enjoying success and infamy in equal measure.

Jochen Peiper was one of the most aggressive and ruthless of all German tactical commanders. Fluent in English and French, Peiper joined the

Above: Although Field Marshal Gerd von Rundstedt was nominally in charge of the Ardennes offensive, he had no faith in the operation and spent much of the time reading his favourite detective novels. Actual field command was exercised by the commander of Army Group B, Field Marshal Walther Model. Model, a committed Nazi, was Hitler's favourite general.

SS at the age of 19. He commanded a company of the *Leibstandarte* in Poland, a battalion in France and was a regimental commander in Russia by the time he was 27. *Kampfgruppe Peiper* consisted of some 5000 troops, including 1st Battalion, SS Panzer Regiment 1; *Schwere SS Panzer Abteilung* 501 armed with King Tiger tanks; a battalion of SS panzer grenadiers; a battalion of SS armoured artillery; a company of armoured engineers; and some anti-aircraft troops from a *Luftwaffe* regiment. Ahead, a unit of *Fallschirmjäger* had been dropped to clear the

169

Above: The dashing Joachim Peiper was one of the glamour figures of the German armed forces. Fluent in English and French, he looked like a recruiting poster, but he was much more than a parade ground soldier. Fearless, aggressive and very capable, he led his troops from the front – but his ferocity all too often crossed the line into atrocity.

roads, in what was one of the last German airborne operations of the war.

The terrain suited the defenders. Narrow roads and gullies, wooded terrain and winding roads made it ideal for ambushes. As Peiper's men advanced, they discovered that the paratroopers had not cleared the roads of mines. With time pressing, Peiper ordered his men to keep going over the minefield, destroying five half-tracks in the process. Once the road was

cleared, reconnaissance patrols advanced to the village of Lanzerath. There, they discovered the paratroopers resting, apparently waiting for dawn before advancing. What most infuriated Peiper was that no sentries had been posted. He angrily demanded that the *Fallschirmjäger* colonel immediately release one of his battalions to his *Kampfgruppe* to press on the advance.

By early morning on 17 September, Peiper and his men had reached the village of Bucholz, which had been abandoned by the Americans. A little later, they encountered light resistance at Honsfeld. There was not the time to eliminate all the American defenders, so Peiper left the paratroopers with a few tanks in support to seize the village.

KEY OBJECTIVE: FUEL

His objective was the American fuel dump at Büllingen, which he captured before the Americans could destroy the fuel stocks. Peiper was thus able to re-fuel his tanks – a much needed replenishment, since consumption had been higher than expected after numerous delays on congested roads. The *Waffen-SS* troops had taken hundreds of American prisoners, some of whom were put to work refuelling Peiper's tanks and armoured vehicles at the fuel dump.

In Russia, Peiper's troops had earned the nickname 'Blowtorch Battalion' after burning their way across Russia, and had also been responsible for slaughtering civilians in two separate villages. Now they were to show that little had changed on the Western Front.

On 19 December an advance party of two Mk V Panther tanks, which were operating ahead of the main body of armour, encountered and overwhelmed an American convoy. The truck convoy, carrying elements of the American 285th Field Artillery Observation Battalion, was intercepted southeast of Malmédy. Upon sighting the trucks, the Panzers opened fire and destroyed the lead vehicles. This brought the convoy to a halt while the deadly accurate tank fire continued. The outgunned Americans abandoned their vehicles and surrendered.

The prisoners were then herded into a field at the main crossroads at Baugnez, as the lead units of the I SS Panzer Corps streamed past. Over a hundred men were under guard when *Oberschütze* Georg Fleps, a *Volksdeutch* volunteer in the *Leibstandarte*, drew his pistol and fired into the mass of prisoners. At his trial at Dachau after the war, Fleps claimed that he was shooting at some of the prisoners who were making a break for the trees. Whatever the cause, his shot was the signal for all of the SS men to open fire on the unarmed Americans. Survivors were killed by a pistol shot to the head, in some cases by English-speaking SS who walked among the victims asking if anyone was injured or needed help.

Below: Members of 12th SS Panzer Division *Hitlerjugend* confer after taking American prisoners in the Ardennes. The American troops manning that sector were not first-line troops – but the stubborn resistance mounted by many isolated units was enough to upset the German offensive timetable, weakening the attack fatally almost from the first day of operations.

Those who responded were shot. A total of 71 Americans were killed in the war's single worst atrocity against US troops in Europe.

Two survivors escaped and reached the Allied lines, where the story of the 'Malmédy Massacre' roused intense fury. News of the massacre strengthened the resistance of even the greenest units.

FOOD STILL ON THE PLATES

Meanwhile, Peiper was racing on to Ligneuville, having received information that a US divisional staff – including the commanding general – was situated there. He missed them by minutes, but he and his men helped themselves to the American rations, which were still hot. Peiper remained in the town to discuss the situation with the commander of the *Leibstandarte*, *SS-Gruppenführer* Wilhelm Mohnke, while his battlegroup continued its advance.

Forward progress was held up by a small group of American engineers, who established a roadblock on the road leading into Stavelot. The

By now, however, *Kampfgruppe Peiper* was considerably behind schedule, and its commander could not take the time to clear up isolated American pockets. Leaving behind a number of fighting groups to secure his lines of communication, he made for his next objective, the town of Trois Ponts. There he found that the Americans had blown the three bridges crossing the rivers Salm and Amblève that gave the town its name. A single 57mm (2.24in) anti-tank gun had stalled the *Kampfgruppe* for just long enough to allow the US Army engineers to do their job.

His way again blocked, Peiper needed to find another crossing. The only option was to head for La Gleize, which the *Kampfgruppe* reached without incident. On reaching the village, Peiper's advance units discovered a bridge intact, and they crossed the river Amblève near Cheneux.

Their good fortune ran out shortly afterwards, when the weather cleared enough for Allied air power to take a hand. The *Kampfgruppe* came under heavy attack by USAAF P-47 fighter-bombers, and it was forced to take cover in the nearby woods for several hours until the weather worsened and the air attacks had to be aborted. Although the damage sustained was minimal, precious hours had been lost and Peiper fell further behind schedule. Nonetheless, the *Kampfgruppe* continued onwards, reaching the Lienne River. Several small bridges at the crossing of Neuf Moulin were captured intact, but all were incapable of supporting the weight of Peiper's heavy armour. A reconnaissance party was sent across in half-tracks, only to be immediately fired upon by American tank destroyers and forced to retreat. With no heavy bridging equipment, Peiper was forced to retreat into the woods, leaving a small force guarding the small bridges.

Meanwhile, an American armoured force had retaken Stavelot. Peiper's troops, who were left

Above: Prisoners of war are always a problem to a rapidly advancing army. Under the terms of the Geneva Convention they should be moved away from the fighting as soon as possible – but doing so means that you have to detach men to guard them. Unfortunately, all too often SS units avoided this problem by eliminating the prisoners.

leading tanks of the column came under fire from the Americans, who were armed with bazookas. Unable to see the small size of the American force, and believing it to be a large tank unit, the Germans decided to pull back for the night. The next morning Peiper returned and immediately ordered an artillery barrage, after which he led an attack that dislodged the outnumbered American defenders. The advance continued.

to hold the road open, were in real danger of being cut off. Even the arrival of the main bulk of the *Leibstandarte* did not prevent the Americans from taking the town. When they did, they discovered the bodies of 26 Belgian civilians, apparently shot by Peiper's men for helping wounded American soldiers.

By now it was clear that *Kampfgruppe Peiper* had made the most significant gains of all the *Waffen-SS* units, so the *Leibstandarte* units still

---

Kampfgruppe Peiper made the deepest penetration of the Allied lines, but fell far short of the objectives specified by the Führer.

---

fighting at Stavelot were ordered to support Peiper. But the Americans, fired by reports of the Malmédy massacre, were fighting as ferociously as the SS, preventing them from disengaging. Small detachments from the *Leibstandarte*'s 2nd Panzergrenadier Battalion did manage to break free, however, and led by *Sturmbannführer* Schnelle broke through to link up with Peiper at La Gleize on the morning of 20 December.

Kampfgruppe Peiper was now spread over a considerable distance and the lead elements, being directed by Peiper himself, were running low on supplies. They were also meeting stiffer resistance as the Allies overcame the initial surprise of the offensive and began feeding more and more strength into the battle. Supply columns sent out to reinforce Peiper were intercepted and destroyed, and the German forces fighting to throw the Americans from Stavelot and open the supply routes to Peiper were held at bay. It looked increasingly possible that *Kampfgruppe Peiper* might be faced with encirclement and have to fight its way back out, but 6th SS Panzer Army refused to allow it to retreat and insisted that the *Leibstandarte* continue its attempts to reinforce Peiper's battlegroup. Concentrated around La Gleize and the river crossing around Cheneux, it was coming under increasingly intense American attack. As a result,

Peiper's forces were becoming perilously low on ammunition and supplies. The *Luftwaffe* did attempt to resupply by airdrops, but the majority of the supplies fell into American hands.

On 23 December the weather cleared and the Allied air forces came out in strength. Fighter-bombers attacked German vehicles and artillery positions, while medium bombers hit the crowded road and rail network in Germany. The good visibility also allowed supplies to be air-dropped by C-47s to besieged American units like the 101st Airborne Division in Bastogne.

Kampfgruppe Peiper, under constant American artillery barrage, was finally ordered to break out of the devastated town of La Gleize. With little fuel, a fighting breakout was impossible. Heavy tanks and equipment had to be destroyed, and any of the wounded who could not be carried on trucks or light vehicles had to be left behind, cared for by volunteer medical officer *Obersturmführer* Dittman. A small rearguard was left behind to destroy the vehicles. After several small skirmishes, the bulk of the *Kampfgruppe* reached the safety of the German lines on Christmas Day.

Despite the ultimate failure of his mission, Peiper had made the greatest penetration of all the German units involved in the offensive, taking thousands of American prisoners in the process. He was awarded the Swords and Oak Leaves to his Knights Cross.

AIRPOWER COMES INTO PLAY

The 9th SS Panzer Division *Hohenstaufen* was sent into action on 18 December, but due to road congestion did not reach the front until four days later. Attacking northwest from Houfalize towards Manhay, the division was held up by an American blocking force at the crossroad village of Baraque de Fraiture. A slight improvement in the weather, which allowed Peiper's men to be hammered by P-47s, also let the Americans launch fighter-bomber attacks on the 9th SS. These, compounded by an almost total lack of fuel, locked the *Hohenstaufen* in place for 24 hours, which had catastrophic effects on the

Above: The most notorious incident to take place during the Ardennes offensive occurred near Malmédy. A truck convoy of the US Army's 285th Field Artillery Observation Battalion was intercepted southeast of Malmédy by a detachment of *Kampfgruppe Peiper*. Lined up in a field, the Americans were shot down in cold blood by the SS men.

German attack timetable and allowed the Americans time to reinforce their positions. A fuel convoy did reach the division on 22 December, and the 9th SS were able to mount an effective attack the next day, driving the Americans back from the crossroads.

To the south, one of Manteuffel's spearheads had success similar to Peiper's, but without displaying the ruthlessness that so often spilled over into atrocity. His forces, in the shape of the Army's 2nd Panzer Division, reached the village of Auw just in front of the vital road junction of St Vith. Here it ran into the tank destroyers and the main artillery of an American infantry division. The American resistance forced the main drive of Manteuffel's army southwards into the gap between St Vith and the other vital road junction, Bastogne. It was here that the attentions of both attackers and defenders now concentrated.

CAUGHT BY SURPRISE

General Bradley's 12th Army Group caught the offensive in its central section. At first, Bradley dismissed it as a spoiling attack to disrupt the First Army's threat to the Roer in the north and the Third Army's to the Saar in the south. But he soon realized this mistake. On 19 December he ordered General Hodges in the north to swing some of his First Army divisions back to hold a flank and then drive down to St Vith. He ordered Patton to do the same in the south and send his crack 4th Armoured Division up to relieve Bastogne. Patton, of course, being Patton, objected, but soon cheered up: 'What the hell! We're still killing Krauts!' With an efficiency that commands the greatest admiration, he swung the bulk of his army through 90 degrees within 48 hours.

In the meantime, General Eisenhower had released his reserves: the 82nd and 101st Airborne Divisions. Recently recovered from their battles at Nijmegen and Eindhoven, they raced north from Patton's lines. The men of the 101st, the 'Screaming Eagles', deployed to begin their famous stand at Bastogne and the 82nd passed on to St Vith.

After the failure of Peiper's *Kampfgruppe*, Field Marshal Model decided to shift responsibility for the main thrust of the attack to Fifth Panzer Army. II SS Panzer Corps was now deployed to support Sixth SS Panzer Army in protecting Fifth Panzer Army's northern flank. As Manteuffel's spearheads probed further and further west, American tank destroyers and artillery worried at the flanks of the advancing *Wehrmacht* formations, while US infantry

Right: Panzerkampfwagen V Panthers move up to confront the besieged Belgian town of Bastogne. Reinforced by the elite paratroopers of the 101st Airborne Division, the American forces in the town conducted an epic defence against everything the Germans could throw at them, holding out successfully until the end of the battle.

units fought doggedly forward into the gaps or held on grimly in isolated positions. The Germans never did achieve their goal of reaching the Meuse River, though the 2nd Panzer Division did almost reach Dinant, where Rommel had crossed in triumph just four years before.

DAS REICH IN ACTION

The 2nd SS Panzer Division *Das Reich* was at Manhay when it was directed southwest towards Grandmenil. The tough SS men brushed aside an American blocking force and took the town. However, American infantry reinforcements blocked attempts to move further west, as did the arrival of the US Army's 3rd Armoured Division – but not before the American tanks had been attacked by their own aircraft, who had mistaken the advancing division for a German unit. Small groups of American infantrymen did manage to enter Grandmenil, but were beaten

back, and further attempts to oust the SS grenadiers also failed.

The day after Christmas the Germans attempted to advance from Grandmenil, but ran head-on into an American attack, which had been launched at exactly the same time. The furious battle that followed saw the Americans suffering heavy casualties, and losing most of their tanks. The Germans then pushed on in two columns. The first was stopped by the American defences on the Grandmenil–Erezee road. The second got bogged down as it advanced through heavily

---

A break in the weather at Christmas allowed Allied aircraft to take to the air. Without Luftwaffe support, Germany had no answer to Allied air power.

---

wooded terrain along narrow winding roads, and was finally blocked by trees deliberately felled by US engineers. Once the armoured column had been stopped, it came under a heavy artillery bombardment and was forced to withdraw.

On that same day the Americans stepped up their efforts to capture both Manhay and Grandmenil, launching intensive artillery strikes and tactical air strikes on the towns. One thing the US Army did not lack was firepower, and the sheer intensity of the assault forced the *Waffen-SS* troops to retreat. By 27 December both towns were in American hands, and *Das Reich* had been forced to retreat as far as the crossroads at Fraiture.

The 9th SS had gone into action north of *Das Reich*, advancing towards St Vith, Poteau and Halleux. Penetrating as far as Villettes, it came up against the elite US 82nd Airborne Division. The paratroopers defended their positions vigorously, forcing the *Hohenstaufen* away from their objective. The 9th SS was now ordered southwards towards Bastogne. There it joined the 1st SS and the 12th SS Panzer Divisions in their battle to take the town from the besieged US 101st Airborne Division, which continued to hold out against all attacks.

By now, the 9th SS was a shadow of its former self, having lost many men and with only 30 surviving tanks. The *Hitlerjugend* was also under strength, not so much through battle damage as through fuel starvation. Many of the division's vehicles, including almost all of its artillery, had been abandoned, left scattered along the route of the offensive. Even with these trials and tribulations, morale remained surprisingly high, and a few *Waffen-SS* units managed to penetrate the defences of Bastogne. Still the Screaming Eagles of the 101st held on.

For most of the time, both sides fought without air cover, with the weather favouring the Germans for days on end. But by Christmas Day, after some of the bitterest fighting seen in Europe, the sting had been drawn from the German onslaught; Allied ground operations now enjoyed air cover. The weather had cleared up and Allied air forces came out in strength, with fighter bombers attacking German vehicles and artillery positions and medium bombers the crowded road and rail network in Germany. The good visibility also allowed supplies to be airdropped by C-47s to the 101st Division in Bastogne. Although Manteuffel mounted a last desperate attack on the town, it was beaten off and on the following day Patton's tanks arrived to break the siege.

ANOTHER OFFENSIVE IS LAUNCHED

In an attempt to draw Allied forces away from the stalled Ardennes offensive, Hitler ordered a new offensive to be launched against the relatively weak French and American forces in Alsace. Launched on 1 January 1945, *Unternehmen Nordwind* (Operation North Wind) involved the 10th SS Panzer Division *Frundsberg*, the 17th SS Panzergrenadier Division *Götz von Berlichingen*, and the 6th SS Mountain Division *Nord*. *Nord* had spent most of the war operating on the northern extremity of the Eastern Front, and was making its first appearance in the West.

The attack made some progress in the first couple of days, with several hundred American prisoners being taken. Within a few days, how-

ever, the attack had ground to a halt due to stiff-ening Allied resistance and a lack of fuel. A second attack by *Frundsberg* collapsed just as quickly. *Nordwind* failed completely, having no effect on the forces being sent by the Allies to the Ardennes.

Meanwhile, Field Marshal Montgomery had taken command of the northern flank. In order to 'tidy up the battlefield', he authorized a with-drawal from the St Vith salient, and brought the British 29th Armoured Brigade down towards the American right flank to hold the deepest pen-etration. On the following day, the whole of the US 2nd Armoured Division came down to join them, and Hitler's last offensive in the West was brought to a halt. On 1 January the *Leibstan-darte* was withdrawn, to be held in reserve. The *Hitlerjugend* followed it on 6 January.

At this stage, it was obvious even to Hitler that the offensive had failed. With a major Soviet offensive brewing in the East, he ordered his SS

Above: SS troops fought with their usual vigour in the Ardennes, but at considerable cost. Units like the 9th SS Panzer Division *Hohenstaufen*, rebuilt after the Arnhem battles, again suffered serious losses in men and equipment. A shortage of petrol forced them to abandon many of their armoured vehicles, and by the end of the offensive they were being used as infantry.

panzer divisions to be transferred to the Eastern Front. The last to pull out was the 9th SS, which withdrew on 24 January. By 10 February 1945 all of the German units were back on the east bank of the Rhine.

What had doomed the attack was the failure to secure the massive Allied fuel dump at Stavelot. Fuel shortages had hampered German operation throughout the war, particularly from the middle of the 1941 campaign in Russia, and in this last offensive Panzer mobility had always depended on capturing the enemy's abundant stocks of petrol, oil and lubricants. The failure to do so meant that the fuel tanks of the Panzers inevitably ran dry.

Such overambition was typical of German planning in 1944/45. As was *Unternehmen Bodenplatte* (Operation Baseplate), which was meant to support *Wacht am Rhein*, but which took place too late to affect the outcome. On 1 January 1945, 800 fighters from the *Luftwaffe* struck at Allied airfields in Belgium and Holland. Like *Wacht am Rhein*, it was a final spectacular gesture that cost the Allies about 500 aircraft, including General Montgomery's personal C47. However, Allied strength was such that losses could be replaced in a fortnight. Few Allied aircrew were lost, while the *Luftwaffe* lost 170 vitally needed pilots, and 67 were taken prisoner.

ELIMINATING THE BULGE

With the coming of the New Year, Allied forces were on the counter-attack. Both the Fifth Panzer Army and the Sixth SS Panzer Army had been halted in the Ardennes, and by 4 January the US First and Third Armies were beginning to counter-attack along the salient that had been christened 'The Bulge' by Allied staffs. On January 8 Hitler acknowledged what the German High Command had realized long before, that *Wacht am Rhein* had run its course. He authorized a withdrawal, and a week later, the Germans were pushed back to their original positions on the border. By 16 January 'The Bulge' was clear, the Germans having lost a further 70,000 men, of which 20,000 had been killed. By 10 February, the German armies had withdrawn over the Rhine.

The failure of this offensive cost Germany dearly. Achieving none of its aims, the offensive had only wasted the precious German reserves of manpower and equipment – which could have been put to much better use and to much greater effect on the other side of the Rhine. Though the Allies had lost 75,000 men dead, captured or wounded, estimates of German losses range from 60,000 to more than 100,000 men. Moreover, the Germans had lost more than 600 tanks, either destroyed or abandoned by their crews

when they ran out of fuel. Allied tank losses were greater, at around 800, but the Allies could replace their losses within days. Where would Germany find the men and machinery to continue the war?

Having wiped out the German reserve, *Wacht am Rhein* hastened the final collapse. In the early spring of 1945, once the thaw had set in, the Allies mounted their offensive across the Rhine. Hitler's exhausted troops were now fighting for the sacred soil of Germany, aware that the war in the West was lost and that it was possible only to delay the inevitable. For the first time, the quality of German fighting troops was inferior to its opponents: it was impossible to counter either the ability of American leadership to deploy guns and armour with supreme efficiency, or the dogged courage of the American infantryman.

Germany and the SS now concentrated their efforts in stopping the advance of the Red Army. In the months that followed, all they could do in the West was to fight persistent rearguard actions to slow the Allies' relentless advance on the *Reich*.

Yet the Allies were still extremely wary of the Nazis. In the Ardennes, the massive German attack had succeeded in wiping out one-tenth of all American and British armour, and the American newsreels were now warning their forces in propaganda films that the Nazi beast had not yet been destroyed. To the East, in Hungary, the Soviets were struggling to wrestle control of the capital, Budapest. In one of the most bitter of all struggles of World War II, an SS Panzer army was attempting to break the siege of Hungary's capital. Further north, the Red Army's offensive of the previous year had ground to a halt on the east bank of the Vistula, before Warsaw.

In Germany, Goebbels' propaganda machine was working at full throttle. German morale had received a huge shot in the arm from the Ardennes counter-blast, coming as it did at the end of a year of calamities for the Reich. Newsreels exhorted the population to renewed and continual sacrifices. For the defence of the homeland, the very old and very young were called upon to place themselves in the path of the Allied onslaught. These 'volunteers' were supplied with the one-shot *Panzerfaust* bazooka, but little else. Although Armaments Minister Albert Speer had dispersed arms manufacture – much of it being carried on underground – the Allied pounding of the marshalling yards and the destruction of *Reichsbahn* rolling stock created difficulties in deploying military hardware from the factories to the front line.

GERMANY UNDER SIEGE

A siege mentality now set in. German mobility was radically undermined. Armour could not be moved by day or night because of Allied fighters and diminishing stocks of fuel. The *Luftwaffe* was now irrelevant. American and British fighter-bombers roamed the skies or hovered over German airfields, ready to pounce

the minute that a *Luftwaffe* aircraft tried to take off.

But at this time of emergency, Hitler retreated further from the public view. From 16 January 1945 he took up residency in Berlin, vowing never to leave. He incarcerated himself in the Spartan underworld of the *Führerbunker*, beneath the Chancellery in the heart of Berlin. Here he continued to play God, moving the pawns of his diminishing divisions around the ever-retreating front lines. But, even though his

Below: In January 1945, German troops were being forced back within the borders of the Reich. A high proportion of SS men like these still fought hard, even though many former believers had lost all faith in the Führer. Now they were fighting for their country's survival, for their homes, for their families and for their comrades in arms.

Above: Men of *Obersturmbannführer* Otto Skorzeny's sabotage commando, captured behind the lines wearing American uniforms, are prepared for the firing squad having been convicted as spies. The plan to spread confusion behind Allied lines had only limited success, though it did raise fears of possible assassination attempts on the life of General Eisenhower.

grip on reality was slipping, the dictator's edicts were still followed on pain of disgrace or execution. Moreover his belief in his own genius remained constant, though many of his orders served only to shorten the life of the *Reich*. His favoured method of defence, in East and West,

was to create a series of *Festungs*, or fortresses. The list of these fortified towns included Stettin, Königsberg, Tannenberg and Breslau in the East and La Rochelle and Rochefort in the West – all of little strategic value. Defending them leeched away German strength by isolating experienced troops who could have been better used in mobile warfare.

Hitler's last military offensive – Operation Spring Awakening – began on 6 March at Lake Balaton, Hungary. A total of 31 divisions, including 11 Panzer and Panzergrenadier divisions took part, although all were substantially below authorized strength. The strike force included some

800 tanks, most being part of Sepp Dietrich's Sixth SS Panzer Army, which had been moved to Hungary from the Ardennes soon after the collapse of the offensive there.

Dietrich soon realized the assault was futile: an early thaw left the Hungarian plain waterlogged, and impossible for his super-heavy King Tiger tanks to cross. The last strength of the Reich's battered armies had been squandered. Hitler had ordered the offensive in a bid to retake the Reich's last source of oil, though it would have been obvious to anyone outside the fantasy land in the bunker that the SS Panzers would have been of more use on the Oder front against the Red armies that threatened Berlin itself.

Few Germans in the West had any desire to fight, though even now there were those who still believed in the Führer. Foremost among these were the young men of the SS training schools and replacement regiments. But even their

fanaticism could do little more than delay an attacker – in the face of the force arrayed against these last defenders of the *Reich*, they had little hope of doing more than dying bravely.

ACROSS THE RHINE

In March, the Anglo-Americans prepared themselves for the final assault on Germany. Eight armies were aligned along the west bank of the Rhine. On 23 March the British Second and American Ninth Armies operations, code-named respectively 'Plunder' and 'Grenade', were

Below: Panthers of SS Division *Das Reich* prepare for their attack on Manhay. The thick forest canopy and poor flying conditions gave the tanks protection against the threat of Allied fighter-bombers, whose 127mm (5in) rockets could destroy them with ease. However the terrain was not ideal tank country, and the lack of fuel hampered operations further.

launched. These were spectacular affairs involving large numbers of amphibious craft, massive air and artillery preparations and the dropping of two airborne divisions behind the German defences on the east bank of the river, and were lightly opposed.

Once through the initial lines of German defence, the Allied armour was free to sweep across the North German Plain. The Allied Liberation army now contained 85 divisions and numbered 4 million men, while the real strength of the German Army in the West was only 26 divisions, mostly made up from the remaining splinters of units shattered in combat, leavened by old men, boys and the walking wounded.

The evolution of Eisenhower's plan in the West had already been changed by the fortuitous capture of the bridge at Remagen on 7 March. A

Above: Even the SS began to falter at the end. At the beginning of the year they still fought hard but, by March 1945, most of the surviving SS Panzer units had been thrown away in futile battles against the Red Army in Hungary. Most of the survivors were fleeing westwards, heading towards the Anglo-American lines to avoid being captured by the Russians.

catalogue of human error had led to its seizure. Hitler was furious and several unfortunate officers were summarily shot, as an example to others. The Allies were unable to exploit this position immediately, but on 22 March Patton led his Third Army in a surprise assault at Oppenheim, where he established another bridgehead.

The German defences of the Rhine were therefore compromised at two widely separated places, in the Ruhr and at its confluence with the river Rhine at Mainz. This threatened the whole *Wehrmacht* position in the West with envelopment on a large scale. Allied plans were now greatly assisted by Hitler, who gave another of his disastrous stand-fast orders. In the real world, German forces would have been better served by a withdrawal form the Ruhr pocket.

The British and Canadian armies pressed on into northern Germany, aiming towards Hamburg, while the Americans aimed for the Ruhr, Germany's industrial heartland. On 4 April the Ruhr Valley was surrounded by the US 1st and 9th Armies. This huge pocket contained the remnants of German Army Group B together with elements of Army Group A's Parachute units. It finally fell on 18 April, yielding 325,000 prisoners. The last few German units surrendered on 21 April. Model, the 'Führer's Fireman', committed suicide.

CONCENTRATION CAMPS

On 13 April the Allies liberated Belsen and Buchenwald concentration camps and Vienna fell to the Red Army. Nuremberg, the spiritual home of the Nazis, fell to the US 7th Army on 20 April, while Dachau was liberated by the US Army on the 25th.

Meanwhile, the US 9th Army was on the move. On the evening of 11 April, it reached the river Elbe, designated the previous year as the demarcation line between the Soviet and Western occupation zones in Germany. At Magdeburg the 2nd Armoured Division seized a bridgehead across the river. The next day the 83rd Infantry Division established another at Barby, and the men then assumed they were on their way to Berlin. After enlarging their bridgehead on 14 April, they were only 80km (50 miles) away.

Orders quickly came down the line, however, that they were not to press for the German capital. Had they done so, Berlin would have fallen to the Americans and not the Russians. Eisenhower, though, was bound by the inter-Allied Agreement reinforced at Yalta. American forces in the central sector had to stay where they were,

while the British and Americans continued to clear Northern Germany and the southern US units and French armies overran Bavaria.

On April 20, the Führer celebrated his 56th birthday. Among his visitors was the pioneering aviatrix Hanna Reitsch, who evaded Soviet fighters and AA fire and landed on the Charlottenburger Strasse near the bunker. The last pictures showing Hitler alive were taken at

---

The last and most fanatical German defenders of Berlin were men of an *SS Kampfgruppe* led by *Leibstandarte* veteran Wilhelm Mohnke.

---

the *Führerbunker* and show him congratulating a line of youthful *Hitlerjugend* 'soldiers', awarding each an Iron Cross for their defence of the *Reich*'s capital. Hitler still had a chance to escape from Berlin by air or road, but on 23 April he declared that he would remain in Berlin to the end. He also confided in his staff that he would commit suicide rather than fall into Russian hands.

Early on 29 April the fighting was less than a quarter of a mile away from the *Reich* Chancellery, which had been demolished by heavy Russian shells. Just 18m (59ft) beneath the surface, Hitler exercised what little authority remained to him. He appointed Grand Admiral Karl Dönitz his successor as Führer. He dismissed Albert Speer for refusal to carry out his orders to turn Germany into a wasteland. He appointed Ritter von Greim as Chief of the Air Force, and he expelled Himmler and Göring from the Nazi Party for acts of treason.

HITLER DISOWNS THE SS

By now, Hitler had even lost faith in the SS. The failure of the battles in Hungary led him to order the *Leibstandarte* and other SS divisions to remove their honour cuff titles – Sepp Dietrich's reaction was to tell his men to collect them in a chamber pot and send them to the Führer.

Then came Himmler's attempt to reach an accommodation with the Allies. If *Treue Heinrich*

Above: On 21 May 1945, Heinrich Himmler was detained at a British check point at Bremervorde having adopted the identity of Heinrich Hitzinger – a dead village policeman. Once he had been identified, Himmler's nerve failed and he crushed a vial of cyanide concealed in his mouth. Unlike millions of his victims, the evil genius of the SS died instantly.

– Loyal Heinrich – was false, then so was the SS. And it was the SS that arranged the first truce with the Allies. On 3 March 1945, an agent from the Office of Strategic Services (OSS, which was to develop after the war into the CIA) met SS General Eugen Dollmann at Lugano, Switzerland. It was the first of a series of secret contacts initiated by *Obergruppenführer* Karl Wolff, the 39-year-old military governor and SS chief in northern Italy. Wolff, a long-time assistant to Himmler, had acted as the liaison officer between Hitler and Mussolini. Recognizing that Germany's cause was beyond hope, he intended to save his own skin. On 8 March, Allen Dulles, the head of intelligence at the OSS, met Wolff and started the process, code-named 'Sunrise', that would lead to the surrender of German forces in Italy. On 19 March Dulles, accompanied by two senior officers from Alexander's HQ, the American General Lyman Lemnitzer (a future head of NATO) and the British General Terence Airey, met Wolff at Ascona on Lake Maggiore in Italy. The Allies were in no mood for anything other than unconditional surrender, so Wolff retired to consult with General Heinrich von Vietinghoff, deputy to *Generalfeldmarschall* Albert Kesselring, C-in-C Italy.

On 25 March 1945, von Vietinghoff succeeded Kesselring. *Reichsführer* Heinrich Himmler ordered Wolff not to leave Italy. The head of the SS had picked up rumours of the meetings and since he was himself involved in tentative negotiations with the Allies, he did not want Wolff to upstage him.

On 23 April, Wolff again approached the Allies, Vietinghoff having agreed that an armistice could be signed without reference to Berlin. On 27 April, Dulles was given authority from Alexander's HQ to resume negotiations.

By now, Hitler had lost the bulk of the SS. In the words of Heinz Höhne:

For thousands and thousands of SS men, their world was collapsing. Small groups of fanatics fought on, hounding themselves senselessly to death, the scourge and the terror of Germany's civil population to the very end. At the Battle of Waterloo, when Napoleon's Old Guard had fired its last cartridge, it was summoned to lay down its arms. General Cambronne is reputed to have said: 'The Guard dies, it does not surrender.' It is the motto of every Imperial Guard; it is the essence and justification of every military elite. But Hitler's Imperial Guard did not fire its last cartridge. The SS surrendered before it was surrounded by the enemy. Little by little, the SS commanders simply gave up the fight.

As for Hitler, he now accepted that all was lost. On his final day, he married his long-time mistress Eva Braun and finally dictated his Last Will and Political Testament. This was a final piece of callous invective carrying the poison of hatred and incite to murder: 'I charge the leadership of the nation and their subjects with the meticulous observance of the race laws and the merciless resistance to the universal prisoner of all peoples, international Jewry.' Hitler committed suicide at around three o'clock on 30 April.

The war in Europe was now almost over. The Germans in Italy had signed a formal surrender document on 29 April, to come into effect on 2 May 1945. On 3 May Admiral Hans von Friedeburg surrendered the German forces in Denmark, Holland and North Germany to Montgomery. On 7 May Jodl, despatched by Dönitz from his makeshift seat of government at Flensburg, signed a general surrender of German forces at Eisenhower's headquarters at Reims in France. Stalin was outraged: he wanted the final surrender to be made in Berlin. Accordingly the next day, Field Marshal Keitel, his arrogance seemingly untroubled by defeat, Marshal Georgi Zhukov and British Air Marshal Tedder signed a second unconditional surrender. Finally the war in Europe was at an end.

After the war, the search for war criminals was most vigorously prosecuted among the former members of the SS. Jochen Peiper, whose *Kampfgruppe* had been responsible for the Malmédy massacre, was tried and found guilty of being responsible. Due to irregularities in his interrogation he was reprieved, jailed and released in 1956. Along with Sepp Dietrich and Panzer Mayer, Jochen Peiper remained a hero to former SS men. He retired to Traves in France, where he lived until 14 July 1976. There, following numerous death threats, French Communists firebombed his home and he was killed.

SOLDIERS – OR WAR CRIMINALS?

The *Waffen-SS* moved a long way in its 25 years of existence. Hitler's personal thugs became the parade soldiers of the 1930s, who in turn evolved into the well-equipped, million-strong army of 1944. They remained the most motivated of German troops, and their fighting abilities saw them being used as elite spearhead forces from Kursk and Kharkov to the Battle of the Bulge. Indeed, their influence on the course of World War II was out of all proportion to their numbers. But their ruthless fanaticism led them to commit many atrocities on both the Eastern and Western Fronts. When the International Military Tribunal at Nuremberg determined that the SS was an illegal organization, many who had considered themselves the elite of the German armed forces faced years of captivity. The victorious Allies judged them to be not prisoners of war, but war criminals.

GERMAN WAFFEN SS KNIGHTS CROSS WINNERS

SS-Sturmann Hermann Alber (26 Dec 1944)
SS-Sturmbannführer Anton Ameiser (1 Nov 1944)
SS-Standartenführer Günther Anhalt (12 Aug 1944)
SS-Obersturmführer Josef Amberger (31 Oct 1944)
SS-Hauptsturmführer Karl Auer (31 Oct 1944)
SS-Brigadeführer Franz Augsberger (31 Mar 1945)
SS-Oberführer Adolf Ax (9 May 1945)
SS-Obergruppenführer Erich Von Dem Bach-Zelewski (30 Sep 1944)
SS-Hauptsturmführer Christian Bachmann (28 Feb 1945)
SS-Obersturmführer Erwin Bachmann (10 Feb 1945)
SS-Hauptsturmführer Josef Bachmeier (23 Aug 1944)
SS-Unterscharführer Ernst Barkmann (27 Aug 1944)
SS-Obersturmführer Heinrich Bastian (6 May 1945)
SS-Hauptsturmführer Karl Bastian (23 Aug 1944)
SS-Obersturmführer Hans Bauer (5 Apr 1945)
SS-Oberscharführer Helmut Bauer (12 Sep 1944)
SS-Sturmbannführer Willi Baumann (27 Jan 1945)
SS-Obersturmführer Wilhelm Beck (28 Mar 1943)
SS-Standartenführer Hellmuth Becker (7 Sep 1943)
SS-Obersturmbannführer Georg-Robert Besslein (30 Apr 1945)
SS-Sturmbannführer Walter Bestmann (29 Sep 1941)
SS-Oberscharführer Fritz Biegi (16 June 1944)
SS-Untersturmführer Friedrich Blond (28 Apr 1945)
SS-Obersturmführer Joachim Boosfeld (21 Feb 1945)
SS-Hauptsturmführer Hermann Borchers (16 Oct 1944)
SS-Obersturmführer Karl-Heinz Boska (16 Dec 1943)
SS-Gruppenführer Karl-Heinrich Brenner (31 Dec 1944)
SS-Hauptsturmführer Siegfried Brosow (31 Nov 1943)
SS-Hauptsturmführer Herman Buchner (16 June 1944)
SS-Oberscharführer Friedrich Buck (27 Jan 1945)
SS-Untersturmführer Franz Budka (19 Apr 1945)
SS-Sturmbannführer Fritz Bunse (30 Jan 1944)
SS-Hauptsturmführer Hans-Georg von Charpentier (29 Dec 1942)
SS-Sturmann Fritz Christen (20 Oct 1941)
SS-Oberscharführer Hermann Dahlke (3 Mar 1943)
SS-Untersturmführer Werber Dallmann (17 Jan 1945)
SS-Hauptsturmführer Werner Damsch (17 Apr 1945)
SS-Obersturmbannführer Fritz Darges (5 Apr 1945)
SS-Oberscharführer Hans Dauser (4 June 1944)
SS-Obersturmführer Heinrich Debus (4 May 1944)
SS-Hauptsturmführer Günther Degen (7 Oct 1944)
SS-Hauptsturmführer Ernst Dehmel (15 Aug 1943)
SS-Sturmbannführer Dr. Eduard Deisenhofer (8 May 1942)
SS-Hauptsturmführer Josef Diefenthal (5 Feb 1945)
SS-Sturmbannführer Hans Diergarten (16 Jan 1944)
SS-Sturmbannführer Bernard Dietsche (17 July 1943)
SS-Oberführer Dr. Oskar Dirlewanger (30 Sep 1944)
SS-Hauptscharführer Sepp Draxenberger (17 Apr 1945)
SS-Hauptsturmführer Franz-Josef Dreike (6 May 1945)
SS-Obersturmführer Hans Drexel (14 Oct 1943)
SS-Obersturmbannführer Oskar Drexler (6 May 1945)
SS-Sturmbannführer Walter Drexler (11 Dec 1944)
SS-Unterscharführer Emil Dürr (23 Aug 1944)
SS-Obersturmbannführer Erich Eberhardt (23 Aug 1944)
SS-Sturmbannführer Georg Eberhardt (4 Aug 1943)
SS-Sturmführer Hans Eckert (4 May 1944)
SS-Rottenführer Fritz Eckstein (18 Nov 1944)
SS-Obersturmführer Paul Egger (27 Apr 1945)
SS-Obersturmbannführer Fritz Ehrath (23 Feb 1944)
SS-Hauptsturmführer Hugo Eichhorn (15 Jan 1943)
SS-Hauptsturmführer Hans Endress (23 Mar 1945)
SS-Sturmbannführer Rudolf Enseling (23 Aug 1944)
SS-Hauptsturmführer Karl-Heinz Ertle (23 Aug 1944)
SS-Hauptscharführer Willi Esslinger (19 June 1943)
SS-Sturmbannführer Alois Etthöfer (17 Mar 1945)
SS-Hauptsturmführer Karl-Heinz Euling (15 Oct 1944)
SS-Obersturmführer Markus Faulhaber (25 Dec 1942)
SS-Sturmbannführer Waldemar Fegelein (16 Dec 1943)
SS-Oberscharführer Willi Fey (29 Apr 1945)

SS-Sturmbannführer Jacob Fick (23 Apr 1943)
SS-Unterscharführer Johann Fiedler (16 June 1944)
SS-Sturmbannführer Alfred Fischer (9 May 1945)
SS-Unterscharführer Gerhard Fischer (4 May 1944)
SS-Hauptsturmführer Hans Flügel (16 Oct 1944)
SS-Sturmbannführer Robert Frank (4 June 1944)
SS-Hauptsturmführer Kurt Franke (3 Oct 1943)
SS-Unterscharführer Egon Franz (16 Oct 1944)
SS-Hauptscharführer Franz Frauscher (31 Dec 1944)
SS-Brigadeführer Fritz Freitag (30 Sep 1944)
SS-Hauptsturmführer Carl-Heinz Frühauf (4 June 1944)
SS-Oberscharführer Wolfgang Gast Gebhard (6 May 1945)
SS-Obersturmführer Walter Gerth (31 Mar 1943)
SS-Obersturmbannführer Karl Gesele (4 July 1944)
SS-Obersturmführer Johannes Göhler (17 Sep 1943)
SS-Panzergrenadier Dr. Erich Göstl (31 Oct 1944)
SS-Standartenführer Herbert Golz (6 May 1945)
SS-Gruppenführer Curt von Gottberg (30 June 1944)
SS-Unterscharführer Heinrich Gottke (17 Dec 1944)
SS-Obersturmbannführer Reiner Gottstein (6 Feb 1945)
SS-Hauptsturmführer Viktor-Eberhard Gräbner (23 Aug 1944)
SS-Unterscharführer Simon Grascher (14 Aug 1943)
SS-Hauptsturmführer Erich Grätz (14 May 1944)
SS-Hauptscharführer Gerhard Grebarsche (24 Jan 1944)
SS-Obersturmführer Horst Gresiak (25 Jan 1945)
SS-Obersturmführer Willi Grieme (17 Sep 1943)
SS-Obersturmführer Franz Grohmann (23 Aug 1944)
SS-Sturmbannführer Martin Gross (22 July 1943)
SS-Untersturmführer Alfred Grossrock (12 Aug 1944)
SS-Unterscharführer Georg-Rudlof Grünner (10 Mar 1945)
SS-Hauptsturmführer Paul Guhl (4 June 1944)
SS-Oberscharführer Alfred Günther (3 Mar 1943)
SS-Hauptsturmführer Martin Gürz (23 Oct 1944)
SS-Hauptsturmführer Heinz Hämel (16 June 1944)
SS-Standartenführer Desiderious Hampel (3 May 1945)
SS-Obersturmbannführer Hans Hanke (3 May 1945)
SS-Standartenführer Heinrich Hannibal (23 Aug 1944)
SS-Obersturmbannführer Walter Harzer (21 Sep 1944)
SS-Obersturmführer Frank Hasse (6 Aug 1944)
SS-Sturmbannführer Hans Hauser (6 May 1945)
SS-Sturmbannführer Ernst Häussler (15 Aug 1943)
SS-Untersturmführer Hans Havik (6 May 1944)
SS-Hauptsturmführer Eberhard Heder (18 Nov 1944)
SS-Oberführer Nikolaus Heilmann (23 Aug 1944)
SS-Hauptsturmführer Heinrich Heimann (23 Feb 1944)
SS-Obersturmführer Willi Hein (4 May 1944)
SS-Oberscharführer Albert Hektor (23 Aug 1944)
SS-Oberscharführer Fritz Henke (12 Feb 1944)
SS-Sturmbannführer Fritz Herzig (29 Apr 1945)
SS-Untersturmführer Konrad Heubeck (17 Apr 1945)
SS-Rottenführer Hans Hirning (23 Oct 1942)
SS-Sturmbannführer Lothar Hofer (5 Apr 1945)
SS-Oberscharführer Josef Holte (27 Aug 1944)
SS-Hauptsturmführer Friedrich Holzer (10 Dec 1943)
SS-Sturmbannführer Werner Hörnicke (1 Dec 1943)
SS-Obersturmführer Willi Hund (20 Apr 1945)
SS-Obersturmführer Georg Hurdelbrink (16 Oct 1944)
SS-Kanonier Walter Jenschke (18 Dec 1944)
SS-Obersturmbannführer Wolfgang Jörchel (21 Apr 1944)
SS-Hauptsturmführer Hans Juchem (12 Sep 1943)
SS-Hauptsturmführer Heinz Jürgens (8 May 1945)
SS-Sturmbannführer Arnold Jürgensen (16 Oct 1944)
SS-Sturmbannführer Helmut Kampfe (10 Dec 1943)
SS-Hauptsturmführer Vincenz Kaiser (6 Apr 1943)
SS-Obersturmführer Alois Kalls (23 Aug 1944)
SS-Obersturmführer Georg Karck (3 Aug 1943)
SS-Obersturmbannführer Friedrich Wilhelm Karl (26 Dec 1944)
SS-Hauptsturmführer Karl Keck (23 Aug 1944)
SS-Oberführer Georg Keppler (15 Aug 1940)

SS-Hauptsturmführer Ludwig Kepplinger (4 Sep 1940)
SS-Hauptsturmführer Dieter Kesten (12 Nov 1943)
SS-Hauptsturmführer Hans Kettgen (14 Feb 1945)
SS-Hauptsturmführer Helmut Kinz (3 May 1945)
SS-Untersturmführer Otto Kirchner (21 Apr 1944)
SS-Sturmbannführer Franz Kleffner (19 Feb 1942)
SS-Obersturmführer Albert Klett (16 Oct 1944)
SS-Hauptsturmführer Heinrich Kling (23 Feb 1944)
SS-Hauptsturmführer Fritz Klingenberg (14 May 1941)
SS-Sturmbannführer Walter Kniep (14 Aug 1943)
SS-Sturmbannführer Gustav Knittel (4 June 1944)
SS-Obersturmbannführer Fritz Knöchlein (16 Nov 1944)
SS-Obersturmführer Alfred Koch (6 May 1945)
SS-Oberscharführer Ludwig Köchle (28 Feb 1942)
SS-Obersturmführer Siegfried Korth (9 Feb 1945)
SS-Sturmbannführer Boris Kraas (28 Feb 1945)
SS-Sturmbannführer Bernhard Krause (18 Nov 1944)
SS-Sturmbannführer Oswald Krauss (27 Jan 1945)
SS-Hauptsturmführer Franz Krombholtz (28 Mar 1945)
SS-Hauptsturmführer Otto Kron (28 June 1942)
SS-Obergruppenführer Friedrich Wilhelm Krüger (30 Sep 1944)
SS-Untersturmführer Joachim Krüger (24 June 1944)
SS-Sturmbannführer Hebert Kuhlmann (13 Feb 1944)
SS-Oberscharführer Josef Lainer (8 Oct 1943)
SS-Oberführer Heinz Lammerding (11 Apr 1944)
SS-Sturmbannführer Paul Landwehr (17 Mar 1945)
SS-Oberscharführer Hermann Lang (23 Oct 1944)
SS-Standartenoberjunker Frtiz Langanke (27 Aug 1944)
SS-Untersturmführer Georg Langendorf (12 Mar 1944)
SS-Sturmbannführer Bernhard Langhorst (5 Apr 1945)
SS-Sturmbannführer Kurt Launer (15 Aug 1943)
SS-Hauptsturmführer Alfred Lex (10 Dec 1943)
SS-Hauptsturmführer Karl-Heinz Lichte (25 Mar 1945)
SS-Obersturmführer Franz Liebisch (9 Feb 1945)
SS-Sturmbannführer Karl Liecke (3 May 1945)
SS-Obersturmführer Dr. Hans Lipinski (2 Jan 1945)
SS-Hauptsturmführer Jakob Lobmeyer (28 Apr 1945)
SS-Obersturmbannführer Gustav Lombard (10 Mar 1943)
SS-Obersturmführer Gerard Lotze (1 Feb 1945)
SS-Hauptscharführer Siegfried Lüngen (16 Nov 1944)
SS-Obersturmführer Hans Malkomes (31 Oct 1944)
SS-Hauptsturmführer Hermann Maringgele (21 Feb 1945)
SS-Hauptsturmführer Arzelino Masarie (3 Apr 1943)
SS-Obersturmführer Walter Mattern (20 Oct 1944)
SS-Hauptsturmführer Walter Mattusch (6 May 1945)
SS-Hauptsturmführer Hans Meyer (2 Sep 1944)
SS-Obersturmführer Werner Meyer (4 May 1944)
SS-Obersturmbannführer Wilhelm Mohnke (11 July 1944)
SS-Obersturmführer Erhard Mösslacher (9 Feb 1945)
SS-Untersturmführer Karl Mühleck (4 June 1944)
SS-Hauptscharführer Albert Müller (6 Aug 1943)
SS-Hauptsturmführer Fritz-Heinz Muller (23 Mar 1945)
SS-Sturmbannführer Seigfried Muller (19 Dec 1944)
SS-Hauptsturmführer Heinz Murr (21 Sep 1944)
SS-Sturmbannführer Eggert Neumann (3 Nov 1944)
SS-Obersturmführer Karl Nicolussi-Leck (9 Apr 1944)
SS-Oberscharführer Alfred Nowak (1 Nov 1943)
SS-Untersturmführer Heinz Nowotnik (14 May 1944)
SS-Obersturmführer Alois Obschil (28 Mar 1945)
SS-Sturmbannführer Erich Olboeter (27 July 1944)
SS-Obersturmführer Harry Paletta (26 Nov 1944)
SS-Obersturmführer Fred Papas (27 Dec 1944)
SS-Hauptscharführer Adolf Peichl (16 Oct 1944)
SS-Obersturmbannführer Heinrich Petersen (13 Nov 1943)
SS-Obersturmführer Otto Petersen (11 Dec 1944)
SS-Obersturmführer Helmut Pfördner (18 Jan 1942)
SS-Hauptsturmführer Harry Phönix (21 Feb 1945)
SS-Obersturmführer Karl Picus (17 Apr 1945)
SS-Hauptscharführer Walter Pitsch (6 May 1945)
SS-Sturmbannführer Adolf Pitschellis (23 Aug 1944)
SS-Obersturmführer Gerd Pleiss (20 Apr 1941)

SS-Obersturmbannführer Harry Polewacz (23 Dec 1942)
SS-Sturmbannführer Hermann Potschka (26 Dec 1944)
SS-Sturmbannführer Otto Prager (29 Dec 1944)
SS-Obersturmbannführer Georg Preuss (25 Feb 1945)
SS-Sturmbannführer Karl-Heinz Prinz (11 July 1944)
SS-Unterscharführer Felix Przedwojewski (16 Dec 1943)
SS-Oberscharführer Erich Rech (23 Aug 1944)
SS-Hauptsturmführer Walter Reder (3 Apr 1943)
SS-Untersturmführer Adolf Reeb (23 Aug 1944)
SS-Sturmbannführer Erwin H. Reichel (28 Feb 1943)
SS-Oberscharführer Hans Reimling (28 Feb 1943)
SS-Sturmbannführer Leo-Hermann Reinhold (16 Oct 1943)
SS-Oberscharführer Paul Reissman (23 Dec 1944)
SS-Untersturmführer Hans Reiter (23 Aug 1944)
SS-Obersturmführer Hans-Albin von Reitzenstein (13 Nov 1943)
SS-Obersturmführer Fritz Rentrop (13 Oct 1941)
SS-Hauptsturmführer Gottleib Renz (12 Aug 1944)
SS-Sturmbannführer Rudolf Rettberg (1 May 1945)
SS-Hauptsturmführer Karl Rettlinger (20 Dec 1943)
SS-Obersturmführer Rudolf von Ribbentrop (15 July 1943)
SS-Sturmbannführer Friedrich Richter (6 May 1945)
SS-Obersturmbannführer Joachim Richter (23 Feb 1944)
SS-Obersturmführer Wilfred Richter (21 Apr 1942)
SS-Obersturmführer Franz Riedel (28 Mar 1945)
SS-Obersturmführer Waldemar Riekogel (11 July 1943)
SS-Obersturmführer Fritz Rieflin (6 May 1945)
SS-Sturmbannführer Julius Riepe (13 Jan 1945)
SS-Untersturmführer Albert-Herbert Rieth (11 Dec 1944)
SS-Obersturmführer Dr. Wolfgang Roehder (1 Dec 1943)
SS-Obersturmbannführer Franz Roestel (3 May 1945)
SS-Unterscharführer Josef Rölleke (16 June 1944)
SS-Unterscharführer Patrick Rosen (14 Mar 1943)
SS-Obersturmführer Rudolf Rott (28 Feb 1945)
SS-Oberscharführer Rudolf Roy (16 Oct 1944)
SS-Obersturmführer Karl Rubatscher (27 Dec 1943)
SS-Oberscharführer Richard Rudolf (18 Nov 1944)
SS-Hauptscharführer Adolf Rüd (23 Aug 1944)
SS-Hauptscharführer Hans Joachim Rühle von Lilienstern (12 Feb 1944)
SS-Oberscharführer Hugo Ruf (16 Oct 1944)
SS-Hauptsturmführer Rudolf Saalbach (12 Mar 1944)
SS-Obersturmführer Johann Sailer (4 May 1945)
SS-Oberscharführer Kurt Sametreiter (31 July 1943)
SS-Sturmbannführer Rudolf Sandig (5 May 1945)
SS-Sturmbannführer Karl Sattler (16 Jan 1945)
SS-Hauptsturmführer Rudolf Säumenicht (13 Oct 1943)
SS-Unterscharführer Hans Schabschneider (27 Aug 1944)
SS-Obersturmführer Max Schachner (14 May 1944)
Major Hans von Schack (27 Jan 1945)
SS-Sturmbannführer Ernst Schäfer (14 Oct 1943)
SS-Sturmbannführer Siegfried Scheibe (9 May 1945)
SS-Sturmbannführer Conrad Schellong (28 Feb 1945)
SS-Obersturmführer Johannes Scherg (23 Oct 1944)
SS-Obersturmführer Anton-Franz Scherzer (28 Mar 1945)
SS-Sturmbannführer Karl Schlamelcher (1 Mar 1942)
SS-Sturmbannführer Wilhelm Schlüter (23 Aug 1944)
SS-Standartenoberjunker Georg Schluifelder (26 Nov 1944)
SS-Unterscharführer Alois Schnaubelt (16 Nov 1944)
SS-Obersturmführer Otto Schneider (4 May 1944)
SS-Rottenführer Alfred Schneidereit (20 Dec 1943)
SS-Obersturmbannführer Georg Schönberg (20 Dec 1943)
SS-Obersturmbannführer Manfred Schönfelder (23 Feb 1944)
SS-Standartenführer Franz Schreiber (26 Dec 1944)
SS-Hauptscharführer Gustav Schreiber (2 Dec 1943)
SS-Hauptsturmführer Helmut Schreiber (30 July 1943)
SS-Sturmbannführer Joachim Schubach (3 Apr 1943)
SS-Standartenführer Hans-Christian Schulze (11 Sep 1941)
SS-Sturmbannführer Hebert Schulze (16 Dec 1943)
SS-Sturmbannführer Karl-Heinz Schulz-Streeck (2 May 1945)
SS-Untersturmführer Kurt Schumacher (4 May 1944)
SS-Hauptsturmführer Oskar Schwappacher (26 Dec 1944)
SS-Sturmbannführer Willi Schweitzer (14 Apr 1945)

SS-Obersturmführer Walter Seebach (12 Mar 1944)
SS-Hauptsturmführer Max Seela (3 May 1942)
SS-Hauptscharführer Emil Seibold (6 May 1945)
SS-Obersturmführer Paul Senghas (11 Dec 1944)
SS-Unterscharführer Karlis Sensburgs (9 May 1945)
SS-Obersturmbannführer Bernhard Siebken (17 Apr 1945)
SS-Hauptsturmführer Hans Siegel (23 Aug 1944)
SS-Obersturmführer Alfred Siegling (2 Feb 1943)
SS-Oberscharführer Hans Sigmund (5 Apr 1945)
SS-Hauptscharführer Willy Simke (16 Dec 1943)
SS-Hauptsturmführer Gunther Sitter (12 Sep 1943)
SS-Obersturmführer Heinrich Sonne (10 Dec 1943)
SS-Sturmbannführer Ludwig Spindler (27 Sep 1944)
SS-Hauptsturmführer Richard Spörle (16 Nov 1944)
SS-Hauptsturmführer Heinrich Springer (12 Jan 1942)
SS-Oberscharführer Ernst Stäudle (10 Apr 1942)
SS-Unterscharführer Franz Staudegger (10 July 1943)
SS-Sturmbannführer Albert Stenwedel (3 May 1945)
SS-Obersturmbannführer Arnold Stoffers (12 Mar 1944)
SS-Rottenführer Stefan Strapatin (16 Nov 1944)
SS-Hauptscharführer Josef Styr (5 Apr 1945)
SS-Obersturmbannführer Friedrich Suhr (11 Dec 1944)
SS-Obersturmbannführer Josef Swientke (16 June 1944)
SS-Rottenführer Lothar Swierzinski (16 Dec 1943)
SS-Obersturmbannführer Martin Tappe (28 Mar 1945)

SS-Sturmbannführer Eberhardt Telkamp (23 Aug 1944)
SS-Unterscharführer Johann Thaler (14 Aug 1943)
SS-Unterscharführer Alfred Titschkus (11 Dec 1944)
SS-Hauptscharführer Paul Trabandt (14 Oct 1943)
SS-Standartenführer Wilhelm Trabandt (6 Jan 1944)
SS-Sturmbannführer Hans Traupe (23 Feb 1944)
SS-Hauptsturmführer Richard Utgenannt (10 Nov 1944)
SS-Oberführer Herbert-Ernst Vahl (31 Mar 1943)
SS-Hauptsturmführer Anton Vandieken (26 Dec 1944)
SS-Obersturmführer Johann Veith (14 Feb 1945)
SS-Sturmbannführer Hans Waldmüller (27 Aug 1944)
SS-Hauptscharführer Alois Weber (30 July 1943)
SS-Obersturmführer Hermann Weiser (28 Mar 1943)
SS-Hauptsturmführer Hans Weiss (6 Apr 1943)
SS-Unterscharführer Helmut Wendorff (12 Feb 1944)
SS-Oberscharführer Gustav Wendrinsky (27 Jan 1945)
SS-Hauptsturmführer Emil Wiesemann (20 Dec 1943)
SS-Oberscharführer Philipp Wild (21 Mar 1944)
SS-Unterscharführer Werner Wolff (7 Aug 1943)
SS-Rottenführer Balthasar Woll (16 Jan 1944)
SS-Hauptscharführer Karl-Heinz Worthmann (31 Mar 1943)
SS-Sturmbannführer Erich Wulff (9 May 1945)
SS-Hauptscharführer Erich Zepper (2 Dec 1943)
SS-Unterscharführer August Zingel (4 Oct 1942)

KNIGHT'S CROSS WITH OAK LEAVES WINNERS

SS-Hauptsturmführer Hans Becker (28 Mar 1943)
SS-Hauptsturmführer Fritz Biermeier (10 Dec 1943)
SS-Obersturmbannführer Fredrich-Wilhelm Bock (28 Mar 1943)
SS-Obersturmführer Gerhard Bremer (31 Oct 1941)
SS-Hauptsturmführer Léon Degrelle (20 Feb 1944) (B)
SS-Gruppenführer Theodor Eicke (26 Dec 1941)
SS-Sturmbannführer Albert Frey (3 Mar 1943)
SS-Untersturmführer Walter Girg (4 Oct 1944)
SS-Sturmbannführer Franz Hack (14 May 1944)
SS-Sturmbannführer Max Hansen (28 Mar 1943)
SS-Untersturmführer Bruno Hinz (2 Dec 1943)
SS-Obergruppenführer Friedrich Jeckeln (27 Aug 1944)
SS-Obersturmbannführer Paul-Albert Kausch (23 Aug 1944)
SS-Brigadeführer Matthias Kleinheisterkamp (31 Mar 1942)
SS-Hauptscharführer Karl Kloskowski (11 July 1943)
SS-Sturmbannführer Hugo Kraas (28 Mar 1943)
SS-Sturmbannführer Ernst-August Krag (23 Oct 1944)
SS-Standartenführer Karl Kreutz (27 Aug 1944)
SS-Sturmbannführer Albrecht Krügel (12 Mar 1944)
SS-Obersturmbannführer Rudolf Lehmann (23 Feb 1944)
SS-Sturmbannführer Hanns-Heinrcih Lohmann (12 Mar 1944)
SS-Untersturmführer Heinz Macher (3 Apr 1943)
SS-Obersturmführer Erwin-Hubert Meierdress (31 Mar 1942)
SS-Obersturmbannführer Otto Meyer (4 June 1944)
SS-Sturmbannführer Johnnes-Rudolf Mühlenkamp (3 Sep 1942)

SS-Sturmbannführer Werner Ostendorff (13 Sep 1941)
SS-Obersturmbannführer Otto Paetsch (23 Aug 1944)
SS-Obergruppenführer Karl Pfeffer-Wildenbruch (11 Jan 1945)
SS-Obergruppenführer Arthur Phelps (4 July 1943)
SS-Hauptsturmführer Werner Potschke (4 June 1944)
SS-Sturmbannführer Alfons Rebane (23 Feb 1944) (E)
SS-Obersturmbannführer Heinrich-Friedrich Reinefarth (25 June 1940)
SS-Obersturmbannführer Joachim Rumohr (16 Jan 1944)
SS-Obersturmführer Max Schäfer (12 Feb 1943)
SS-Obersturmführer Heinrich Schmelzer (12 Mar 1944)
SS-Hauptsturmführer Walter Schmidt (4 Aug 1943)
SS-Untersturmführer Helmut Scholz (4 June 1944)
SS-Oberführer Max Simon (20 Oct 1941)
SS-Hauptsturmführer Otto Skorzeny (13 Sep 1943)
SS-Brigadeführer Bruno Streckenbach (27 Aug 1944)
SS-Sturmbannführer Christian Tychsen (31 Mar 1943)
SS-Sturmbannführer Karl Ullrich (19 Feb 1942)
SS-Obersturmführer Fritz Vogt (4 Sep 1940)
SS-Oberführer Jürgen Wagner (24 July 1943)
SS-Hauptsturmführer Kurt Wahl (23 Aug 1944)
SS-Hauptsturmführer Heinz Werner (23 Aug 1944)
SS-Sturmbannführer Fritz Witt (4 Sep 1940)
SS-Sturmbannführer Max Wünsche (28 Feb 1943)
SS-Brigadeführer Joachim Ziegler (5 Sep 1944)

WINNERS OF THE KNIGHT'S CROSS WITH OAK LEAVES AND SWORDS

SS-Sturmbannführer Otto Baum (8 May 1942)
SS-Oberführer Wilhelm Bittrich (14 Dec 1941)
SS-Hauptsturmführer Georg Bochmann (3 May 1942)
SS-Sturmbannführer August Dieckmann (23 Apr 1942)
SS-Hauptsturmführer Hans Dorr (27 Sep 1942)
SS-Sturmbannführer Helmut Dörner (15 May 1942)
SS-Standartenführer Hermann Fegelein (2 Mar 1942)
SS-Obersturmbannführer Heinz Harmel (31 Mar 1943)
SS-Obergruppenführer Paul Hausser (8 Aug 1941)
SS-Brigadeführer Walter Krüger (13 Dec 1941)
SS-Obersturmbannführer Otto Kumm (16 Feb 1942)
SS-Sturmbannführer Kurt Meyer (18 May 1941)

SS-Sturmbannführer Joachim Peiper (9 Mar 1943)
SS-Oberführer Hermann Priess (28 Apr 1943)
SS-Oberführer Fritz von Scholz (18 Jan 1942)
SS-Obersturmbannführer Heinrich Schuldt (5 Apr 1942)
SS-Sturmbannführer Sylvester Stadler (6 Apr 1943)
SS-Oberführer Felix Steiner (15 Aug 1940)
SS-Sturmbannführer Otto Weidinger (21 Apr 1944)
SS-Sturmbannführer Theodor Wisch (15 Sep 1941)
SS-Sturmbannführer Theodor Wisch (15 Sep 1941)
SS-Sturmbannführer Gunther-Eberhard Wisliceny (30 July 1943)
SS-Untersturmführer Michael Wittmann (14 Jan 1944)
Oberst der Schupo Alfred Wünnenberg (15 Nov 1941)

WINNERS OF THE KNIGHT'S CROSS WITH OAK LEAVES, SWORDS AND DIAMONDS

SS-Obergruppenführer Josef 'Sepp' Dietrich (5 July 1940)   *SS-Oberführer* Hebert-Otto Gille (8 Oct 1942)

NON GERMAN KNIGHTS CROSS (OR BETTER) WINNERS

Belgian
SS-Hauptsturmführer Léon Degrelle (20 Feb 1944)
SS-Untersturmführer Leon Gillis (30 Sep 1944)
SS-Untersturmführer Jacques Leroy (20 Apr 1945)
SS-Sturmmann Remi Schrijnen (21 Sep 1944)

Danish
SS-Obersturmführer Johannes Hellmers (5 Mar 1945)
SS-Untersturmführer Soeren Kam (7 Feb 1945)
SS-Unterscharführer Egon Christophersen (11 July 1944)

Dutch
SS-Rottenführer Derk-Elsko Bruins (23 Aug 1944)
SS-Sturmmann Gerardus Mooijman (20 Feb 1943)
SS-Unterscharführer Kaspar Sporck (23 Oct 1944)

Estonian
SS-Hauptsturmführer Paul Maitla (23 Aug 1944)
Waffen-Unterscharführer Haralt Nugiseks (9 Apr 1944)
SS-Sturmbannführer Alfons Rebane (23 Feb 1944)
SS-Obersturmbannführer Haraldt Riipalu (23 Aug 1944)

French
Legion-Unterscharführer Francois Apollat (29 Apr 1945)
SS-Hauptsturmführer Henri-Josef Fenet (29 Apr 1944)
Legion-Unterscharführer Eugene Vaulot (29 Apr 1945)

Latvian
Legion-Untersturmführer Miervaldis Adamsons (25 Jan 1945)
Waffen-Untersturmführer Roberts Ancans (25 Jan 1945)
Waffen-Hauptscharführer Zanis Ansons (25 Jan 1945)
Waffen-Obersturmbannführer Karlis Aperats (21 Sep 1944)
Waffen-Hauptsturmführer Zanis Butkus (21 Sep 1944)
SS-Obersturmführer Andrejs Freimanis (5 May 1945)
Waffen-Obersturmführer Roberts Gaigals (5 May 1945)
Waffen-Obersturmbannführer Nikoljas Galdins (25 Jan 1945)
Waffen-Sturmbannführer Voldermar Reinholds (9 May 1945)
SS-Unterscharführer Alfreds Riekstins (5 Apr 1945)
Waffen-Standartenführer Woldermars Veiss (9 Feb 1944)

SS ORDERS OF BATTLE

1. SS Panzer Division
Leibstandarte Adolf Hitler

2. SS Panzer Division
Das Reich

3. SS Panzer Division
Totenkopf

4. SS Panzer Grenadier Division
Polizei

5. SS Panzer Division
Wiking

6. SS Mountain Division
Nord

7. SS Vol Mountain Division
Prinz Eugen

8. SS Cavalry Division
Florian Geyer

9. SS Panzer Division
Hohenstaufen

10. SS Panzer Division
Frundsberg

11. SS Freiwilligen Panzer Grenadier Division
Nordland

12. SS Panzer Division
Hitlerjugend

13. Waffen Gebirgs Division der SS
Handschar
(Kroatisches Nr. I)

14. Waffen Grenadier Division der SS
(Galizisches / Ukrainisches)

15. Waffen Grenadier Division der SS
(Lettisches Nr. II)

16. SS Panzer Grenadier Division
Reichsführer SS

17. SS Panzer Grenadier Division
Götz von Berlichingen

18. SS Freiwilligen Panzer Grenadier Division
Horst Wessel

19. Waffen Grenadier Division der SS
(Lettisches Nr. II)

20. Waffen Grenadier Division der SS
(Estnisches Nr. I)

21. Waffen Gebirgs Division der SS
Skanderbeg

22. Freiwilligen Kavallerie Division der SS
Maria Theresa

23. Waffen Gebirgs Division der SS
Kama (Kroatisches Nr. II)

(Disbanded in late 1944 and the remnants became part of the new 23rd SS Division.)

23. SS Freiwilligen Panzer Grenadier Division
Niederland / Nederland

24. Waffen Gebirgs Division der SS
Karstjäger

25. Waffen Grenadier Division der SS
Hunyadi
(Ungarisches Nr. I)

26. Waffen Grenadier Division der SS
(Ungarisches Nr. II)

27. SS Freiwilligen Grenadier Division
Langemarck
(Flämische Nr. I)

28. SS Freiwilligen Panzer Grenadier Division
Wallonien

29. Waffen Grenadier Division der SS
(Russisches Nr. I)

29. Waffen Grenadier Division der SS
(Italienisches No. I)

30. Waffen Grenadier Division der SS
(Russisches Nr. II)

31. SS Freiwilligen Grenadier Division

32. SS Freiwilligen Grenadier Division
30 Januar

33. Waffen Kavallerie Division der SS
(Ungarisches Nr. III)

33. SS Waffen Grenadier Division der SS
Charlemagne
(Französisches Nr. I)

34. SS Freiwilligen Grenadier Division
Landstorm Nederland

35. SS Polizei Grenadier Division

36. Waffen Grenadier Division der SS

37. SS Freiwilligen Kavallerie Division
Lützow

38. SS Panzer Grenadier Division
Nibelungen

39. Gebirgs Division der SS *
Andreas Höfer

40. SS Freiwilligen Panzer Grenadier Division *
Feldherrnhalle

41. Waffen Grenadier Division der SS *
Kalevala
(Finnisches Nr. I)

42. ??? *
Niederschsen

43. ??? *
Reichsmarschall

44. SS Panzer Grenadier Division *
Wallenstein

45. SS Division *
Waräger

* Existed on paper only.

INDEX